# FRESH START SUCCESS

# FRESH START SUCCESS

*Gail Z. Martin*
*Larry N. Martin*

DreamSpinner Communications
Charlotte, North Carolina

Cover Art: Vaughn Davidson
http://www.killercovers.com

Interior Design: Susan H. Roddey
http://www.shroddey.com

ISBN: 978.1.939704.35.1

Published by DreamSpinner Communications
Charlotte, North Carolina

# INDEX

# Welcome to Fresh Start Success!

How to use this book, who is in it, what you'll learn, how to apply it.

ARE YOU READY for a change? Or has change come looking for you? Whether you're initiating a big shift or reacting to an unexpected set of circumstances, you'll find plenty of ideas, inspiration, and possibilities in this book to help you design your own Fresh Start Success.

Within these pages, you'll meet forty-one people who made successful big changes in their lives and work. They come from all different industries and career paths, following a wide variety of interests, and redefining "success" for themselves along the way. They hail from all over the world, represent a range of ages, and came to the decision to make a change in their own unique ways, but every single one found success from following his or her passion.

Our Fresh Start Success profiles include Katana Abbott, Amber Allen, Christine Bové, Debbi Dachinger, Melissa Darnay, Teresa de Grosbois, Jo Dibblee, Barbara Edie, Sheri Fink, Dawn Fleming, Marla Goldberg, Tamara Green, Oksana Gritsenko, Christine Hassler, Steve Hobbs, EdD, Wendy Ida, Mike Jaffe, Lisa Jendza, Grace Kelly, Karen Kessler, Poonam Gupta-Krishnan, Lisa Manyon, Sharon McRill, Lisa Mininni, Faith Monson, Sheevaun Moran, Loriann Oberlin, Debbie Peterson, Lauren Brett Randolph, Danielle Ratliff, Sherri Richards, Cha~zay Sandhriel, PhD, LeeAnn Shattuck, Pierette Simpson, Susan Sklar, MD, Gail Watson, Patryk Wezowski, Lisa Woodie, and Wendy Woodworth. We round that number out to forty-one since we made our own big personal and professional reinventions, and the experience sparked our interest in finding how other people coped with change and reimagined their lives and work.

We asked each person we profiled the same set of questions and were fascinated with the similarities and differences in their answers. Each person followed his or her own path, and you'll get the behind-the-scenes stories complete with triumph and tragedy, and our experts share what they learned the hard way. If you take nothing else away from this book (but you will, we promise), please remember that the path to reinvention rarely runs straight or smoothly. Challenges, unknowns, set-backs, and detours are part of the journey, but persistence is the key to Fresh Start Success.

Your own path will be unique, but look for similarities between your own journey and those of the successful reinventors in this book. You're likely to find ideas to help you envision your own big shift, encourage you through rough times, and think big about the possibilities that lay before you. Each of the profile chapters is framed with an introduction and a "take-away" section to share insights we gained in getting to know these amazing entrepreneurs. While their individual paths may have differed, the true power of their stories shines through the commonalities. Let them be your inspiration as you chart your own course toward a successful reinvention.

# Change is Uncomfortable

## Gail Z. Martin and Larry N. Martin

EVERY TIME WE tell an audience that "change is uncomfortable," Gail thinks of the parakeet her friend Lorraine used to own. Lorraine's parakeet was very tame. She would let it out of its cage, and it could fly around the house. One day, the parakeet landed on the floor in the middle of the kitchen. Lorraine's springer spaniel swallowed the bird in one gulp.

In the next instant, Lorraine's teenage son dove across the kitchen and tackled the dog, giving it the Heimlich Maneuver. Up came the parakeet—alive and unhurt—but looking rather bedraggled and confused.

Change often makes us feel a lot like Lorraine's parakeet.

Today's work environment is constantly changing, making us feel bedraggled and confused, especially when the shifts send us into unknown territory. The trick to making a Fresh Start Success is to learn how to make those changes work for you.

What do we mean when we say "change"? In our parents' and grandparents' generations, people often retired after working for the same company for thirty years. Now, the average time in a job is around two years. Just a few years ago, the average person made seven job changes in a lifetime—now, that's up to thirteen. That's a whole lot of change going on.

For the purposes of this book, let's define what we're counting as a change. Maybe it's getting a new job with a new company. That's a big change. But getting a promotion or making a lateral move—especially from one division or department to another within the same organization—is also a big change. Getting reassigned to a different manager or project is a change. Relocating—either as part of your job, or to get a job, or for personal reasons—is a change. Leaving or returning to the workforce for health or family reasons is a change.

And then there are life changes—marriage and divorce, giving birth or adopting, having a sick child, hitting the empty nest phase, taking care of older parents or a sick partner, facing a health challenge—lots of "changes" that affect your work life. The strategies we cover might provide insights that are the difference between being able to leap nimbly from change to change or being snowed under.

There's a powerful skill that lies at the heart of dealing with change. It's the ability to reinvent yourself and reimagine your future. That reinvention skill determines your personal brand and your expert platform, and it's the secret behind taking control of your career future.

## Gail's Story

Gail learned about the power of reinvention in her own life the hard way. She earned her MBA and worked for corporations for seventeen years, and she'd been a vice president of corporate communications several times over. A Fortune 10 company hired her to head up a web marketing department. But then the industry hit a downturn, and the budget got cut and the sponsor got reassigned, and in the winter of 2002, Gail was one of close to 400 people who got a pink slip right before Christmas.

"You can't really put a smiley face on that. In fact, when I called Larry to tell him I'd been laid off, before I'd said more than his name, he picked up on the stress in my voice," Gail says.

"I worked with an outplacement counselor while I interviewed and looked at options. And I realized a couple of things. First, I realized that every aptitude test I'd ever taken had said I should be an entrepreneur, and I had ignored them," Gail recalls. "And secondly, I had to admit that I had the skills needed to make that leap." In fact, it didn't take long before Gail's corporate colleagues were calling her to hire her back for projects, and pretty soon, she had a profitable consulting practice. DreamSpinner Communications was born.

Gail kept busy writing all kinds of business brochures, magazine articles, and video scripts, along with consulting. But there was something missing. "I wanted to write fantasy adventure novels," Gail says. "That had been my dream since I was fourteen years old. Every time I went into a bookstore, I would go to the fantasy aisle and find where the George R. R. Martin books were and move them over to the side, just enough to put my hand in the place where my book would sit. I would close my eyes and picture putting my hand on the spine of my very own novel."

So she decided that part of taking control of her career would be making that dream come true. The book was written. She'd been working on it for years, and every time life got busy, the manuscript would go back in a drawer, but she always came back to it. Gail would work on it before dawn on Saturday mornings and after the kids went to bed. It was finally ready. She found an agent who landed the book with a publisher in London. A year later, her first novel, *The Summoner,* came out internationally and sold so well, it went back for a reprint in just two months.

"I had a book and a publisher, but I wanted to use my marketing experience to help the books succeed. Social media was new, and I taught myself how to use it because my publisher and many of my readers were in the UK, and I wanted to be able to connect and engage with people no matter where they were located," Gail recalls. Gail used social media to reach out to readers, reviewers, and bloggers all over the world, which helped her find her raving fans. "Other authors and publishers started asking me what I was doing, and if I tell them how to do it because it was working."

That got Gail thinking about how she could teach her marketing clients about social media and put what she had learned with her fiction books to use on the other side of her professional life. Ultimately, that led to contracts to write several marketing books about social media and online marketing, as well as to webinars and international speaking engagements around social media marketing.

"The idea of professional reinvention is near and dear to my heart because I've done it numerous times, and I've helped others communicate their reinvention successfully," Gail says. "We're constantly reinventing both DreamSpinner Communications and our fiction series, since every new book and new series is a completely fresh start. I enjoy using what I've learned the hard way to help others make an easier transition."

## Larry's Story

Larry Martin had no idea of what he wanted to be when he grew up, but he assumed he would work in business. His parents owned their own company, and he just assumed "that's what people do." He spent a couple years working in retail after graduating with a bachelor of arts in business and saved up enough to go back to graduate school for his MBA "It was the thing to do if you wanted to be successful in business. I went back to my college advisors and they all said the same—get your MBA—and so I did," he says, looking back. "I really loved marketing and advertising, so that's what I pursued and I was fortunate to get into a young, growing software company."

The company was doing a lot of mergers and acquisitions, which gave Larry the opportunity to try out new areas, and before long, he moved from sales support to finance. Responsibilities changed regularly, and the job was never the same two years in a row. A hostile takeover ended a great run, and because it happened during an economic downturn, Larry and Gail decided they had no choice but to consider relocating.

A friend and former co-worker saved the day. He'd joined a fast-growing financial services company, and they needed help. A new chapter began in a new city, and things were looking up—and then came the next buyout. Yet again, Gail and Larry decided to move for his job. Fortunately, it worked out well, but three companies and three states in three years (with small children in tow) was taxing.

Larry was in the corporate fast lane. The new financial services company was growing and changing rapidly. Mergers, acquisitions, and travel added to Larry's responsibilities in finance and operations. But after surviving so many mergers, corporate life was starting to take a toll. "My staff used to get scared when I came in wearing a dark suit, especially if my human resources business partner was with me, because they thought it meant layoffs. They joked that I was the Grim Reaper," Larry recounts. "But sadly, that's how it often felt. Not usually for my own teams, but for the companies acquired—absolutely."

"There were aspects of my job that I absolutely loved, and I had a tremendous and very talented team," he remembers. "We always hired with the mantra: pick someone who can be your replacement. Coaching and development of our teams was a priority. However, corporate politics and turf wars wear you down." Fortunately for Larry, one of his senior managers saw an opportunity and recommended that he become a diversity consultant—helping the enterprise build an inclusive environment for its team members.

"It was a tough and yet rewarding experience," Larry says. Though the position was in addition to his normal day-to-day responsibilities, it gave him the opportunity to coach and assist leaders and their teams. "It kept me going as the company hit some hard times and the politics, cost-cutting, and efficiency exercises went into overdrive." But, in hindsight for Larry, it was the beginning of the end—those were the indicators things were falling apart, and change really hit when the company, a top bank, was bought.

"It was a tough period and one that made Gail and me sit back and re-evaluate," Larry says. The acquiring company did not plan on keeping the diversity initiative, and Larry's job was split between multiple divisions. "While they wanted me to look within, the company's culture was very different, and it likely meant relocation—again. We sat down as a family and talked about possibilities." The children (who were, by then, in or nearing high school) didn't want to move and really wanted Larry to leave the company. Up to this point, they had always given his job and its demands priority. It was time for a shift.

Larry and Gail had always planned for him to come into the marketing and writing business at some point, and they decided that maybe now was the time. The business had reached the point where it needed both of them to take it to the next level. So, with a little trepidation and a lot of prayers and planning, they took the plunge, and Larry became a partner in both the coaching/consulting as well as the writing.

The reinvention was learning how to take the training in diversity consulting and the experiences of being a senior manager for more than twenty years and applying those lessons to small businesses and entrepreneurs—and doing it without all the systems and staff of a corporation to help. Now, after having a few years under their belt, Larry and Gail are doing more than twice as much as they did before. As part of the shift, Larry took a number of classes and got to add some creative pieces to his work, giving him a better balance in life. In his corporate days, Larry sometimes traveled fifty percent of the time, while Gail chose jobs without travel. With the books, Gail often is on the road while Larry keep things on an even keel at home.

## The Take-Away

Reinvention is often incremental and evolutionary. The vision you have for your new business or the outgrowth of your passion is likely to change as you learn, grow, and test the waters. Your audience's tastes may shift, or the economy may push you to expand, refocus, or branch into other streams of income. Don't fight it: embrace the opportunities. You may well find that the path you didn't plan to take turns out to be the best of all!

# Reinvent, Grow, Repeat

CAREER SUCCESS IS all about reinvention, which creates your personal branding and expert platform.

But here's a secret: you don't always get reinvention—or branding—right on the first try.

Gail's friend Alex learned this lesson from a golden retriever named Ralph.

Alex lived in a nice suburban neighborhood, and when he let Ralph out in the morning, Ralph would jump the fence and not come back until he had retrieved all of the neighbors' newspapers. That was cute the first time, but pretty soon, it got to be a problem. As fond as Alex was of Ralph, he thought maybe Ralph would do better with a little more room to roam.

He found a great home for Ralph with a friend who had a farm out in the country and no newspapers around for miles. But… the farmer had a pond filled with turtles. Ralph soon decided it was fun to swim out and retrieve the turtles and then bring them to shore and flip them over. Before long, the Fish and Wildlife ranger was unhappy with Ralph's turtle "hobby."

Alex and the farmer decided that since Ralph was so smart, maybe he should work for law enforcement and be a drug-sniffing dog. They got Ralph an interview with the FBI and the DEA. When Ralph's big day came, they both took Ralph to where the agents would put him through different scenarios. Finally, the DEA agent came out with the news. On one hand, Ralph had proven that he could sniff out drugs in every package. But… Ralph was such a friendly dog, he wouldn't turn anyone in. He washed out as a narc. In the end, they found Ralph a great home on a farm without any turtles or newspapers, and he lived a long and happy life.

Sometimes it takes more than one try to get your branding right. That's okay. Keep at it until you find your sweet spot.

Our company, DreamSpinner Communications, is more than a decade old. Gail began doing project work for her former corporate colleagues. A lot of that involved writing marketing plans and managing projects like annual reports, in-house publications and media, as well as writing freelance articles for local, regional, and national magazines. But the market was changing, and that meant our focus had to change. Gail's success using social media with her fiction books led to the publishing contracts to write several books about social media and online marketing.

Those books led to new opportunities which included writing articles for magazines and blogs, speaking for live events and webinars, and coaching individual clients. As social media has evolved, our work has taken us toward enabling other "corporate refugees" to find their own Fresh Start Success and develop their personal branding and expert platforms, using social media to widen their influence. It's continual reinvention.

## The Take-Away

Reinvention isn't a once-and-done occurrence—it's continual. Over the years DreamSpinner Communications has been in business, our work has shifted as the market changed. In some years, magazine editing and writing magazine articles were big parts of what we did—under Gail's byline and for clients. In other years, consulting and ghostwriting took the majority of our focus, then live events speaking about social media, then books. Being nimble means changing to meet what the market needs.

Don't let that scare you. After all, if you were working in a job for someone else, your job description and daily tasks would change over time, too. The company might be bought or merged, and you'd get moved to a new boss or a new division. Creating a Fresh Start Success doesn't insulate you from change, but it *does* give you control over *how* you change and which direction you go.

As you create your own Fresh Start Success, chart your course, but realize that you're likely to hit some detours along the way!

# Five Essential Steps to Fresh Start Success

THE PEOPLE PROFILED in this book came from different careers and found their path to reinvention in different ways, but there was one thing they all agreed on: marketing was a key element in their success.

Realize that "marketing" is actually a different way of saying "communication." Does that make you feel better? Put the idea of hard-sell infomercial spokespeople out of mind. That's not what we're talking about. When we say "marketing," we're covering a wide range of activities that can include social media, newsletters, in-person conversations, networking (in-person or online), speaking to groups, direct mail, traditional advertising, public relations, video, and more.

What's essential is that you find a way to do two very important things: redefine yourself to the world, and create a personal brand to stand out and be remembered. Creating a personal brand will take you a long way toward getting colleagues, customers, and the media to see you in a new light.

So how do you do it? Glad you asked!

## Step One: Identify the Change

Who do you want to be now that you've grown up? Do you want to keep working in your area of expertise, but for a different industry? For yourself? For a not-for-profit? Or do you want to build on your skills and experience and do something entirely different?

If you aren't clear about who you are becoming as you reinvent yourself, no one else will know, either. They'll either continue to see you as "Joe, who used to do such-and-such," or "Joanna, who is thinking about her options."

Maybe you left your old job with a long-desired change of direction already clear in your mind. Perhaps you've been saying "no" for a long time to an internal voice that's been trying to lead you in a particular direction, and now you're starting to listen and consider alternatives. Or you might have a clearer idea of what you don't want to do than what you're passionate about doing. That's okay—thinking things through is a natural part of the Fresh Start process. But before you can more forward, you need to have an inkling about the direction you want to go.

Think about it this way: An international airport has flights to hundreds of cities all over the world. You could get on any plane and end up in any one of those places. But odds are, some destinations will suit you better than others, and all destinations are not created equal. You've been to some places before and don't need to go back. You might like to revisit others or find new places with similar charms. Some don't attract you at all. But you can't go anywhere until you pick a destination and buy your ticket.

So… where is your reinvention "ticket" going to take you?

Once you have a destination in mind (in other words, a fairly clear idea of what kind of work you want to do and the type of structure—corporate, not-for-profit, self-employed—you want to do it in), you can start moving toward it. As long as you have a clear destination in mind, don't worry yet if you aren't sure exactly how to get there. That's what nav systems are for—and this book is your Fresh Start Success GPS.

## Step Two: Communicate the Change

So you've picked your destination. Great! Now it's time to shift people's perception of you. That's important because if they don't know you've made a change or can't see you in a different light, they can't help you succeed.

There's a reason for stereotypes and pigeon-holes. They are ways our brains categorize people in our mental map of the me-centered universe. "Bob the accountant," "Jane the teacher," "Bill the dentist," "Anna the engineer"—these are all short, easy ways we keep straight all the hundreds of people we meet and know. Stereotypes come in when we create a one-size-fits-all description of what someone who is in a certain job or profession is like. "Accountants are risk-averse and detailed-oriented" or "IT people like to solve problems and are introverts"—you probably could fill a page with your own version of professional stereotypes if you gave it some thought.

Have you ever considered how the people you know have already pigeon-holed and stereotyped you?

Just for fun, ask your significant other, your best friend and a former colleague to tell you how they'd introduce you professionally to someone you didn't know. It's usually an eye-opening experience. Odds are, if that's the way people who know you well see you professionally, your business acquaintances, neighbors, social friends, and club buddies have an even fuzzier grasp on what you do.

Now that you know how people view you after years—or half a lifetime—in your prior job or career, your task is twofold: to get them to understand the change you're making and to be able to articulate it clearly, briefly, and accurately so they can tell others (correctly) what you do and thereby help you make connections to succeed. Fuzzy introductions like "Joe's a great guy—you should talk to him sometime" aren't as powerful as "Joe knows more about supply chain processes than anyone in the city. I bet he could help you with what you need."

Other people won't come up with those great descriptions on their own. You have to communicate your new preferred description of yourself to them.

Remember when we said this book includes forty-one Fresh Start Success stories of reinvention? There's a reason for the story-telling format. Stories are powerful teaching tools. People are hard-wired to listen to and remember stories. Stories stick. That's why a crucial part of creating your Fresh Start Success is learning to tell your own story in a powerful way. Tell people who you were and who you are now. Let them know what's changed and what you create for them in your new role.

Tell us how you got where you are now and what you learned, saw, and overcame. Your story differentiates you because no one else has exactly the same story you do. Because of your story, you'll resonate more with people who are a good fit for you to work with, attracting the right kind of clients, partners, and team members. Your story reinforces your expertise and is an essential part of building your brand.

Use your story to communicate the change you're making and shift the way others remember you and what you do.

## Step Three: Demonstrate the Change

Start to live your Fresh Start Success in public. Go to networking events in your field and introduce yourself with your new specialty (and your new business card). Join the professional associations and business groups for your type of business. It will feel strange at first, especially if you spent many years in your former role and your old position was a big part of your personal identity. But as you slip into this new person you're becoming, repetition will make it easier to represent your new self to others (and see yourself in a new light).

Make sure your online persona matches your reinvention. Do you have a website for your new business? How does it represent you and what you offer? Have you updated your Facebook, Twitter, and LinkedIn profiles to accurately reflect who you are now and what you're doing?

Social media sites are a key way to demonstrate the change you've made. Tweet about the business events you're attending. Take a photo of yourself at the event with one of the speakers or other colleagues and post it to Facebook, mentioning where you are, who you're with, and what it means to your business. Use LinkedIn to let others know what conferences and business events you'll be at so you can meet for coffee. When you meet someone at one of these events and have a great conversation, connect on LinkedIn and Facebook to keep that acquaintance warm. Traveling for business? Snap some photos of city landmarks, the airport, or your hotel and talk about where you are and what you're doing.

As people see you living out your Fresh Start Success, they will start to transition you from their old mental pigeonhole to a new one more in line with who you are becoming. Of course, what you choose to post, comment on, retweet, and link to should all be carefully curated to put your best online foot forward. Gail covers creating an effective, no-stress social media strategy in more detail in her book *30 Days to Social Media Success*.

Blogging is another great way to demonstrate the change you're making. A well-written and frequently updated blog can be a cornerstone of your expert platform, sharing information that establishes you as a knowledgeable subject matter expert. Share the link to your blog posts on LinkedIn, Facebook, and Twitter to drive traffic to your site. Embed the blog link in your web page so it automatically updates there, too.

The key here is to provide visual evidence that you are in the process of becoming the "new you." You are always on display, so anticipate that and make it work for you.

Part of demonstrating your change is creating a personal brand that sets you apart as you establish yourself in your new area of expertise. A brand is the intentional creation of a mental pigeonhole so that your customers remember you in the way you want to be remembered.

Think of the most famous brands in the world: Coca-Cola®, Nike, Apple, Microsoft, Google, and more. When you read those company names, I'm betting that you immediately saw their logo, thought of their tag-line, and perhaps heard their signature song. In other words, they have successfully created a mental pigeonhole in your mind and crafted your memory of them in the way they want you to remember them. Pretty smart, huh?

Now think of their competitors. In most cases, I bet that if any branding for the also-rans comes to mind, it isn't as clear or immediate. That might be part of the reason they're the competitor and not the top dog.

What is your personal brand? Think about what you do the most, what you're good at, who you work best with, and what you'd want to do more of. Then add one more thing: what outcome do you produce? Put those together, and you have the beginning of a personal brand.

## Step Four: Live the Change Consistently

How do you prove your Fresh Start Success is the real deal? Consistency. Show us day-in and day-out that you're who you say you are and that you're making steady progress on your Fresh Start Success goals.

That's why it's so important to be consistent, both in how frequently you post on social media and in what you say. Let me break those two ideas down because they're related and important.

No one likes to be stood up for an appointment. That's what it feels like when someone who is interested in learning more about you, going deeper into your content, or connecting with you personally, goes to your Facebook page or your blog and finds out you haven't been there in months. They made the effort to show up—and you've got to show up, too.

That doesn't mean you have to create all your own content all the time. Invite guest bloggers to send you posts related to your blog's theme. Retweet and repost links to interesting articles, events, and photo quotes by other people. But be present on a regular basis so that your consistent commitment enables other people to feel they can rely on you and that you're serious about your new focus.

Consistency in what you say is also a big part of building your online tribe. Your "tribe" is made up of the people who come back time and again because they want to hear what you have to say. Curate your topics and tone with care. Every interaction either adds to or detracts from your personal branding. Avoid rants—political or otherwise. They won't change the situation, and they can easily alienate people on issues that have nothing to do with your core business. It's not worth it. Be your best self on social media because you never know who is watching, and what you say and do in cyberspace lasts forever.

## Step Five: Keep On Changing

There's no such thing as standing still anymore. The world is changing fast. Reinvention never stops. Updating your personal brand and your expert platform never ends.

You are never too old to reinvent yourself. One of the people who made a huge impact on my life was my high school history teacher, Mr. G. He wasn't the average teacher. He had attended—and dropped out of—that same high school when he was a teenager. He enlisted in the army and retired with the rank of colonel. Then he took the GI benefits and went to college to become a teacher. And just like that old *Welcome Back Kotter* TV show, Mr. G. came back to the same school where he'd been a drop-out to teach and inspire a new generation.

But that wasn't the end of the story. Two years after I graduated, Mr. G retired from teaching and decided to fulfill a lifelong dream… he went to law school at age sixty-five.

## The Take-Away

You are never too old to reinvent yourself and take control of your career! Not only that, but you can keep on reinventing yourself and creating new Fresh Start Successes all through your life. The remarkable people profiled in this book made their big change at all different ages, from late thirties into their sixties and beyond. Many succeeded at several careers before making this latest shift, reinventing themselves as their interests and life circumstances evolved.

Don't get hung up over your age, your past, or what others may or may not think. This is your life—seize the opportunities!

# Pitfalls on the Way to Fresh Start Success

As you reinvent your work and reimagine your life, you'll find some potential pitfalls and potholes in the road to Fresh Start Success. Here's your "road map" to avoid some of the most common things that trip people up as they create their reinvention.

## Four Common Pitfalls and Platform Problems

The first pitfall is an **unclear platform**; people aren't sure who you are or what you do. This can happen in several ways. If you haven't been clear about making a big change, people who have known you for a while personally and professionally may still have you mentally pigeonholed in your old area of expertise. The quickest way to fix this is to be loud and proud about what you're doing now, in person and on social media.

The second platform problem can be that **people know you for too many things** and can't get a mental fix on what you do. Have you ever met someone at a networking event who tells you that he/she is a coach and a Reiki healer and sells jewelry and has a line of nutritional supplements? You walk away with a mental blur because you don't know how to classify the person in your memory, which means you aren't likely to remember him or her for anything. The easiest fix is to pick your target audience and limit yourself to being known for one thing with each group if you have multiple businesses or multiple unrelated streams of income. So be a coach at coaching events, a healer at holistic events, a jewelry salesperson at weekend craft shows, and a supplement dealer at health fairs. If you have individuals who get to know you in one venue and express an interest in something else you do, then by all means, tell them about your "secret identity."

The third pothole is a **lack of evidence**. Have you demonstrated your new expertise publicly and online? If there's nothing to back up the "new you" platform—e-book, audio, video, testimonials, case studies, etc.—then it isn't "real." Fortunately, this is also easy to fix. Blog about topics that provide insight into your approach and mindset. Ask every customer to give you a testimonial. Pull your best blog posts together into an e-book. Do a video series highlighting key tips on how to do something better. The possibilities are easy and endless.

The fourth and final way to trip up is by **leaving your reputation to chance**. Have you Googled yourself lately? You might be surprised—pleasantly or unpleasantly—to see what's out there linked to your name. Not showing up at all is a bad thing—people need to be able to find out about you. Googling should lead to your website, blog, Facebook posts, videos, and other sites. But you might find that you share a name with a *nogoodnik*, and you definitely want to make sure your audience knows you're not that person. Or you may find that something negative posted years ago is still floating around near the top of the search results. Creating more recent content will push that back into history where it belongs. But it all begins by taking ownership of your online reputation.

Gather recommendations and endorsements on LinkedIn. LinkedIn is one of the first places people go to check you out, so make sure what they find there is current and put your best online foot forward. Connect with former colleagues and accumulate recommendations from prior positions, and encourage new clients to endorse and recommend you in your brand new role. Build up your LinkedIn connections by inviting new people into your circle when you've made a good connection. Be generous in endorsing and recommending others. And use your status updates to share links to your latest blog posts, videos, and new projects. Help people see the "new you" you want them to remember.

Finally, manage your reputation by telling your own reinvention story. Talk about the choices you made, the reasons you've made a shift, and how what you're doing now pulls together threads from your life experience that might not be obvious to others. Stories are more memorable than data, so tap into the power of your personal story—like the forty-one stories of awesome people in this book—to celebrate and share your own Fresh Start Success.

## The Take-Away

Every one of the people profiled in this book agreed that marketing is essential to a successful reinvention. The ways they market their businesses and the audiences they seek may vary, but there was no dispute over the importance of intentionally shaping how people perceive you and your new venture. Remember, if you don't define yourself, someone else will, and they are likely to get it wrong! Take control of your message, and use it to shape your Fresh Start Success.

# The FRESH System to Help You Rock Your Reinvention

CREATING YOUR OWN Fresh Start Success is exciting and frightening, both at the same time. There are plenty of unknowns, and it's easy to focus on the risk. Or, it's tempting to be so entranced by the opportunities and possibilities that you might downplay serious concerns. The best course is in between those two extremes, but as logical as that sounds, most people on the road to reinvention swing back and forth from day to day.

Here's a simple acronym to keep you on track: FRESH

- **F**ind your passion
- **R**e-think your skills and look for how they can be re-purposed for your new career
- **E**xperiment to find the right message and the ideal audience tribe; then expand your offerings to meet demand
- **S**tart building your platform, branding, and audience right away
- **H**ave systems in place so you don't need to stress over basic business functions

## Find Your Passion

Don't be so focused on security that you trade one prison for another. Take a good look at the parts of your old job that made you feel alive, and the parts you hated. Inventory what you love to do, including lifelong hobbies and interests. Don't be quick to decide that "I can't make a living from that." You'd be surprised how determined reinventors have found ways to marry their passion to their profession when they get the chance to design their future.

If you're not sure what your passions are (and if you've been denying them for a long time to fit the corporate mold, you might need to be reminded), ask the people who know you best. Odds are, they'll have ideas on the tips of their tongues based on what they've seen you enjoy and gravitate toward. Listen closely without dismissing anything. Make a list. Let your subconscious percolate on ideas. Investigate the kinds of careers associated with different traits and interests.

Even if you can't figure out how to fit all your favorite things into your new job, don't make the mistake of shoving those interests back into the mental closet. This is your Fresh Start Success. Make time for what matters most to you. Have you always loved performing but didn't want to be an actor? That same skill set can be honed to make you a dynamite motivational speaker or video presenter. Enjoy photography but don't want to make it your livelihood? Volunteer to take photos at conferences and events (where plenty of interesting people will come looking for you for a photo), or turn your "pretty pictures" into backgrounds for quote memes to promote yourself and your business on social media. Whatever your passion, look for ways to incorporate it into your new career. You'll be happier and healthier if you follow your heart.

## Re-think and Repurpose

Stop and take an inventory of your skills. That can include computer proficiency, specialized training and testable abilities, as well as "soft skills" like being good with people, having excellent organizational abilities, or a knack for hiring good people. Don't judge whether you think a skill is valuable or not—if you're good at it, write it down.

Next, note which skills you're good at and enjoy, and which ones you can do well but hate doing. This is your reinvention, so you want to maximize using the skills you enjoy and minimize using the ones you don't enjoy (even if you're good at them). Things you don't like doing should be the first to be delegated at the earliest opportunity. You'll be happier, and the tasks will get done better and faster by someone who actually likes to do them.

Now look at your list and think about how you can re-use, re-think, and re-purpose your skills to support your Fresh Start Success. For example, skill doing budgets for your department has direct carryover to setting up spreadsheets to track your expenses and income. Speaking skills honed at corporate meetings might pave the way to incorporating training or motivational speaking into your new career. No skill is ever wasted! Look for ways to make the most of everything you've learned from your prior experience.

## Experiment

There's a picture on Facebook that shows two lines. One rises in a straight line diagonally from the bottom left corner to the top right corner. It's marked, "What people think success looks like." The other is a squiggly tangle with a line that backtracks and goes in circles and wobbles all around but gradually rises to the same height. It's marked, "What success really looks like."

That's a good message to keep in mind as you create your Fresh Start Success. You will have days with brilliant breakthroughs and days of disappointing setbacks. It will feel like "two steps forward, one step back." That's how it goes. Just remember, a bad day of being in charge of your own future is better than a good day of being at the mercy of someone else's agenda.

The best way to build as straight a line as possible toward the success you want is by being open to experimenting. Start with an idea of your best message, based on the benefits and results you produce. Try it out on people. Ask for their feedback. Ask clients what they think the biggest benefit was from working with you. You might be surprised that what others identify and value is completely different from what you thought it would be. Try out two different messages to different audiences simultaneously and see which gets a better response. Direct marketers refer to this as "A-B testing," and it's the best way to refine headlines, content, and offers—based on repeated experimentation.

Revise your message and retry it until you've got something that resonates and moves your listeners to action. It's safe to say that no one gets it right on the first try and that the impact of a message can change as the market

31

changes, so even a brilliant message will need to be updated periodically to remain resonant.

Do you think you know your ideal audience? Here's another place where experimenting is essential. Go after that first audience, and see how it works. Are they as interested as you expected? Can they pay for the services they want? Are they motivated to take action? If the audience isn't quite right, experiment by presenting to different groups, attending a variety of networking events, and participating online with people from all different professional backgrounds. You may discover that your real ideal audience is a group you never would have thought of but who desperately needs what you have to offer and is ready to move forward. Changes in the economy can shift your ideal tribe over time, so continue to experiment to bring in new people from new areas.

Don't be afraid to experiment with product and service offerings to find what your audience wants. Digital production reduces the cost and risk of creating e-books, webinars, and online events to help you stoke interest and gauge response. Some will succeed beyond your wildest dreams, while others will fizzle. That's okay. You'll learn something from each foray that will make the next one even better. Even when you find your breakout hit, realize that you'll have to keep innovating (that's another word for "experimenting successfully") to keep from becoming outdated.

Experimentation is the lifeblood of successful reinvention. Embrace it as a key to your own Fresh Start Success.

## Start Building

Today is a good day to start building your expert platform, branding, and credibility. Right now is the perfect time to begin attracting an audience, exploring resources, networking professionally, and asking for references.

Whether you're planning to start your business tomorrow from scratch or ramp it up gradually part-time, it takes longer to get pieces in place than anyone ever expects. All of these areas are essential for success, and they lend themselves well to gradual evolution.

Your expert platform is made up of the knowledge and results on which you are staking your professional claim. What are you best at doing to create amazing results for your clients? Help others get to know you and appreciate your knowledge through blogging; writing articles for professional magazines; being interviewed on radio, TV, and specialty-topic podcasts; and speaking to business audiences. You'll simultaneously build credibility and get your name known, while attracting an audience you can invite to remain in touch by subscribing to your newsletter, following you on social media, attending your events, and reading your blog.

Branding goes hand-in-hand with your expert platform since it's the way your audience will differentiate you from all the other experts out there in the same field. It can take a while to hit on the right logo and tagline to make yourself memorable and secure your "mental pigeonhole" in the minds of your audience, so start sooner rather than later!

As you gain experience, blog about what you have learned and talk about topics of interest to customers and colleagues. Create a Facebook business page and set up a Twitter account. Experiment with creating YouTube videos, and take a course or two if the idea of getting in front of a camera gives you the willies. Attend webinars and learn how to host them. Every opportunity to write a blog post or article, speak to a local group, or be interviewed on a radio show or podcast builds the content online that establishes and reinforces your expert credibility in your new field.

You'll need resources of all kinds, from materials to suppliers to online platforms and software. Now is a great time to begin identifying what you need and exploring your options. Do your research to get the best price and performance. Ask the people with whom you're networking for recommendations. Scout locations, read product reviews, do your homework. This is exciting because it's tangible evidence that you are making progress toward your reinvention goals. Due diligence is time-consuming but worth the effort, so start on this crucial piece as soon as possible.

Start asking people who know you for recommendations. Gather recommendations from people who work with you and with whom you've worked in prior positions. Have you held volunteer roles? Ask your volunteer coordinator to recommend you. Ideally, you'll want to document these comments on LinkedIn where everyone can see them. Since many people use LinkedIn as a professional networking tool while they're working for a company, this shouldn't seem awkward even before you make your move toward reinvention. People are busy, and even when people love your work, it can take longer than you'd think to get them to write you a recommendation, so begin the process early.

If you have the opportunity to get these crucial steps in the works before you have to step out into your new opportunity, you'll feel more confident and better prepared, and you'll shave time off the learning curve toward your Fresh Start Success. Reimagining your life is exciting, so dive in now!

## Have Systems

Systems aren't sexy, but they are essential. The sooner you put good systems into place, the fewer headaches you'll have down the line. It's a lot easier to build small systems right than to go back and retrofit them after they are larger and not working properly. Be sure to plan for success and build in scalability so that you aren't constantly needing to switch over to different software or systems with more capacity as you grow. If you're not a systems kind of person, hire someone. Bad systems will come back to bite you, and they can get you in big, expensive trouble.

No matter what kind of business you run, you'll need to have systems in place for accounts payable and accounts receivable. You'll need to track invoices and billing, handle payroll, administer benefits (even if you're a sole proprietor), and manage your time. Depending on what kind of business you have, you may also need to manage inventory or document version control, product and supply ordering, and lead generation and follow-up.

If you plan to hire help, even if it's part-time or virtual, you'll have human resources issues and at the least need to track wages for tax purposes. Odds are, you'll need a resource for handling computer problems and setting up your network. Every business needs resources for legal questions and accounting help, as well as handling taxes. Some industries also have mandated reporting that will require good tracking systems. And you'll need good calendar and filing systems or chaos will quickly ensue.

Plan how you'll handle marketing, social media, and public relations (PR) so they are executed consistently and professionally. Take a hard look at what you're good at and where you'll do much better hiring help. As the saying goes, there's never time to do it right, but there's always time to do it over!

Whether you plan to handle these issues yourself, hire help, or outsource, you'll have some work to do getting your systems set up. Don't wait. You can research providers and software before you make your jump and have everything ready to go when you flip the switch. Once you are hip-deep in alligators, you won't want to take the time to build systems, so do yourself a big favor and get them set up right from the start.

## The Take-Away

Embrace your Fresh Start Success by getting started right now. You can take action today to begin laying the foundation for your reinvention so that your transition will be smoother and less stressful and your learning curve will be less steep. By wading in before you have to sink or swim, you extend your ramp-up time before the clock is ticking. Anything you can do before you make a full-time switch will pay enormous dividends later when you're busy with day-to-day tasks.

Tackling these tasks can help build your enthusiasm for your "new you" and enable you to overcome fear and doubt through early, small successes. Every time you get positive feedback from a networking event, have an article published, or get good comments on a blog post, you are receiving reinforcement. Your dream is becoming reality. Ideas are taking shape and becoming tangible. Your reinvention is happening—and every step, no matter how small or how early in the process, takes you closer to Fresh Start Success.

People talk about "building the plane while you're flying it," and that's an apt description for the continual process of experimenting and reinvention, but any chaos you can avoid makes life that much easier and increases your chances for success. Your best bet for a problem-free flight is to "build your plane" to the best of your ability while you're on the ground, so you can enjoy the view once you're flying!

# Creating Your Own Fresh Start Success

YOU'RE READY FOR a change. What now? That depends on you and your circumstances—and the passion you want to follow. Based on the interviews in this book, our personal experience, and what we've learned from our coaching clients, we can offer some touchstones as you create your own, unique reinvention to help you succeed.

If you have the opportunity, **try before you dive in**. Look for opportunities to work on your dream part-time while you're still employed to see if you like the reality of the new role as much as you liked the idea. If it's right for you, experience will yield confirmation, even if you discover some unexpected obstacles along the way. On the other hand, if the reality of the work doesn't hold the appeal you expected, or you learn something new that fundamentally changes the attractiveness of the business opportunity, you can walk away and chalk it up to a learning experience.

**Talk to people** who are already doing what you think you want to do. Your best bet is to find people outside your market (who won't be tempted to consider you competition) and see if you can pick their brains. Ask what they learned the hard way, what surprised them, and what they wish they had known when they started. Find out how long it took them to become profitable, so you can factor that into your financial planning. Make sure you know what kind of investment you'll need to make in certifications, facilities, licensing, and equipment. Don't be afraid to find out what your interviewees love about their work and what drives them crazy. Make sure you can accept and deal with the common rough spots that go with the business because they're going to happen to you.

**Start networking now**. Attend industry conferences, subscribe to publications, read and comment on blogs, and join online professional groups related to the type of business you want to shift into. Not only will this begin to give you an unvarnished idea of what the realities of the business are like, but you'll also meet lots of people who can share their experiences, recommend resources, and help you shave off time spent in the school of hard knocks. Build relationships by being willing to give of your own expertise and be helpful without expectation of *quid pro quo*, and you're likely to build strong, mutually-beneficial relationships.

Professional networking takes time to create results. People need to get to know, like, and trust you before they make referrals or sign on as a customer. Expect to put time into becoming a known entity in the groups you join. Volunteer to help with events and behind-the-scenes roles. Be nice to everyone (that should go without saying, but it's important). You'll need several months of consistent commitment (at least) before your networking begins to pay off in a big way, so get started now!

**Learn.** Devour everything you can find about your new career. If you need to earn certification (or a whole new degree), now is the time to make the investment. Read blogs and professional magazines. Find a coach to help you with aspects that don't come naturally. Use this time to sharpen your skills and acquire new abilities. You'll need everything you've learned once your business takes off.

## Volunteer, Intern, Apprentice

Lots of professions sound glamorous, but what about the side no one sees? For example, speakers spend a lot of time traveling and in hotel rooms. They schlep their books and materials into conference rooms and sweat the details getting the audio and video set-up right, often at the last minute. Life is full of delayed flights, misprinted handouts, lost shipments, and laryngitis. Income is often unpredictable, especially in the early years. That's just one example, but the truth is universal. Every career has its dark side. If you truly love the work, you can live with the hard parts. If not, you'll be re-thinking your choices in short order and chalking it up as an expensive lesson.

You can reduce your risk by creating the opportunity to get an insider's look at the behind-the-scenes side of a business through volunteering, interning, or apprenticing. Look for a part-time job in a new field before you make the choice to buy or start a business. Get to know people who do that work for a living and ask what they love—and hate—about it. There's nothing like first-hand experience to validate your choice of reinvention—or steer you in another direction.

Look for a mentor in your new field who won't feel threatened by your success. Ideally, this would be someone who is still active in the business, so he or she knows the current economic environment, competitive threats, technological impacts, and regulatory issues. Even if you only have the chance to sit down for coffee or dinner once, you can learn a lot from someone who is already established in the field. Realize you're hearing one person's perspective, so if you hear something that really might change your mind, search for validation or insight from other sources.

Give first. Make giving back part of your reinvention by contributing your time and talent to help others make their own Fresh Start. Passion encompasses more than what you do for a living. Look at what kinds of charitable causes are close to your heart (preferably non-controversial, non-political causes to avoid alienating potential clients). Have you or someone you know had a health problem? Raising money for a cure might tie into your passion. Love animals? There are plenty of rescue and veterinary organizations to choose from. Want to change the world through clean water, access to economic opportunities, or reducing preventable disease? Make it part of your Fresh Start Success. You'll meet a wide variety of people, make a difference in the world, and be part of reinvention on a greater scale. Paying it forward always yields long-term benefits. Reimagine yourself as part of the solution.

What if you've been thrown into change without the opportunity to ease into your reinvention? The same steps in this chapter and the previous chapter still apply. You may be able to move through the steps more quickly because you can focus on them full-time. If you have to pick up part-time or transitional employment, you're back into building your future career in your spare time. Keep your eye on the future you want in order to create your own Fresh Start Success.

## The Take-Away

Preparation creates successful change. Don't leave anything to chance—dive in and learn. See it as the first test of your passion. Make it a priority to build relationships—those will be essential to your success. Give first by volunteering, helping others through your current expertise, and providing a signal boost on social media for experts you admire. If you find that your enthusiasm grows as you learn and meet people in your field, take it as confirmation that you're heading in the right direction.

# Keep What Works
## Gail Watson

FRESH START SUCCESS looks different for different people. For some, it means striking out in a whole new field, using skills or interests that the prior career didn't fully utilize, or which didn't take center stage. For others, it's a sidestep, shifting the focus from one area to another—like sales to event promotion, in Gail Watson's case. The key to remember here is that you are the architect of your own reinvention. How big a leap it is—or whether it's just a reprioritizing and subtle shift—is up to you and what brings *you* satisfaction.

Give yourself permission to create the Fresh Start Success that best suits your own interests, skills, talents, passion, background, and personal network. If you chose your first career in order to please your parents or mentors, pick a "secure" job, make a lot of money, or any other external factor, make this career about satisfying your soul as well as supplying your financial needs.

## It Chose Me

Gail Watson loved being in sales. She soon realized that she was a "thrill of the kill" type who loved working on one hundred percent commission, and she loved the thrill of the risk. Gail went into executive-level selling, and she earned a high six-figure income focused on products that she could introduce into Canada. She built her territory and was exceptionally successful, earning a seven figure income, with the addition of real estate, to her business portfolio.

"I'm really good at preparation and at learning new skills," Gail says. She didn't get a college degree, but she did take a lot of evening courses. She was adopted at birth by Scottish immigrants to Canada. Their example taught her about grit and hard work, as she saw her parents work at jobs they didn't want to do, but they had a strong fighting attitude and were highly empowered to go after their dreams. That "worker bee" mentality and a frugal lifestyle helped Gail later on, when she had her own tough choices to make. "I learned that you can do whatever you want to in your life—those words carried me through every day with a new perspective. I knew that my hardest day was nothing like what my parents had dealt with, and that helped me carry on," Gail recalls.

As she looks back on it, Gail liked products or services she could introduce that were brand new to the market. She enjoyed breaking down the doors of traditional thinking. That experience created a shift toward strong entrepreneurial thinking, but Gail didn't realize it at the time. "Entrepreneurship was the blood that was running through my veins," she says.

Gail was making a lot of money. Then her company bought the leading competitor, and as a result of the merger, she lost her job. It took her two years to recover from the blow to her ego because she took it personally. "Looking back, I realize that losing my job there was absolutely what I needed because I was caring for my mother, who had Alzheimer's," Gail recalls. She was in the Top 50 salespeople of her company one May and fired ninety days later, at the height of her mom's illness. "I do think that my responsibility for caring for my mother factored into the decision to fire me," Gail says.

Gail had always put money aside from her windfalls. She invested her cash and owned real estate, so she had a cushion when she was finally let go from corporate. But the biggest problem was overcoming the mental part of separation. "Someone in my network finally told me that it was okay to say 'fired,' and that made a huge difference," she recounts. "Once I could do that, I could start finding ways to turn a negative into a positive. Here's what's so sad—no one out there teaches you how to deal with something like this in advance. So you learn from the community, one person at a time. There is no community in corporate life; people just want you for your title."

"As for the next career, it chose me," Gail adds. A friend introduced her to the world of female small business owners with a company that promoted women's business networking groups across the United States and Canada. At that point in her life, Gail didn't even know what an entrepreneur was. "I started meeting these women who were brilliant, fantastic people with great ideas and a sense of freedom, and I started to build a community that had my back," she recounts. "In corporate, as an executive-level salesperson in one of the most aggressive areas, with hundreds of thousands of dollars in commissions riding on deals, your partner would often undercut you. In the entrepreneurial world, I found people standing together, sharing resources, helping each other. When life happens, nobody should go down." Entrepreneurs are community-driven, and Gail thrived in the discovery that she no longer had to be out on her own.

Gail saw that belief in action when she supported a friend with breast cancer who had been given a life-threatening diagnosis. "My friend said 'keep me busy,'" Gail says. "I committed to supporting her business by finding customers because I was going to see her through it." The friend recovered and came out of her health crisis with more business than she had before she got sick, thanks to Gail's resolve. "The community can get you through anything, and the community has the power to not let you fail," she says. "Everything improves outside of corporate life. The more you empower entrepreneurial attributes, so much is born from it. You've got access to anything you need from the community."

Some of the people Gail knew from her corporate days didn't understand the shift she had made, walking away from the big salaries and prestige of her prior sales jobs. "The naysayers figure value based on money," she says. "They were the people who didn't understand the idea that a job might not just be about chasing the dollars. It was the happiest I had ever been in my life, and I wasn't making a dime."

Gail was fired, so she didn't have a choice about timing her leap into her new Fresh Start Success. "It's better to choose your transition if you have the opportunity," she adds with a laugh. "That lets you work on it before jumping right in, if you have a choice. But at some point, you have to take the leap and ask yourself what you have to lose. I figured that if worst came to worst, I could always get another job."

"My husband saw me being so happy, and he was supportive. We were lucky; he was head of a concrete company and had a good nest egg," Gail recalls. Gail stayed with the women's networking group for several years, climbing the ranks and winning awards. But the entrepreneurial bug bit her again, and she began to long for something that was completely her own. Gail started an email marketing company and added a second business with a speakers' association for women five years later. She co-founded Women Speakers Association in 2011, committed to helping women express themselves authentically and step into leadership roles that inspire others.

Building her own dream came with some rough patches. "We drained some of that nest egg and lived off a line of credit," she admits. "There were some hard times financially, but we were willing to take the risk, and things started to turn around." Fortunately, Gail understands how to financially structure a company. "It's not a lemonade stand. No one teaches you how to wear multiple hats: you have to learn it on your own. Setbacks are part of the process. I decided that I'm going for it. I know it takes time to build up."

## The Take-Away

Gail chose to make a fairly radical shift, stepping away from a big-salary sales job. At the same time, she used many of the same skills in her new role that had propelled her to success in her former career. The difference: personal satisfaction, re-arranged priorities, and a new self-confidence that focused less on what other people thought and more on what she found to be important in life.

When you're creating your own Fresh Start Success, separate the skills you have from the job you had. Jobs come and go, but you retain skills forever. You are likely to find that the skills are versatile and can be applied to a wide range of potential new careers. Use your creativity to identify the right combination of interests, skills, and ideal clients to find—or create—your next career.

## Q&A with Gail Watson

**Q: How did you decide what was important to you in your Second Act?**
A: "I wanted sustainable income. Women Speakers Association created income

and impact. I really wanted to find a new way to help others succeed, and to shorten their timeline to success, to stay independent and let go of things that didn't work. Entrepreneurs are gifted with a spirit of sharing, and there is so much power from that collaboration that you don't get in corporate life, which is very restricted by comparison."

## Q: What did you learn the hard way?

A: "Getting fired was hard. I had put everything into my old job, handed over my identity to a public company that was all about the stock price. I had a nanny instead of taking six months off for my baby, and I traveled every two weeks. It wasn't until later that I realized that how a corporation treats people has the power to destroy. Never again will I sell my soul. I chose a lifestyle-driven business versus a business that drives my lifestyle, so I can be available for my kids."

## Q: To what do you attribute your Fresh Start Success?

A: "Support. My husband and kids empowered me to not go and get another job. They helped to make sound, smart choices about money. My biggest naysayer was myself. You have to have a commitment to yourself and learn to let go of what you think. It's not a failure if you have to supplement what you're doing with consulting."

## Q: How are you a different person? What did you learn?

A: "I learned that I am in control, I can create and see things through. I have a much stronger commitment than I thought I had, and I'm truly happy without faking it. I've learned that it's okay to ask for help: you don't have to know it all. I learn something new every day. Life can be fun, not like you're taught in school. Schools drive you into professions, but that's not necessarily what your gift is to do."

## Q: If you had a superpower, what would it be?

A: "I wish I could just have people stop and remove the resistance and pain and baggage that are holding them back. I wish I could give them that freedom."

**Q: What role has marketing and branding played in your success?**
A: "Marketing and branding have meant the world to my business. Women Speakers Association was only launched through my newsletter and blog posts and grew to five hundred members in only three weeks. It is absolutely critical to be in touch and engaged with your customer community. You have to build the community first and listen to their needs to create the brand promise. It's so important to remain in touch with the community because at the end of the day, your database is your number one asset."

# The Organizer
## Sharon McRill

SOMETIMES, AS THE saying goes, life is what happens while you're making other plans. When a twist of circumstance leaves you flat, start with what you know. One of the most empowering tools for making a Fresh Start Success is a list. Sit down with several clean pieces of paper, and make a list of all the things you're good at. What do you know how to do? Write it down.

Next, make a list of the things you enjoy doing. Don't censor yourself. If you like doing it, write it down. You're not going to show this to anyone. On the third list, make a list of the things you hate doing. Finally, make a list of the people you know who have specific expertise or connections who might be able to help you with various aspects of your Fresh Start Success. Now look at what you've created. In those lists is the sprout of your reinvention and the tools to help you get there.

## Organizing Chaos

Sharon earned a degree in general studies but had no idea what she wanted to do. She took a lot of English, film/video, and women's studies credits while in school, then decided she wanted to work at Borders Books' headquarters. "I banged on the door every week until they hired me," she says. At Borders, Sharon was hired to be a vendor liaison and helped buyers track shipments and purchase orders, handled special deals, and managed corporate accounts. She also was in charge of new media, CDs, video, and DVDs.

Borders as a chain got into financial trouble, and Sharon was downsized. By that point, she had been part of Borders' dot com group, which grew from five people to seventy in the time she worked for them. After being let go, she discovered the company had sold the website, which was a complete surprise to the employees. Although Sharon got a buy-out package and severance, she was very bitter for a while as she looked for a new job.

At first, Sharon wasn't interested in being an entrepreneur because she had seen her parents and grandparents run businesses and thought being self-employed seemed hard. She landed another corporate job, but it didn't last. At that point, she sat down and made a list of what she knew how to do and was good at, what she trained to do, what she didn't want to do. She liked project management, working with people, and simplifying things, so that was where she put her focus as she decided to create a company of personal organizers, which is now The Betty Brigade.

Sharon's company was a hit, helping people clean out their homes, pack up to move, and generally clear out clutter and organize their lives. She hired her first employee after eleven months in business but really wasn't sure what came next. "I had no idea how to grow my company," Sharon admits. "My parents and grandparents had bought existing companies, so I didn't know how to do that part."

She went looking for resources and received coaching from local entrepreneur groups. Then she created a volunteer board of directors as advisors. She bought them dinner on a quarterly basis and talked candidly with them about the business's numbers and the issues she faced. That's when she realized her company's growth was being slowed by her own difficulty letting go and delegating. "I didn't trust my staff to do it as well as I did, but they could actually do it better. Now I delegate like crazy," Sharon says.

Most of Sharon's family was very supportive of her shift to self-employment. She gave herself a year to make it work, using her unemployment benefits and severance. "I think my family initially underestimated the size of what I was doing," she reflects with a laugh. Other business owners were very supportive, and she found her tribe of like-minded entrepreneurs.

Sharon's work and planning paid off, and she broke even her first year. "That was shocking because of how much I didn't know," she admits. "We have a goal of thirty percent growth every year, and so far it has been reachable. Everything still goes back into the business because it's still growing. The big thing I'm working on is how to get new employees up to speed faster. I want to get them in gear in thirty days instead of ninety, so we hit profitability faster. Eventually, I'd like to license the business," Sharon adds.

Along the way, Sharon learned what was really important in her Fresh Start Success. "It has to do with who you are as a person," she says. "I wanted the company culture to reflect who I was as a person of service. I wanted to create a community of family, co-workers, and vendors. Every person you contact, you can be of service. Bring that commitment into your business and hire people who share it," she advises.

In 2013, Sharon was very proud that The Betty Brigade was able to donate more than $31,000 of unwanted items from clients. To put that in perspective, their donations included recycling forty-seven cubic yards (almost eight forty-yard dumpsters) of glass, plastic, metal, and paper. They also recycled household toxic waste like paint, cleaners, and unwanted medicine. Sharon enjoys finding unusual ways to recycle. For example, her people often find old fur coats that are unwearable because they were not stored properly. Sharon discovered a "Coats for Cubs" program that makes fur beds for rescued wild animal babies, which recover faster when nestled in real fur. Unwanted wigs are recycled for cancer patients.

"What can you do that helps the community at large?" Sharon asks. She encourages the staff to take part in volunteer activities every week. At the end of the month, the staff member with the most volunteer time gets a small prize, like movie tickets or candy.

As Sharon's vision has grown and she's become attuned to meeting customer needs, The Betty Brigade has grown, too. Her vision has expanded to include not only organizing and de-cluttering services, but also specialized corporate relocation assistance and other niche services.

## The Take-Away

Are you denying your inner entrepreneur? If all of your work experience has been in corporations or working for other people, you may view owning your own company as being "too scary" to contemplate. Maybe it's time to take a second look, especially if entrepreneurship creates the opportunity to use your gifts, follow your passion, and build the lifestyle you desire.

Entrepreneurship can be learned. Many colleges offer seminars and degree programs that cover all aspects of running a small business. Community colleges also offer workshops and courses on various aspects of being an entrepreneur, and so do many local business centers. Don't let fear of the unknown hold you back. Like Sharon, you might discover that your vision takes you to amazing places and grows into something much bigger and even more satisfying than you ever imagined.

## Q&A with Sharon McRill

**Q: What did you learn the hard way?**
A: "Paying taxes on time matters!"

**Q: To what do you attribute your Fresh Start Success?**
A: "Perseverance, hard-headedness, believing that failure was not an option. The staff supports what I'm trying to do and takes that out to the clients."

**Q: How are you a different person?**
A: "When I was in corporate life, I believed that the corporation owed me because they were big and I was small, that I didn't need to do extra. Now I entirely get the idea that I am a human on a big planet, and what I put out comes back, the more I am of service, the more I am kind, the more it comes back. In the end, it isn't about me. It's about clients and taking care of people, being a company they love to do business with."

**Q: What new skills or knowledge did you learn?**
A: "I learned how to be a leader. In the beginning, I didn't know what I didn't know. I developed patience. When you work with people, you need to be patient: not everyone gets it at the same speed. Now I focus on the team, building our community, managing our growth rate."

**Q: What did you learn about yourself?**
A: "The more vulnerable I am, the more I get what I really want. I need to show who I am as a human. I've learned that we need to be honest about the things we want in our lives."

**Q: What lessons from your old life helped prepare you for your Fresh Start Success?**
A: "I discovered that corporations are not all the same. There are ways to keep a business intimate and small even as it grows, which is what keeps people coming back. Borders had been more about profitability than people. But what I learned there made a difference. Project management, marketing, and learning how to treat people were all valuable lessons."

**Q: What traits are critical to your Fresh Start Success?**
A: "Really listening to what people want is important because they will tell you every time. In corporate life, it was more about me and what I got out of it, and less about listening. Now, the more I listen and reflect back so customers feel heard, the more they are open to different ideas."

**Q: If you had a superpower, what would it be?**
A: "I wish I could blink and be anywhere in the world instantaneously."

**Q: What advice would you give to someone considering making a change?**
A: "Pick something you love. Make sure it isn't a hobby, that it's something you can do for years and not get bored. The first two or three years are the hardest. There will be a lot of successes and failures, so learn from it. Failures have to happen."

**Q: What roles has marketing played?**
A: "It's been huge. We pitch the media about what we do, and I've been through media training to learn how to identify press opportunities. We're in a natural business for storytelling, and once or twice a month, the media runs

stories about the company. People read those stories and learn about us, but it's more credible because it's not traditional advertising. I'm constantly on social media, doing one or two posts daily, every day to stay visible. I keep it light, fun, professional. We also work with a web designer and a marketing expert to help us increase our online presence through our website, social media, search engines, and business review sites."

# Serial Entrepreneur
## Lisa Woodie

**OFTEN, IT TAKES** more than one try to find where you really belong. Many of the people interviewed for this book are serial entrepreneurs. They have owned more than one business, with varying degrees of success. Sometimes the market shifted or the economy changed, but in many cases, the entrepreneur realized that his or her passion and opportunity lay elsewhere.

To put it a different way—being good at something doesn't lock you in to having to do that type of work for the rest of your life. It's okay to be good at more than one thing and to "graduate" from running one kind of business into another. The work that satisfies you at one age may grow stale a decade or two later. The demands of one profession may become more than you want to put up with at a different stage in your life, and so you forge a new career better suited to your current needs.

As you're considering your Fresh Start Success, think about the jobs you've had, the roles you've played, maybe even the companies you've owned. What common traits did the best—and the worst—share? When you plan your next move, factor in the value of the experience you've gained from your prior entrepreneurial efforts, and put that self-knowledge to use as you map out your future.

## Cooking Up New Opportunities

Lisa Woodie earned a degree in journalism from the University of North Carolina at Chapel Hill, with a specialization in marketing and public relations. She spent the first half of her career in corporate and non-profit marketing, and as the owner of a marketing business.

Lisa found the creative and strategic planning part of marketing to be very satisfying. She liked starting with a challenge and coming up with a program to address the problem, and then seeing success. The variety kept the work fresh. What drove her crazy was the industry's volatility. When business was bad, companies laid off marketing people. Lisa had been with a major business newspaper, but when her boss retired and the paper got a new publisher during an economic slump, the new publisher laid off multiple staff members across many departments, including Lisa.

Lisa always loved to cook and enjoyed using her creativity in the kitchen. At one point, she left marketing to own and run a restaurant, only to discover that while she loved cooking, she didn't like running a restaurant. The day-to-day management issues took too much of her focus away from cooking.

Then, Lisa hit several life transitions in a row. After the layoff, her sister died, and her mother was diagnosed with terminal cancer. Lisa was the caregiver for both her sister and mother until they passed away. For a while, she went back to marketing, putting her marketing skills to use as a consultant, and she did some soul searching over her next move.

When Lisa began marketing a wellness company, the experience led her to research holistic nutrition, natural medicine, and environmental toxins. Health was uppermost in her mind, after her recent caregiving experience. Lisa decided to marry her interest in health with her love of cooking. Lisa considered going to culinary school, but decided against it because classic French/gourmet food wasn't a good fit for her business vision. She decided to explore becoming a personal chef and took a personal chef course at the local community college to see if it would be a good fit. Lisa was confident that between her prior entrepreneur experience and her marketing background, she had what it takes to run a successful business.

At the end of 2011, Lisa founded Homemade Fresh Chef Service to provide personalized meal planning and preparation in client homes. She was still caring for her mother at that time and then needed to provide care for her father. Even with those other responsibilities, Lisa started planting and watering the seeds of her new career in 2012. The slow start frustrated her because she was eager to follow her passion, but she knew she had to be patient.

Lisa's father and grandparents were entrepreneurs. "It was in my blood," she says. "This time, since it wasn't my first time starting a business, I knew what to expect. I believe everything happens for a reason. Hard work and passion lead to success."

In the end it worked out, and several years later, she is even more passionate about healthy cooking than she ever was about marketing. Now Lisa is a personal chef. She has regular clients, and she goes to their homes once or twice a month to prepare meals for them. She customizes the meals to each family's personal taste and dietary requirements. Then she packages, labels, and freezes/refrigerates the meals, provides reheating instructions, and cleans up the kitchen. Her company also provides in-home catering, and Lisa works with wine consultants to pair food and wine for tastings.

Her income has grown steadily. In 2013, Lisa's company did four times the business of the previous year, and in 2014, her revenue jumped one and a half times that of the previous year. "Business started to explode, especially in 2015," she said. "I'm on track to get the business where I want it to be." Lisa knew that personal satisfaction was key to making her next career jump. "I've been a business owner for half of my career," she says. "Money is important, but it's not the only thing. Happiness is key, along with a supportive partner who has a good job!"

Lisa's clients either don't like to cook or have no time to spend in the kitchen. "My food makes my clients happy, and it helps them experience the benefit of fueling their bodies with real, high quality food instead of processed ingredients," Lisa says. "I get personal satisfaction out of helping people eat better, be happier, enjoy meals and time with family, and be healthier. I make it possible for my clients to enjoy real food made from scratch with heat-and-eat convenience."

In 2015, Lisa won the Rising Star award from the National Association of Women Business Owners, Charlotte Chapter. The award is presented annually to someone who has demonstrated entrepreneurial creativity and determination in successfully managing a business that is less than five years old.

After all her career shifts, Lisa sees work philosophically. "I've never understood people who were unhappy with a job and kept on doing it," she says. "We get one go-round at life. It's short and there are no guarantees. I am blessed to be able to work at what I enjoy."

## The Take-Away

If you're planning your own Fresh Start Success, take a moment to view your past experiences as stepping stones to your next opportunity. Life rarely moves in straight lines, and we often encounter setbacks and obstacles as we pursue our dreams. Sometimes the most valuable insights we gain are from the things we've done that didn't quite turn out the way we planned. Lisa's prior experience with marketing meshed with what she learned about herself from her previous entrepreneurial endeavors helped her to figure out where she really needed to focus. Look for ways your own past experiences—good and bad—can help you define and refine your path to the future.

## Q&A with Lisa Woodie

**Q: How are you a different person now?**
A: "I'm happier. I'm at a good place in life. I love to tell people that I whistle while I work. And I feel healthier since I changed my diet to focus on food from nature, not science."

**Q: What did you learn about yourself?**
A: "I'm grateful to know that I have what it takes to make a complete mid-life change and succeed. I've learned that I'm as creative as a chef as I was as a marketing professional. I'm certain that I'm wired to be an entrepreneur because that's what makes me the happiest and most fulfilled."

**Q: What new skills did you gain?**
A: "I have always been a sponge when it comes to learning new things. I love

to read, I enjoy researching new concepts, and I even enjoy practicing to hone skills. I've gained skills beyond just the ability to cook, like learning how to cook in different kitchens, how to be creative designing meal plans to fit various dietary requirements, and how to do multiple things at once. I'm better now at multitasking. There has been lots of trial and error, and gaining new skills and knowledge is an ongoing process."

**Q: What one trait is crucial to your success?**
A: "Drive—never giving up, getting past obstacles, having the right mindset. I'm not afraid of hard work and long hours. Another trait that is crucial is resourcefulness—I use this almost every day in my business."

**Q: If you had a superpower, what would it be?**
A: "The ability to wrinkle my nose and clean up the kitchen like the character Samantha Stevens on the TV show *Bewitched*. There's a lot to clean when you make several meals simultaneously! I've added a part-time assistant, and as business grows, I plan to add more assistants and chefs."

**Q: How has marketing and branding played into your success?**
A: "It's made a tremendous difference. I used my marketing skills to create my website, knowing it's the first place people go. Branding was very important, so I hired a designer to redo my logo and rebrand myself once the business began growing. Social media is incredibly important. One client had posted on Facebook looking for a chef because she needed someone who could work with a very limited diet. She got half a dozen replies recommending me. Clients have also found me from the guest posts I've written for various blogs. My business is growing by word of mouth, through referrals, via networking, and from sites like LinkedIn, Facebook, and Yelp. I don't do traditional advertising. My marketing background was a big help in more ways than I can say. I've seen other personal chefs whose businesses haven't grown as fast, and I think it's due, in part, to them not being as comfortable with networking and marketing."

# Jump or Pivot?
## Susan Sklar, MD

**MAKING A FRESH** Start Success doesn't always mean completely leaving the old behind to make room for the new. Sometimes it's a lateral shift, staying within a profession but changing the focus. When we come to a career/life crossroads, the idea that we have to jump instead of pivot can make us afraid to move forward. While some people embrace the idea for a complete reboot and the chance to do something completely different, pivoting allows you to keep one foot in the familiar while gaining a completely new perspective.

If the fear of making a huge change is holding you back from Fresh Start Success, stop feeling like you need to make a big jump and look for an opportunity to make a strategic pivot!

## From Birth to Renewal

Dr. Susan Sklar, MD, wanted to be a doctor since she was fifteen years old. She knew she wanted a career where she could be of service and considered being a teacher. Her mother, a survivor of the Great Depression, told her doctors never went hungry. Convinced that she had found a calling that was both secure and enabled her to be of service, Susan earned her medical degree and practiced obstetrics and gynecology for over thirty years.

Her relationship with patients was deeply satisfying. Susan liked helping people feel better, enabling them to become healthier, and making emotional connections. It was satisfying for her to reassure people and reduce their worry. But while the medical side of her work was satisfying, the business side was stressful. Forms, billing, insurance, and regulations meant more time focusing on paperwork and less time for patients. The overhead necessary to handle all the paperwork meant she had to see more patients to break even, reducing the time spent per patient and squeezing the relationship-building Susan valued. The frustration built up over ten years, but eventually, Susan felt like a rat on a wheel.

Susan was afraid she would have to leave medicine in order to get away from the aspects of her practice that were driving her crazy. That was a frightening prospect because after investing so much time in her education and building her practice, she wasn't really equipped to do something outside of medicine. She wanted to be engaged with people in a helping field and still have financial success. Then her son introduced Susan to another doctor who specialized in anti-aging medicine. This field of restoring poor health and promoting healthy longevity through prevention fit Susan's professional interests as well as her own stage of life.

Susan was intrigued. This was an emerging medical specialty that was relatively new on the market. Most people didn't know what it was. Susan liked the emphasis on helping patients in ways they didn't dream they could be helped. Because anti-aging medicine tends to be direct-pay, that reduced Susan's frustration with paperwork and insurance.

Susan was sixty years old, with a lot invested in her long-time career. She weighed her options carefully. She needed to finance her education in anti-aging medication and set up her new practice. One way would be to borrow from her retirement accounts and get bank loans. Borrowing from her retirement accounts and taking on debt was scary. The other option was to work part-time for the Veterans Administration. That would keep her from needing to tap into her savings, but it would slow down her progress. Susan felt a strong desire to begin learning and growing. That need for fulfillment won out over the risks, and Susan let go of the part-time opportunity to embrace her new calling wholeheartedly.

Going into anti-aging medicine meant Susan had to do new medical training. It took her a year to learn the medicine. But what was really new was the need to market her specialty and educate prospective clients that the types of services and the benefits they produced even existed. Everyone knew what an OB/GYN doctor did and what type of medicine and services obstetrics/gynecology included. But anti-aging medicine was so new, the people who needed it most didn't know that help was even available.

Susan didn't know anything about marketing, branding, or social media because her former specialty had not required her to focus on promotion. "It took me one year to learn the medicine and five to seven years to learn marketing," Susan says. "It was faster to learn the medicine than the marketing!" Her new practice started out slowly, but Susan was motivated by the results she saw. She was helping people feel better and turning lives around. Gradually, word of mouth spread. Susan found experts to help her with marketing and also found a mentor who directed her training and helped her develop a workable salary.

Susan was fortunate to be able to tap into savings and apply for loans to finance her switch. Her husband's income was an additional safety net. "The first three or four years were really hard," she says. All told, it took eight years to get what Susan considered to be very good cash flow, but she began to take a salary comparable to her old income at five years. Now she is practicing a type of medicine that she loves, helping patients, and continuing to learn and grow as a person while meeting her financial goals.

## The Take-Away

Susan loved the core aspects of what she did—helping people, seeing results, making people better. The industry infrastructure, such as insurance paperwork and regulatory demands, took her away from the core aspects she found fulfilling and produced enough stress that she thought about walking away altogether. What is noteworthy is that she found a way to make a strategic pivot that enabled her to keep the core aspects she loved—medicine and helping people—and do it in a setting that had far fewer of the pieces she found frustrating.

Did you notice that Susan was sixty years old when she decided to go back for additional medical training, strike out in a new medical field, and start a whole new practice? It's never too late to follow your heart and find your Fresh Start Success!

## Q&A with Dr. Susan Sklar

### Q: What did you learn the hard way?
A: "The marketing. It always felt like trial and error, like I was shooting in the dark without guidance. This year, it's so much better. I have wonderful guidance from a supportive group of colleagues, I've found a mentor, and I've decreased my stress by learning how to do more strategic marketing planning."

### Q: To what do you attribute your Fresh Start Success?
A: "Willpower, determination, bullheadedness. I do amazing things for people. I can't let this fail because I lack marketing knowledge. I have so much to offer; I've got to do this. I believe in what I'm doing."

### Q: How are you a different person now?
A: "I'm somewhat humbled by what all has happened, and proud of what I've done. I still have a strong desire to learn, grow, and contribute. I'm tougher now than I used to be. I used to feel I was a personal failure if I had a bad month, but I've got thicker skin now!"

### Q: What did you learn about yourself?
A: "I'm really tough, really determined, really smart."

### Q: If you had a superpower, what would it be?
A: "I'm a very visual person, so I'd love to have the ability to have x-ray vision, be able to see to the inside of a patient and know what's wrong without needing to use equipment."

### Q: What role has marketing and branding played in your success?
A: "Huge. I'm in a new medical field that most people don't know about. Marketing gets the message out. Most people don't know the anti-aging field exists. I rely on both traditional marketing and social media to help spread the word."

# Mentors and Legacy
## Stephen Hobbs, EdD


MENTORS AND ROLE models aren't exactly the same. A role model can be someone you admire from afar for that person's success or ability but never interact with personally. A mentor, on the other hand, takes an active role as guide and sometimes as champion and advocate as well. Mentors shepherd more junior people who often remind them of their own younger selves. A good mentor can help you accelerate your learning curve and avoid costly mistakes. A great mentor can change your life.

Mentoring is a form of giving back and paying forward, and it's also a way to leave a legacy in the form of a successful next generation. A personal relationship with a mentor can build confidence, encourage judicious risk-taking, and improve the ability to assess situations and learn from mistakes. Mentors gain something too—including personal satisfaction, the chance to pay back a kindness done by their own long-ago mentors, and a sense of touching the future by shaping a life or career.

As you're considering your own Fresh Start Success, consider finding a mentor for yourself who has demonstrated excellence in an area in which you feel lacking. Making a big career or life shift can be intimidating; it helps a lot to have a seasoned guide. Once you get your feet under you, think about becoming a mentor to someone else. Skills and perspectives you take for granted could be invaluable to others seeking their own Fresh Start Success.


## Leaving a Legacy

Stephen Hobbs planned to be a civil engineer, then went into forestry. When neither fulfilled him, he went on a six-month overseas trip. However, he came back four years later. That trip was his first experience with personal re-creating, and Stephen gained insights into recreation.

When he returned, Stephen completed two undergraduate degrees plus his master's degree. Ten years later, he earned his EdD in adult education, what he calls "people navigation." Now Stephen builds bridges, metaphorically. "I started with science and math 'structure me' and became people and connections 'relationship me,'" he says.

"I'm up to about thirty-plus careers now," Stephen says. "I started in the recreation industry and moved through all sorts of organizational arrangements in Canada and internationally. I find it rather funny that I'm returning to my roots with a focus on 're-creation,' the creation of a life lived freely and abundantly. And all that structure background still helps!"

Stephen enjoyed a varied career. He was an educator and consultant for over forty years and spent fifteen years as a senior manager and executive. Stephen has worked on six of the seven continents. He served as a CEO of a workplace education company; worked for for-profit, non-profit, and public organizations; was a university professor; and served as a delegate for overseas missions in Eastern Africa.

Over the course of his career, Stephen realized that his biggest satisfaction came from seeing people enjoy themselves. He loved working with groups and creating programming, as well as organizing people. A big change happened for him in the mid-1980s while he was working in Africa for the Red Cross on the HIV/AIDS epidemic in Uganda. Stephen stopped at a roadblock and a fourteen-year-old soldier shoved a machine gun through the window of his vehicle. Aside from looking point-blank up the muzzle, it was who was holding the gun that caught his attention. It was a young woman, about fourteen to fifteen years old. This experience, and more, cut to his core. "I found myself thinking that there has to be a different way to be in this world," he says. "That changed my paradigm forever." A year later, he returned to Eastern Africa working as Air Operations Coordinator in the war zone in South Sudan.

Stephen knew that the kinds of jobs he loved weren't the best way to make a living. He had an idea of what "recreation" should be, but it didn't seem to be a viable full-time career choice. Then Stephen changed the way he viewed the organization of work. He created and successfully implemented several programs to test his vision and opened his business in 1990. Stephen didn't go full-time into his business until 1996. "I gave up paid employment and corporate benefits with no transition plan," he recalls. "I stepped right off the ledge."

Once Stephen made the leap to pursuing his business full-time, it took close to a year and a half to become successful, with some loss/gain, step-up/step-back moments on the way. "I had a couple of problematic business partners, learned some hard lessons, and rebuilt in a better way," Stephen reflects.

Mentors were important for Stephen's success. His first mentor gave him exposure to the creative process, opening up opportunities for innovation and creativity in his work. This mentor showed Stephen how to use television to re-create, how to incorporate creative play, and how to use multiple modalities to bring stories to people. It sparked Stephen's interest in play and leisure, which served him well during a career as a team development facilitator.

His second mentor was the soldier in Uganda, who he calls his "Three Minute Mentor."

Stephen's third mentor focused on organizational psychology and culture, helping Stephen put together a paradigm of what guides people in working together. This led to a deeper understanding of organizations and culture with a focus on re-creating the structure of work, building bridges between people for better understanding, and using technology to create a structure that benefits both the individual and the organization. Stephen also gained the ability to be better at getting a quick read of groups of people in order to match programming to their interests.

The most recent version of Stephen's vision is Wellth Movement, a company helping older adults create a legacy as eco-conscious grandparents and elders in their communities. It is a whole new take on Stephen's long-time passion for recreation, evolving "re-creation."

## The Take-Away

As you make your personal and professional reinvention, be sure to think about the long term legacy you leave behind in terms of your impact on the people around you; your lasting contribution of wisdom or beauty in books, art, articles, and other tangible records; and your ability to make a change in the larger world. You enrich the world when you leave your story and accumulated knowledge behind in a form others can learn from and use. Think about how you can make a difference in the lives around you. You can begin leaving a legacy of your own right now.

## Q&A with Stephen Hobbs

**Q: What did you learn the hard way?**
A: "I learned that unfortunately, there are no friends in business, so one should be careful doing business with friends and family—it can go sideways big-time. I also identified what I call my 'shadow self' around the concept of rejection. I realize now that I avoided difficult conversation with my business partners out of a fear of rejection. I know that I can be intimidating, between my physical height and my advanced degrees, and now I realize that I often used my intelligence as a buffer to keep people at arm's length. Since I've learned that I need to be truly present, I no longer need to use a 'mask.' My whole world shifted."

**Q: What traits are critical to your Fresh Start Success?**
A: "Aside from patience, flexibility, and discretion, it's important to step up, stay found, share wisdom, shine light. Step up—challenge yourself to make more of a difference, fulfill your commitments. My word for how to live in the world is 'magnificence,' but I challenge everyone to find his or her own meaningful key word. Stay found—maintain your presence, stay mindful. I take this aspect from my time leading wilderness programs because we always told people that if you get lost, stay where you are, 'stay found.' Share wisdom—focus on education. When you listen, you learn; when you share, you educate. In everything you do, you educate. Shine light—you light the path for others through lightening their burden and through helping people to ground themselves all while having fun. I share, 'Make it so/so IT is' and encourage them to find their 'IT,' which, for me, means 'I Transition.'"

**Q: If you had a superpower, what would it be?**

A: "Flying. When I was a kid, my imaginary companion was a flying turtle. I have an affinity to the North American First Nations' turtle clan because the turtle carries his home with him. I recently sold my home and vehicle and gave nearly everything away except for what I can carry with me in a few boxes—so now, I am Super Turtle."

**Q: What advice would you give someone considering making a Fresh Start Success?**

A: "Determine your sense of seriousness, urgency and growth requirements and requests. There is growth potential for you and those with whom you interact. Write your intentions down and create a story about the direction of where you want to go. Look at what your IT (I Transition) is. Create a community with the people you love and love to know. Your friends and family are important, so be willing to hear what they say and sense their contribution. Most people don't share their vision story widely enough and miss out on awesome people who could help them make their shift faster/smoother/cheaper/safer."

**Q: What role did marketing play in your success?**

A: "I've been dabbling online since 1996, but I didn't really leverage it until two years ago. Most of my work is face-to-face. Now I've hired help to share my social media branding and story. I've joined three complementary masterminds to do it better. Return on Investment (ROI) while hard to calculate is doable with effort. And I believe direct response marketing does create valuable returns. You've got to be systematic and systemic in your approach to starting fresh. Systematic in how you manage and systemic in how you lead."

# Prestige or Peace?

## Christine Hassler

IS YOUR EGO killing you? Have you acquired prestige at the expense of peace of mind? Many of the people interviewed in this book had high-paying, glamorous jobs with perks and privileges that were the envy of those around them. If the cost of your "success" is depression, isolation, unhappiness, poor health, and damaged relationships, you may be ready for reinvention.

When everyone else thinks you "have it all," it can be difficult to give up the job or lifestyle others covet, even when you're miserable. Listen to your body and pay attention to what your soul is telling you. Others may think you're crazy for walking away from what appears to be the pinnacle of career success. Your intelligence, drive, and intuition got you to your level of prominence; trust it to be sufficient to guide your Fresh Start Success.

## Illusion and Reality

Christine Hassler went to Northwestern University and majored in TV/ film and communication studies. Studio mogul Sherri Lansing was her idol. Then Christine moved to Los Angeles at age twenty-one and four years later, she was a Hollywood agent making a six-figure salary.

It was a high-profile, exciting life. Christine liked the entertainment industry. She spent her time with celebrities, attended the Academy Awards and the Golden Globes, and had a wardrobe full of great clothes. But as glamorous as the work appeared, it was only temporarily satisfying.

"I was driven by insecurities," Christine says. "All my achievements were only momentarily satisfying, not fulfilling, because the bar was always raised. The turning point came when I was in an elevator with a woman who was the head of a company, and I found out that the woman's daughter's first word was 'hola' because she spent more time with the Spanish-speaking nanny than with her parents." Christine found the woman to be cold and hard, and she didn't want to be like that. She was already thinking of resigning, even though she did not know what else she was going to do. Having the realization that she was also becoming cold and hard scared her. She decided to quit her job three days later, in 2003.

"I had a coveted job," Christine says. "Everyone thought I was crazy, but my family supported me. Now, people tell me I was courageous."

Christine had no clear plan, thinking at first that she might want to be a health and fitness/workout guru. "I tried out close to a dozen jobs, including being a hand model, as I figured out what I wanted to do. That was depressing and a huge adjustment because I had a lot of my identity tied up in my job," she says.

That's when Christine hit a wall. "In one year, my engagement broke up, there was a rift in my family, I was in debt with no job, and I became deeply depressed," she recalls. This was all part of her "quarter-life crisis." She felt like she hit rock bottom. And one night, at one of her lowest points, she experienced what she calls a "God moment" and dedicated her life to helping others. That decision helped her turn a corner, and her life took a turn for the better. Christine had the idea for her first book, people wanted to coach with her, and she began speaking at colleges and then to companies. Christine went back for her master's degree in spiritual psychology, health and healing and began speaking on the motivational stage, coaching more people, and leading retreats around the world.

"I learned to change fear into inspiration and found the ability to take risk," she recounts. "I studied hypnosis and trained to be a life coach. Other skills like selling, writing, and being charismatic on camera, I learned from the entertainment industry."

By 2006, she quit her part-time jobs and has since replaced and surpassed her former income while working fewer hours. Now, Christine is the author of three books: *Expectation Hangover, The 20 Something Manifesto*, and *20 Something, 20 Everything*. For the last decade, she has pursued her passion as a speaker, retreat facilitator, and life coach.

"I got out of my own way, aligned with my purpose, and things started to show up," Christine says.

## The Take-Away

If your current, demanding-yet-glamorous job is sucking the life out of you, it's time for a change. Pay attention to the times your intuition "pings" you with interest about a different kind of work or when an idea grabs your imagination and won't let go. That's your inner self, trying to hatch an escape plan. Listen to it, nurture it, and do your homework, then rescue yourself before it's too late.

Sometimes we remain in a coveted position because we have confused ourselves with our title and job. If you are defining your worth—to yourself and to others—by the size of your paycheck, the perks of the job, or the impressiveness of your title, take a step back and spend some time discovering who you are outside of your career. Look for your unique strengths and talents, and note patterns where others have repeatedly turned to you for guidance and leadership. Ask your closest friends and family to tell you what they value about you unrelated to your job. When you learn to see your intrinsic human value outside of your job, you will discover the building blocks you can use to create your Fresh Start Success.

## Q&A with Christine Hassler

**Q: What did you learn the hard way?**
A: "Fulfillment isn't 'out there'—it comes from inside, not from your job or from others. It requires finding what's true for you. My ego was louder than my intuition for a long time, and when I didn't listen to my intuition, it led to suffering. I also learned that passion doesn't come automatically, and profitability takes work. And I discovered that just because you're good at something doesn't mean you should do it as a career."

**Q: To what do you attribute your Fresh Start Success?**
A: "Personal growth. People are drawn to me because I'm authentic and vulnerable, and I share my struggle with them. I'm dedicated to helping others.

I'm also disciplined. I've blogged weekly since 2006. And I invest in myself by training with business and spiritual coaches. I've also learned to invest in a team and not to try to do everything myself."

**Q: How are you a different person? What did you learn about yourself?**
A: "I am way more self-accepting now. I didn't become that woman I met in the elevator. I'm softer and focused on love instead of hustling for the next promotion. The key is in my relationship to myself. I'm no longer hard and driving to myself, and I show love to myself and others."

**Q: How did your prior experience prepare you for what you're doing now?**
A: "I understand the pain of Expectation Hangovers, working at a job and not being fulfilled, being heartbroken, feeling the disapproval of others disagreeing with your decisions, being worried about money, getting diagnosed with an illness, etc. I understand what my clients are feeling when they work so hard and don't get what they want or their outcome isn't fulfilling."

**Q: What trait is critical for your Fresh Start Success?**
A: "Being a constant student of life and my industry. I set intentions, and I pursue my goals with high involvement but low attachment. And faith!"

**Q: If you could have a superpower, what would it be?**
A: "To fly. I've always dreamed of flying. I want to get my pilot's license."

**Q: What role has marketing played in your success?**
A: "Relationships and referrals are essential. I have a niche in which I do good work and provide value. My marketing strategy has been about being authentic and connecting with people. Also continuing to produce free content and be of service. This has been crucial to my success."

# Essential Branding
## LeeAnn Shattuck

**WHO ARE YOU?** To the world, you are the brand you create for yourself. That can be scary if you're new to thinking of yourself as a brand. But to put it another way, you are the product, and products need a brand to stand out. So what's yours?

One approach to coming up with your brand is to think about who you serve, what you do for them, and what result you achieve, and then distill it down to three or four words. If you try that and struggle, here's an exercise we use with clients. Describe what you do flippantly. Now look at what you wrote down. Is there truth in what you've said? How could you tweak it and make it work for you? That's exactly what LeeAnn did—and her branding propelled her business far beyond her initial expectations.

As you create your Fresh Start Success, make sure that branding is on your list of essentials!

## The Car Chick™

LeeAnn Shattuck went to college and earned degrees in quantitative economics and industrial engineering at Stanford. She followed in the footsteps of her father, who was a managing partner at Ernst & Whinney, and became an IT consultant for Anderson Consulting (which became Accenture).

"I learned a lot of different businesses and industries," LeeAnn says. "I learned something new every day. There was always a lot of interesting new information. But the travel got old. I traveled so often that I knew all about the flight crews and their families. When the crew started to comment when I wore a new outfit, I knew it was too much."

LeeAnn left Accenture and went to IBM, doing the same work at the same pay but working from home. After 9/11, IBM wanted her to move to New

York City, and she refused. She moved to different IT jobs with smaller and smaller firms. "It was always the same hassles," LeeAnn says. She got divorced, and her life began to shift.

"The last straw came when I asked my boss if I could work a day at home—same billable hours—to meet a repair man, and he said, 'Why can't your wife just handle all that for you?' It didn't even hit him what he was saying until it was out of his mouth," LeeAnn says. "He and his male friends all had wives who didn't work. It was very chauvinistic."

LeeAnn reevaluated her goals. "I asked myself why I was working eighty-hour weeks to build a business for this idiot," she recalls. "I wasn't getting treated the same as the men, and they had zero-percent respect for work-life balance." LeeAnn realized she was burned out and began looking for other options, including franchises.

Then the universe intervened. "I was in the bathroom when I saw a brochure about car shopping—a company that helped women shop for cars," LeeAnn says. "I called the owner and fell in love with the concept right then. I have always loved cars; I've raced cars all my life. It was fate stepping in." The company at the time was called Women's Automotive Solutions.

"I had no idea of what I was getting into," LeeAnn admits. "Customers don't magically show up. I didn't know what I didn't know about marketing, sales, etc. I hadn't thought about being an entrepreneur. Working with a business partner was new, since it was just the founder and me. I went from a cushy six-figure salary to nothing for a long time."

Thus began a journey of learning how to run and market a business. "My first customer was a young, single mother who had been taken advantage of by a con artist and was stuck in a bad lease. She was terrified of going to the car lot. I helped her get out of her old lease, found her a car she loved at an affordable price, and got her out of a bad situation," LeeAnn recalls. "This wasn't really about cars. It was about empowering women. Cars were something I knew well. People started calling me 'The Car Chick™' and it stuck. That's who I really am, and this is what I was meant to do."

LeeAnn had to create her own support network. Her ex-husband wasn't supportive of her venture, but her father believed in her. "Mom was a worrier," she adds. She found groups of other women entrepreneurs and gradually found her way. "I was empowering other women, but I empowered myself, too," LeeAnn says. "I just ignored the naysayers."

It took about five years for the business to become profitable. "There was a big learning curve," LeeAnn says, "and I had to get over my fears and out from under the limitations of my business partner, who had a small view of what the company could become."

She hired a good business coach and tripled what she was charging while also increasing the services clients received. "My business is different now," LeeAnn says. "I provide so much more value than I did originally."

"I am not even remotely the same person that I was before," LeeAnn says. "I was very risk-averse, and I didn't see myself as an entrepreneur. Now I'm seen as one of the most influential women in the auto industry. I used to be afraid to speak to groups—now I'm on radio and TV."

She's learned a lot, but there's always something new to master. "I still get scared of a lot of things, but my fear of failure is less than my fear of not trying," LeeAnn adds. "I don't need a boss or a partner to be a leader. I know that this is my purpose on Earth, and if I didn't do it, I would regret it forever."

## The Take-Away

Brands help busy consumers find a mental "filing place" to remember you. Have you ever noticed how you can remember the tag lines of old advertisements decades after the products disappeared? That's how well we remember brands—and why creating a catchy and memorable brand is an essential element in your Fresh Start Success.

## Q&A with LeeAnn Shattuck

### Q: What did you learn the hard way?

A: "Everything. 'If you build it, they will come' is crap. You've got to keep stoking the fire. It takes time to build traction. You just keep trudging forward."

**Q: To what do you attribute your Fresh Start Success?**
A: "My brand. I didn't set out to build The Car Chick™ as a brand; it built me. It started as a joke. I called myself 'Chief Car Chick' instead of CEO. The name just took off. I used media, sent out press releases, talked about the unique business model. I got good at speaking about car buying and was asked to be on radio and TV. I ended up building a personality brand by keeping open to opportunity."

**Q: What is the one trait that is crucial to your success?**
A: "Passion. Not being afraid to form an opinion, state it, make it my platform. I take a stand. I have opinions, and that gets attention. I'm just being myself. I'm not worried about offending people."

**Q: If you had a superpower, what would it be?**
A: "I would be able to teleport and go visit anywhere easily."

**Q: What role has marketing played in your success?**
A: "Huge. Radio and TV are big for me. I am now a TV host and producer with a nationally-recognized brand. I spent less than $2,000 on classic advertising— it's all been word of mouth. Social media is on my list of things to improve. It has helped me spread worth of mouth, and I need a more solid, comprehensive strategy. I'm working on two reality shows right now. One is about my business as The Car Chick™, and one is 'Rust Rescue' where my co-host and I find an old classic American car out in a field and renovate it, teaching viewers how to do it themselves for ten thousand dollars or less."

# The Inspiration of a Role Model

Patryk Wezowski

WHO ARE YOUR heroes? The people who inspire you may have made an impact in a variety of ways: business, literature, art, religion, politics, music, sports, etc. What can you learn from their journeys that you can apply to your own quest to create a Fresh Start Success?

Most of us have read Napoleon Hill's *Think and Grow Rich*, in which he interviews the Gilded Age captains of industry and looks for common traits that led to their success. Stephen Covey's *The 7 Habits of Highly Effective People* is a similar compilation. Both are good reading, but don't stop there. Assemble a list of your own heroes, people you admire for their accomplishments, and read their biographies. Study the paths they took to achieve their success. Get to know the ways they thought and how they dealt with set-backs and adversity.

Now assemble your own imaginary board of directors and draft your role models to sit around the table. When you face a challenge, reach a dead end, or simply need encouragement, imagine going to your "board members" for advice. Drawing from what you learned about their lives, thoughts, habits, and experiences, what wisdom would those luminaries share with you?

Don't dismiss this as fantasy. It's a technique many successful people have employed, and it works because it forces you to think through your own problems from the vantage point of someone who struggled with similar issues and succeeded. While you may live in a different time period and face different challenges, the similarities usually outweigh the differences, especially when you distill wisdom to its essence.

## Getting to Yes

Patryk Wezowski earned a bachelor's degree in economics but discovered he didn't like that field of study. He had a passion to study psychology and did so on his own. He was unsure what he wanted to do with his life, but he remembered reading, at twelve years of age, the story of the man who founded Mercedes-Benz and that the founder had a vision of bringing mobility to the world. Patryk knew he wanted to do something important and meaningful like that someday.

Patryk, who is Belgian, remembers walking down the main street in Antwerp as a teenager and wanting to buy the things he saw in the store windows, but he did not have the money. "Up to that time, I had worked in factories, at low-paying, horrible jobs," he recalls. "When I was nineteen years old, I started managing events for a company and felt my entrepreneurial spirit stir. That led me to a clear vision of wanting to do something meaningful in life."

When he came out of university, his goal was to find a job that was interesting and paid well. Patryk sent out hundreds of resumes, and he got an excellent job as an information technology project manager, setting up the internet presence for a large company. "I was so blown away that the whole world connected through the servers, and it was my responsibility to connect Belgium with the whole world," he remembers.

There was a lot to learn in a short time, and he studied on his own, learning quickly. But Patryk was still looking for a mission. His job was very flexible, and Patryk looked into how to affordably travel around the world. He spent all of his lunch breaks setting up sponsorships for him to travel around the world interviewing people about what made them happy so that he could write articles, a book, maybe even a film about the answers.

"If you have to finance yourself, getting a lot of 'no' answers is discouraging," Patryk says. He had many companies that declined to sponsor him, but he kept on going and his 'yes' answers came in the end. "People have to think about the requests you make. Too many people give up too quickly. It's not about being 'safe' in your goals; it's about going for your dream until you reach it." Two years later, the trip was set up, and Patryk took a six-month leave from his job.

Those early lessons stuck with Patryk. Today, together with his wife, Kasia Wezowski, he is the producer of *Coaching*, the first documentary about the coaching profession. As the Founder of the Center for Body Language, Patryk developed over a dozen non-verbal communication training programs tailored for Sales, Recruitment, Leadership, and Negotiation. His methodologies and conversation strategies are being taught in local languages by forty-five international representatives in fifteen countries. Patryk is also the author of *The Micro Expressions Book for Business.*

"I believe it's important for everyone to have a clear vision and mission for your life, a clear answer to 'why am I here in this world?'" Patryk says. "Even if your vision is borrowed or incomplete, you can grow into it. Immerse yourself in it with all the power of your life. Put in the hard work. Go for what you want."

## The Take-Away

Study the lives of successful people written by good journalistic biographers, and you'll find a track record of failures, disappointments, dead ends, and hurdles. You'll also discover the amount of hard work, tenacity, and stubborn determination that went into creating what might have appeared to be "overnight" success. When your own road is rough and you don't achieve your goals as quickly or painlessly as you had hoped, look to the examples of your imaginary board of directors for inspiration and encouragement.

As you create your own Fresh Start Success, look for your own vision and mission of why you are in the world and how you can make it different and better through what you can contribute, and chart a course to make it happen.

## Q&A with Patryk Wezowski

### Q: What did you learn the hard way?

A: "Start with anything that is in your full power. I had several corporate jobs, and I wanted to set up my own company, but I didn't know where to start. So I took a piece of blank paper and wrote down two ideas for companies/products that would help people. One was about recruiters being able to learn body language, and the other was on how to travel around the world. I decided to compile all the knowledge and research about body language I studied until then and threw myself into becoming a body language expert. Then I created a DVD, which is still available in Dutch. I sent emails to people who were job-hunting and offered a free seminar about body language. At the end of the seminar, I promoted my DVD, and sixty percent of them bought the DVD, even though they were unemployed. That's when I realized I could quit my full-time job and focus on body language."

**Q: How are you a different person than before? What did you learn about yourself?**
A: "When you stick to your vision/mission in whatever you do, your tactics change, but one thing you should never go away from is your clear vision/ mission. When you lose your vision on the way, everything else falters."

"The question is, how can you be different from what is out there, to lead and influence and get others to follow you? For the Center for Body Language to become the world's leading organization of its kind, we developed the world's first program on micro expressions, which reveal true feelings through video. No one else had done it before. All of marketing and social media is based on communicating what is new, special, unique and useful, what is totally different from what exists. It's important to teach by example."

**Q: If you had a superpower, what would it be?**
A: "Every person can develop a superpower. You might already have a superpower, but you just need to identify it. Getting a good coach is a great way of discovering your superpower. That's just what happened to me, and that's why we're so dedicated to making a film about coaching. My ability to read facial expressions grew out a hearing problem when I was a child, so I had to pay close attention to body language. From that experience, I learned about body language. If you can read micro expressions, you see more than everyone else, and know what people need and expect. You know whether someone is lying or telling the truth. It's more than just intuition."

# Introvert or Extrovert
## Danielle Ratliff

ARE YOU AN introvert or an extrovert? Does working with people power you up or drain your battery? Do you crave company and enjoy the bustle of a busy workplace? Or are you in your happy spot where it's quiet and you can work with solitary focus?

Most of us are a mix of introvert and extrovert traits. You may be able to turn up the wattage and shine on stage or at a social event, then come home and collapse because you're utterly worn out. Or you might be able to work alone on a project for hours, but then go looking to recharge by going to the mall and surrounding yourself with people. Often, we've learned to adapt to school and work demands for us to be either more outgoing or more solitary than we truly prefer.

As you consider your options for your own Fresh Start Success, it's important to gauge the amount of interaction you need to feel energized and happy. For example, if being in the public eye drains you, a new career where you're constantly on the road and making presentations is unlikely to satisfy you, regardless of the money. On the other hand, if you thrive on having people around, you may feel lonely and restless working from home with no one but the dog for company.

## Positive Interaction

Danielle trained to be a registered dietitian and worked as a dietitian for seven years. Although she was doing what she went to school to do, very little about the job was satisfying. "I'm a people person," Danielle says, "and it was good to meet people and help them on their journey, but the lack of compliance made me crazy."

She faced an uphill battle trying to help clients change dysfunctional food habits, self-destructive behaviors, and deeply-rooted emotions. Long-term successes were few and far between. "There was a lot negative energy," Danielle recalls. The last straw was when she was sexually assaulted and faced her own emotional struggle and post-traumatic stress disorder from the assault. Fortunately, Danielle had a good support network, so she didn't have to deal with the situation alone.

As she considered leaving her role as a nutritionist, Danielle researched her options. "Emotional health was my number one priority, along with a job that created positive energy," she says. "For me, that was all part of being happy." Danielle also reassessed why she went into being a nutritionist, and what she wanted out of her reinvention.

"In my first career, I did what I thought I was supposed to do. My parents led me in that direction as a safe choice," Danielle says.

Her husband suggested looking at becoming a massage therapist because he said she was good at giving amateur massages to family and friends. Danielle enrolled in a part-time program at the North Carolina School of Massage and loved it. Her old job gave her plenty of experience interacting with people. Massage requires a high degree of personal interaction and communication, and it's hands-on, requiring good rapport with clients.

"Massage is a positive profession because people smile when they're finished with a massage. I could provide immediate gratification to my clients, and making them feel better gratified me," she says.

Unfortunately, one teacher left mid-way through the program. Danielle didn't like the replacement teacher as much, but she stuck with it, and her clinical practice providing public massages went very well. She interned with the teacher who had left the school and planned to work at the same massage practice after she graduated, but then the owner of the shop moved and offered to sell it to her.

Danielle bought the practice out of her savings and plunged into learning the business end. The old owner had been losing money. Danielle only needed six months to turn a profit and take a paycheck. "It took three years, but I've surpassed my old income," Danielle says. She kept the name of the practice ("Serenity Now") and differentiated herself by positioning the studio as the premier provider of therapeutic massage, as opposed to sheer relaxation. "I put a lot of thought into appealing to my local audience. I made sure I knew the demographics," she adds.

What would she tell others considering making a big change? "Just do it. Jump in with both feet. You'll surprise yourself," Danielle says. "Find the courage to take the first step. Baby steps are okay."

## The Take-Away

If you thrive on a certain type of work that uses your gifts and satisfies your soul, consider the options you have for how to deliver your services to fit your introvert/extrovert personality. Don't assume that the way you've seen others do something is the only possibility. With today's technology, you can be connected to the world without leaving home. At the same time, our computer addiction leaves many people hungry for personal, high-touch service that requires intensive interaction. Make your new Fresh Start Success suit you!

## Q&A with Danielle Ratliff

### Q: What did you learn the hard way?
A: "Make sure you do background checks on people before you hire them. One person interviewed well, and I hired the person on the spot, then found out there was a criminal record, so I had to let the person go. That was difficult. Also, be very careful with coupon programs like Groupon® and LivingSocial. They make it hard to keep the cash flow even. It's much better to build on word of mouth."

### Q: To what do you attribute your Fresh Start Success?
A: "I credit it to having really good people around me and working for me. I hire positive, go-getters, people who will make sacrifices for the company. Our employees and mentors form a circle of support for each other."

**Q: How are you a different person than before?**
A: "I'm much happier. I'm stronger, not afraid to put my foot down, better with boundaries."

**Q: What did you learn about yourself?**
A: "That I'm a heck of a lot stronger than I thought I was. I never would have believed that before. I have confidence and strength to live my dream every day."

**Q: What is one trait that is critical to your Fresh Start Success?**
A: "Having a positive attitude, believing that you can do things that seem difficult or impossible, and having patience."

**Q: If you had a superpower, what would it be?**
A: "I would be a mind-reader. It would make things easier if you knew what people are thinking and what their agendas are."

**Q: What role has marketing and branding played with your success?**
A: "Social media, branding on Facebook, Twitter, and LinkedIn are all very important to help build word of mouth."

# From High Tech to High Touch
## Lisa Jendza

OUR CULTURE ENCOURAGES us to think of ourselves as one-dimensional regarding our skills. We overlook the fact that people can be good at more than one thing. School and corporate human resources professionals pigeon-hole people with a tendency to focus on just one aspect or skill set. If we're not careful, we internalize those views and begin to see ourselves as only good at one type of work.

The reality is more complex. We may enjoy doing very left-brain work during one period in our lives and crave more creativity during another phase of life. Putting in long hours and never having time to indulge our "other side" through hobbies can make us feel burned out, restless, and used up inside.

When you're creating your own Fresh Start Success, pay attention to where you feel dissatisfied about your current work and life. Are you traveling too much or too little? Do you get the right amount of social interaction? Do you feel like you are using and being rewarded for both analytical and creative abilities? If you sense an imbalance—or if you already know that too much of one thing and the lack of something else is making you miserable—build your reinvention in a way that helps you regain balance and work-life satisfaction.

## Overcoming "Soul Sickness"

Lisa Jendza always planned a career in business. Her first job at age sixteen was in an office, followed by high school co-op clerical work at General Motors. When she was eighteen, Lisa was hired full time at Electronic Data Systems (EDS) while going to college at night. She worked her way from administrative assistant up to management.

EDS, at that time, moved people around to do a lot of different jobs during a period of massive growth, which provided Lisa with tremendous experience. But she saw that processes and procedures that worked when the business was a start-up did not work long-term. Lisa was working 100-hour weeks, often on swing shift, meaning she didn't sleep. She built EDS's GM Truck network and then the OnStar network during those years of tremendous growth.

But the hours were bad for her health, and she realized that she was not getting to spend time with her young children. She had to get her health back and regain family time. Lisa moved to the corporate audit department and worked on several special short-term projects while investigating holistic health to heal herself and help her experience spiritual growth.

"I felt soul-sick," Lisa recalls. "I was too far from my soul's purpose, and I was weary of the left-brain, masculine default for thinking."

Lisa made a huge jump into starting a day spa and creating her own line of body wrap products, Skin & Tonic. She joined a Holistic Chamber of Commerce and now offers advanced training programs on body wraps and detoxification treatments, and she offers business consulting to holistic practitioners.

"I had to relearn a lot," Lisa says. "I took all kinds of classes, workshops, seminars, and training on how to run a spa. I also had to learn to use spa management software. I didn't end up using a lot of my old corporate skills, except for my ability to learn technology. Not much else transferred. But I am a huge believer in the power of good IT and also in the power of internet marketing."

Lisa learned that building her new business on the side while working full-time makes success take longer. "I had my spa for five years part-time, and then I realized it would never really earn a living for me until I went into it full-time," Lisa says. She increased her profits four hundred percent when she restructured into a boutique business model, and she regained half of her corporate income. Her line of body wrap products has been a labor of love. "The lesson I learned is that if you're not fully invested in your business, you may never reach your goals," Lisa adds.

## The Take-Away

Who says you can only be good at one kind of work? If your heart is calling you to do something completely different, don't rule it out. Notice that Lisa did a lot of homework and retraining before she made her move. That's important because there will always be unpleasant aspects regardless of what line of work you're doing, so you need to know the good and the bad before you leap and be sure you can live with the whole package.

Note also that Lisa reinvented her spa to serve a niche clientele. Reinvention is a continuous process. Lisa added new products and services, retooled to serve a more profitable audience, and started her own skin care line. When you're considering your Fresh Start Success, think about short-term, mid-range and long-term goals so you always have a target to grow toward.

## Q&A with Lisa Jendza

**Q: What did you learn the hard way?**
A: "Everything! I have four degrees in business and managed multi-million dollar accounts for HP and EDS, but I didn't feel completely prepared for self-employment. For small business, it's how well you network and who you know."

**Q: How did you decide what was important to you?**
A: "Freedom. Freedom means something different with your own business—you're in control of your schedule. I also wanted personal satisfaction and personal spiritual growth/impact. Being free from bureaucracy and politics, owning what you build, going the extra mile for yourself and your clients, putting money back in the local economy—those were all important to me."

**Q: To what do you attribute your Fresh Start Success?**
A: "Perseverance. If something doesn't work, try something else. If you don't know what you don't know, hire a coach. Do the stuff you don't want to do.

I needed to make my business more exclusive so I could charge a premium. I needed fewer clients who paid well. Now I work with clients two days a week, ten clients at a time, no discounts. I reduced my schedule and downsized my space."

**Q: How are you a different person? What did you learn about yourself?**
A: "I've always been persistent. Now, I have more empathy, and I'm more spiritual than when I was in corporate work. In the corporate world, everyone has to fit a certain model. It's easy to lose yourself in who you have to be to be successful. That wasn't really me. Now I'm more authentic. I realized I didn't have to be someone else to attract clients because they come to me."

**Q: What one trait or habit is crucial to your Fresh Start Success?**
A: "Self-esteem. Whenever you beat yourself up, you need to let it go. Also learning and practicing not losing hope when things go wrong. I'm still working on that. The optimist goes on to try again. The pessimist ruminates. You need to learn to ruminate for a shorter period of time before you get back in the game. I counsel my clients to let things go."

**Q: If you had a superpower, what would it be?**
A: "I would like to be clairvoyant, to know intuitively that I'm on the right track."

**Q: What role does marketing play in your success?**
A: "Huge. Marketing was something I didn't take seriously at first. The marketing firm had tried to get me into social media and branding, but I hadn't listened. Now I understand the importance of marketing and social media. I see that a huge part of increasing visibility is to target the correct audience and support the brand. Sometimes smaller is better. When I cast a big net, I had smaller sales than when I cast a small net and got the right people and dramatically increased my sales. Targeting matters!"

# Walk Away
## Amber Allen

WORKING FOR BIG companies—especially the famous firms with names everyone recognizes—has traditionally been considered the "holy grail" of employment. Whether we were nudged toward huge companies by parents who wanted us to be secure or driven toward them by ambition to prove ourselves by getting to the top of the heap, many people would see being wooed by companies like Google and Disney as the pinnacle of a career. Amber Allen walked away. Here's why.

## The View from Inside

Amber wanted to do marketing and sales. When she worked at Reebok, she had a great boss who was very involved in events and partnerships, and his example inspired her to follow a similar path. She got involved in events in ways that were outside her job description and loved what she was doing. Amber tried other paths, including corporate sales, but she kept coming back to her love of event planning. The work was very visual, and sometimes crazy, but Amber liked the adrenaline and the chance to create something tangible. She decided event planning was her career destiny.

As the internal company liaison who contracted outside event planners, Amber had often been disappointed with the contractors' service and delivery. In her experience, many outside event agencies made big promises they couldn't fulfill and got contracts with low prices that suddenly inflated with hidden increases. Most of the people in the outside contract agencies had never sat in Amber's chair on the inside of the organization, and they didn't understand all the internal processes that the in-house event producer had to navigate. Amber realized there was a gap between what in-house planners needed and what outside agencies were providing and claimed that need as her opportunity.

Amber always had good bosses and flexibility, but she longed for freedom to do events her way. She likes seeing what needs to be done and doing it efficiently. In corporations, she had to use the resources that were in-house or already under contract. Now, she can get the best people for each job and make certain that every event gets what is really needed.

When she left to start her own firm, Double A Events, people in the industry thought her new-found entrepreneurship was something she had to get out of her system, that she would eventually return to corporate life. "In the beginning, I would get offers from some of my past bosses for a job at one of the larger companies like Google and Disney," she said. "When I turned down a final round of interviews at Google because it was either now or never for my company, I knew I was committed to this dream. Many of my friends and old colleagues have hired Double A Events over the last two years and have shown amazing support."

Amber built her company based on her former corporate business model and the possibilities she saw to improve performance. Her company functions as if it were an in-house department with fixed prices that eliminate surprise extra costs, and she allows clients to see the receipts, assuring no hidden mark-ups. Double A Events specializes in product launches and global summits for three markets: technology, video games, and entertainment.

Making the transition from being part of a big company with lots of support systems to being an entrepreneur was a learning curve. "You know what you love," says Amber. "But you're not always sure what goes into it. You don't realize how many things you don't know, like insurance, worker's compensation, stock options, etc." She is learning continually and finds support and resources by surrounding herself with other entrepreneurs who are "crazy enough" to be out in the market building their dreams.

Now in its third year, Double A Events has grown beyond Amber's wildest expectations. What started as a small idea to operate as an independent producer has turned into an agency that was voted among the Top 100 event companies worldwide by *Event Marketer* magazine. Amber has a growing staff of thirty across four offices, and she now spends her time focusing on how to create an environment where people on the team can create great experiences for their clients. She replaced her old salary and then some, enough success to put her emphasis on service and satisfaction. "It's not about the money but the quality, and that shows."

## The Take-Away

Many people are so focused on the prestige of working for a big, well-known company (as well as the steady paycheck and great benefits) that leaving that brand name firm creates a loss of personal identity and validation. That dependence on status-by-association can become a trap, keeping you in a job or company even when there are no more good opportunities to grow.

Amber was brave enough to leave a big-name employer and turn down "dream job" opportunities to commit to her vision. It's likely that she had friends and colleagues who thought she might be making a mistake or who feared that she was taking on too much risk. That's when, as an entrepreneur, you need to assess cautionary advice, make sure you've done your homework, and if your plan is solid, trust your heart and your vision to see it through. There will always be risk—even if you choose to remain with that brand-name company. A solid business plan and constant education can go a long way toward reducing that risk to manageable proportions. Don't let risk or status keep you from going for what you really want.

## Q&A with Amber Allen

### Q: What did you learn the hard way?
A: "So many things! Management techniques, especially managing Millennials. How to make them feel valuable when I can't pay a lot. Learning which projects to turn down."

**Q: To what do you attribute your Fresh Start Success?**
A: "I credit the people I've had in leadership positions above me, and the really good bosses who are now my mentors. They're available to answer questions and get me over the rough spots. I surround myself with people I want to be like, and we build things together."

**Q: How are you a different person now?**
A: "I get a lot less sleep! I work twice as much as I used to, but I feel more refreshed. The business is like my baby. I'm looking forward to the next twenty years. This thing I'm building consumes me. Everything you build is like Lego blocks, one piece connecting to every other piece."

**Q: What did you learn about yourself?**
A: "I'm more passionate than I thought I was. I have a lot more weaknesses than I thought I did. There are a lot of ways to learn and grow."

**Q: What new skills/knowledge did you gain?**
A: "I've learned so much! Let's see: patience, skills with interviewing people, knowledge about profit and loss, cash flow projects, finance in general. Lots!"

**Q: What one trait/habit/behavior is crucial to your Fresh Start Success?**
A: "I'm extremely organized and detailed. I believe the client is always right. I get my ducks in a row to come up with solutions that work for the client. I build the events the way the client wants, instead of doing it in a different way behind the client's back or cutting corners without regard for the end result, which is something I often saw other agencies do when I was the client."

**Q: If you had a superpower, what would it be?**
A: "Flying. I've been skydiving, and I've flown planes. I hate LA traffic."

**Q: What role has marketing and branding played in your success?**
A: "Given that events are very visual, the way that the company presents itself

has to feel cutting-edge but polished, just like the events the company produces. That means the company website, business cards, and social media presence has to be representative of what the company can produce for its customers. It adds a lot of additional consideration to everything we do, but luckily everyone's genuinely excited about new tech, like advanced web and app development, social media, and so on. We create sizzle videos showcasing highlights of our events, and we put the videos on social media. I want to see the same level of quality on our marketing materials as we create in the end products we provide for clients. Quality makes a difference. So do relationships and word of mouth. We never do cold calls. I'm always networking and meeting with people—a minimum of two meetings a day."

# Transferrable Skills

### Karen Kessler

WHAT IF YOUR career skills were the equivalent of a Swiss Army knife, adaptable to almost every situation? That might just be truer than you think. We're brought up to believe that different careers require unique skills, like specialized tools. Our lifetime of being herded into high school academic tracks and college majors reinforces the idea that skills map to particular careers, with very little overlap.

But what if your skills were more of a web connecting abilities to more than one possible career? We believe that's more accurate than our educational system leads us to believe. The reality is that our skills are multi-purpose tools, adaptable to many uses, and that means they are transferable to a greater degree than you may initially think. As you plan for your Fresh Start Success, review your personal skills inventory often and ask yourself how your abilities could be applied to the needs and challenges of the new career you want to pursue. You may find that you need fine-tuning rather than a whole new tool box!

## Choose Your Course

Karen Kessler went to college to be a paramedic and pursued that career for a decade. She managed restaurants, then served as an ambulance and 911 dispatcher, and was later hired as a project manager at a government office. "I've had five careers," Karen says. "My skills are highly transferable."

Now, as a coach and trainer, Karen owns her own company, ChooseRESULTS. She uses principles of Neuro-Linguistic Programming (NLP) to help clients leave the past behind and overcome the thoughts and behaviors holding them back from success. She enables people to "choose results" and take responsibility through her coaching and mentorship programs. Karen left her government job behind three years ago, and her husband is now full-time with the business as well.

Karen lost $75,000 her first year by rejecting her mentor's advice. "I was afraid of success," Karen says. "I was hiding from the magnificence of the outcome I could produce because I didn't feel ready." Then she committed to "The Expert Model," as created by Dr. Kim Redman, and to do the steps of the model in order. She met more people, changed how she used social media, and found that her message resonated more deeply.

She trained and was board designated in NLP, hypnosis, Time Line Therapy®, coaching, and project management. "All those tools are great for coaching and leadership because they help to put the 'big why' together," Karen says.

Not everyone was supportive when Karen decided to make a change. "Some people were like the proverbial crabs in the bucket, dragging others down," she says. "People who depend on your dance—even out of love—can become uncomfortable when you change." Karen stepped out to make new friends and a new circle of people who affirmed her and found a mentor in Dr. Kim Redman, who committed to guide her to make solid business decisions for her growing company.

"I get so excited seeing people 'get' what I teach," Karen says. "I wanted to help people avoid making the big mistakes I made initially, and I also wanted to create a company that provided me with flexibility."

## The Take-Away

As you consider your next move in your Fresh Start Success, look for common threads among the jobs, careers, and volunteer positions you have held. When you look closely, a pattern is likely to become clear, helping you identify the skills, types of tasks, and rewards that draw you again and again. That's your natural center of gravity, and you'll find the most satisfaction in your reinvention if you plan to build them in and make them a core part of your new career.

## Q&A with Karen Kessler

**Q: What did you learn the hard way?**

A: "I learned that you have to create the building blocks of your business in the right sequence and in order to get the maximum benefit. I also learned how to get comfortable with being uncomfortable. As a business owner, you learn to do what makes you feel uncomfortable—new skills are always uncomfortable in the beginning—without exception. Entrepreneurship is a new skill set. Even though I had skills, they weren't entrepreneur skills. In a corporate setting, other people were around to do specific tasks. As an entrepreneur, it's up to you, or you have to hire someone. I did a lot of training and webinars and spent $35,000 on training when I was five years away from being able to use it."

**Q: To what do you attribute your Fresh Start Success?**

A: "I decided to make ongoing personal development a priority, working with a mentor to hone skill gaps, working on my next moves, focusing on the numbers. It's essential to look at the numbers and the external measurements, and not just feelings. Honor your feelings, but don't make decisions based on them."

**Q: How are you a different person?**

A: "I am so much more self-empowered now. I have better boundaries and more congruence. I love what I do."

**Q: What did you learn about yourself?**

A: "I know now that I can do anything; I just have to focus. Focus determines behavior, and behavior determines results. I also realized that everything in my life that I didn't like was my own doing, which was empowering."

**Q: What traits are critical to your Fresh Start Success?**

A: "Perseverance, the ability to make quick decisions by using opportunity/cost models, the ability to find the resources you need fast, and get out of isolation and work interdependently for bigger win-wins."

**Q: If you had a superpower, what would it be?**
A: "I am a universal translator. I help clients communicate between the conscious and unconscious mind and connect the dream and the details."

**Q: What role has marketing played in your success?**
A: "I use social media to keep my community engaged. To grow my community, I connect personally with people and invite them to discover more about their own journey. When I am the right person to guide them, then we have a win-win. The next thing that happens is magical: people who are moving forward on their journey refer fabulous people to me who want the same journey—it's a win-win."

# Finding Your Alignment
## Christine Bové

WHEN DO YOU feel most at peace, most like you are in total sync with the universe as it should be? Most people would be unlikely to say "at work," which is a shame, considering how much of our lives we spend at the office.

What if you could change that? Why not look for a Fresh Start that brings you into that feeling of alignment, of working on your "zone," of being at the top of your game? Wouldn't you be doing the best work, providing the best outcomes, bringing your best energy if you felt in alignment with what you do for a living?

As you create your own Fresh Start Success, look into ways to monetize business services related to the settings and activities in which you feel most aligned with your own best self. Not only will your work become a joy, but you will be better able to serve your customers with passion and energy.

## Harmonizing Energy

Christine Bové went to school to study speech pathology and worked as a speech teacher with disabled children. She made good money, made friends, and had fun, but the work was not fulfilling. She knew that as valuable as the service she provided was to her clients, it was not her passion.

"I didn't know what I wanted to do, but I was sure of what I didn't want to do," she says. Christine had started her master's degree and thought about going into the corporate world. That was back in 1998. She got a job with a technology company in the World Trade Center during the dot com boom and learned a lot about start-ups. The start-up couldn't pay much money, and it wasn't stable.

"I found a headhunter who helped me get a job in a software company in New York City," Christine remembers. That position lasted for five years, but she was miserable. On the plus side, the job provided stability while she explored the city to figure out what she wanted to do next.

Christine networked diligently, looking for her next step. She had an opportunity to talk about "How to Feng Shui Your Office" that was well received. Her co-workers encouraged her to look deeper in into this career path. It was the first time in a long while that anything felt easy or that she felt truly contented, and her life changed.

As she began her studies in Feng Shui, she was shifting internally and recognizing that she couldn't stay in her old work environment because she was really unhappy with the company. "I was impatient and couldn't spend another minute in a place where I didn't feel respected or valued. I quit my job and relied on my savings to support me for a couple of months." This was a big transition that brought on emotional stress, which created resistance as she was finishing her Feng Shui certification. She discovered an opportunity that would support her new career path working at The Container Store®. It was a perfect fit. The store's customers were her ideal Feng Shui clients. The work at the store aligned with her goals, and she enjoyed organizing and closet design. Working for The Container Store® provided financial ease as she grew her business. She saw results with clients right away, but financial success took several years to achieve.

"People were very supportive," she says. "Everyone was surprised that I was a risk-taker—even me. Some friends were nervous on my behalf." The biggest struggle was with her inner self. "I get disappointed if I don't hit a home run right away. I had to overcome that to grow my business."

Christine consistently studied other people's success and how they achieved their goals. "I trusted my inner self, listened to my intuition, did my inner spiritual work, and got back up when I fell down," she recalls. "I'm continually evaluating and learning to be less judgmental of myself. I let go of what isn't working, take risks, and evaluate step-by-step."

## The Take-Away

Chronic unhappiness with your job or your work environment takes a toll in your mood, health, relationships, and quality of life. You don't have to accept being miserable as a requirement for earning a paycheck. If you're reinventing yourself, why not create a job you love?

While it's true that every type of work has its less desirable facets and down days, that's a far cry from a job that is pure hell. You deserve better. As you're making plans for your own Fresh Start Success, reimagine your work and reinvent your life so you can come from a place of service and passion, giving your customers your very best.

## Q&A with Christine Bové

**Q: How are you a different person now?**
A: "I'm a whole new person. I'm happier, I enjoy my work, and I found a place in the universe that works for me. I'm not trying to fit in, and I've gotten to the place where I don't have to be liked by everyone. Before, I had tried so much to fit in with other people. Now, I am who I am. I'm not afraid to talk about my intuitive side, gifts, and talents."

**Q: What did you learn about yourself?**
A: "I learned I'm a sensitive person. I didn't realize that before. I used to see sensitivity as a weakness. Now I realize that I am very tuned-in to other people's energy, and sometimes I took on emotional baggage that wasn't my own. Now I work to stay grounded in my own beliefs and be who I am with my friends and family to support me without giving up who I am."

**Q: What new knowledge did you gain?**
A: "Life is all about experiencing the good and the bad to lead you to what you truly desire. You have to be flexible to experience a bump in the road and learn how to turn around so you can grow faster. Commit to the goal and find the path to achieve it! It's worth it in the end."

**Q: What one trait is crucial to your success?**
A: "Self-confidence. I know now that I have to be strong, believe in myself, and know when to say no. I've learned to depend on my intuition and to brush off failures and move on."

**Q: If you had a superpower, what would it be?**
A: "I wish I could walk into a home and organize it in a second."

**Q: How did marketing and branding contribute to your success?**
A: "Social media is a tool to build relationships. I use it to create virtual sessions for clients all over the world and create relationships with people I wouldn't otherwise meet. Social media helped me to spread the word about what I do, connect and collaborate with other experts, and find people who share the same interests and enjoy what I do. Branding also helped me meet other experts."

# Voyager
## Pierette Simpson

IF LIFE IS a voyage and we're the ship, along the way most of us hit rough seas, spring a few leaks, and do our best to evade icebergs. Sometimes, despite our best efforts, we get hit amidships and life leaves us adrift. If we're fortunate, rescuers find us, or we swim to shore. Then the question becomes, how will we allow that shipwreck to affect the rest of our lives? How do we deal with tragedy and trauma, and where in ourselves do we find the strength to rise above—and inspire others?

We may not all have stories as dramatic as Pierette's, but we do each have a personal story of wins and losses, triumphs and low points, successes and failures. How we choose to interpret those events shapes what we make of our lives. How we frame the narrative we create around the things that happen to us not only affects our personal worldview, but also the legacy we leave in the world and how we touch the lives of those around us.

As you consider your Fresh Start Success, don't be in too much of a hurry to jettison the hardships and disappointments of the past without examining them for chances to learn, grow, and springboard toward something new. Opportunities are often hidden among hardships, waiting for us to reframe our narrative and see the chance to fix a problem, right a wrong, provide a better solution, or help others make the same journey to a place of strength and healing. What kind of legacy will you leave? How can the Fresh Start Success you create help you draw on your personal narrative of transcending hardship to leave a meaningful, lasting legacy? Like Pierette, you might be amazed at where the journey takes you!

## Shipwreck Survivor

Pierette Domenica Burzio was nine years old when her family set out from Pranzalito, Italy, with her grandparents in 1956. It was to be a dream life in

America where Pierette's mother had immigrated eight years earlier. They were aboard the *SS Andrea Doria* ocean liner, the pride of the Italian Line. On July 25, 1956, the *Stockholm*, a ship from the Swedish American Line, struck the *Andrea Doria* in waters just off the coast of Massachusetts. Fifty-one people died, but over sixteen hundred—including Pierette—were saved before the Andrea Doria capsized and sank. The sinking of the *Andrea Doria* is one of the worst maritime disasters and one of the most well-known aside from the *Titanic*.

After the rescue, Pierette and her grandparents settled in Detroit, Michigan. Pierette went to Wayne State University and studied to be a foreign language teacher. She taught languages for thirty-seven years to high school, junior high, and elementary school students.

Pierette found teaching to be very satisfying. She loved working with young people, loved teaching, and loved being in the academic world. Pierette was named Michigan Foreign Language Teacher of the Year and was inducted into the Farmington Teacher Hall of Fame. Even now, she's still in touch with dozens of her students on Facebook.

When Pierette reached the age when she thought she would retire, she planned to finish her master's degree in education and become a consultant. Instead, she received a call from a prestigious private school to substitute for a year and ended up staying for ten years.

While Pierette was teaching, she decided she was going to write survival stories about herself and others related to the sinking of the *Andrea Doria*. The shipwreck was something she remembered vividly, although she was only nine-and-a-half-years old when the *Andrea Doria* went down. Pierette started to network with survivors, then reached out to naval experts. The circumstances leading to the wreck had always been controversial, with various versions, but most placed blame on the Italian captain and crew. Due to unscrupulous politics, the case never went to court, and no verdict was ever reached.

As Pierette got to know naval experts, she began researching information that was in technical journals about the shipwreck, but had never been made public, and experts in the field shared what they believed "really happened."

The information Pierette learned cast the situation in a very different light from the popular understanding portrayed in the media. Her research vindicated the Italian captain, crew, and builders, all of whom had been blamed in the press and in other publications.

She exposed the scientific facts regarding the collision, sinking, and rescue, and about diving to the ship in her first book, *Alive on the* Andrea Doria! *The Greatest Sea Rescue in History.* The book was filled with survivor stories and naval science and was published in both the United States and in Italy. She became an authority on the topic and worked with the Society of Naval Architects and Marine Engineers, and with the divers, getting the whole picture.

From that book and her research, Pierette stepped into public speaking. Her presentations ranged from historical discussions about the shipwreck to motivational speeches about transcending life's crises to reaching the American Dream as an immigrant. She retired from teaching in 2006 and became a full-time author/speaker, presenting to community groups and scientific organizations. Then one of her audience members, who was an advisor for Ameriprise Financial, recommended Pierette to the company as a motivational speaker. Ameriprise employed her, and she traveled throughout the Midwest speaking to their employees and clients.

Audiences loved Pierette's presentations and were fascinated by the story of the *Andrea Doria.* That's when Pierette realized that nothing but documentaries had ever been made about the disaster. She decided to make a movie to bring to light the new information she had presented in her book. Pierette had no prior moviemaking experience, but she was passionate about her topic and determined to find a way forward.

After working on gathering the elements needed to make her movie, Pierette took a hiatus from her project to promote a photographic exhibition by her fiancé, photographer Richard Haskin, which was touring in Detroit and Turin, Italy. She founded an international project to support the exhibition, and then co-curated it as part of Project Detur. A documentary came out of that partnership called "Art Within Art· From Italy to Detroit and Vice Versa." That project dropped in her lap when the person originally in charge couldn't finish it, and it fell to Pierette as the curator of Haskin's photography. (Haskin won two national awards for his photography.) Pierette completed the documentary and brought the film and the exhibition to Turin, Italy.

Pierette's success with the photography documentary spurred her ambition to tell the "real" story of the *Andrea Doria*. At age sixty-eight, she decided to go full-speed ahead into movie production and learned to be a screenwriter. She took on the role of producer in Detroit and Italy. "I am definitely younger than my chronological age," Pierette says in jest. By her own admission, Pierette can be intense. "I like learning a craft and challenging myself by doing things for the first time, like writing a screenplay, learning to be a producer, and even an actress," she adds. She and her crew filmed in Italy for the *Andrea Doria* movie, putting in sixteen-hour days in hundred-degree heat.

Most heartening was the support Pierette garnered for the movie. "Many people supported me," she says. "Friends in Detroit were actors. Other friends who owned local businesses sponsored the filming and catering. A local salon did the actors' make-up and hair. It was so amazing," Pierette recounts.

"I was astounded by the response from the village in Northern Italy where I was born," Pierette says. "We went back there to film, and those people pulled through for me. It's a village with one hundred and eight people, at the foot of the Alps. They organized so much to help us film the project, like closing restaurants to feed the crew, providing lodging and transportation. Some pitched in to find period costumes or cars for the filming. It was above and beyond expectations."

Along the way, the film had plenty of hurdles to overcome. "Every day, there were setbacks," Pierette says. "We couldn't find period cars—in Detroit, of all places! The cars that were right for the period were too busy with other things or too expensive for our budget. We finally got five cars lined up for a shoot, and only two showed up. Then the worst storm of the whole summer was headed our way, and after all that, we only had two hours to film. But we made it work."

Pranzalito honored Pierette with a tribute for bringing the project to the village. "They gave so much to me," Pierette says. Villagers were the actors in the film, playing their own ancestors who had sailed on the *Andrea Doria*.

Pierette's seventy-nine-year-old cousin played her great-grandmother, and that woman's daughter played Pierette's mother. "They did everything to make it successful," Pierette recalls. "The crew from Rome became best friends with the village. We woke up a village in a way it never expected it would wake up. The village rediscovered itself by re-enacting its history and personal experiences."

Pierette's movie, Andrea Doria: *Are the Passengers Saved?* is currently in post-production, while gathering the funding necessary to push it over the finish line. The movie is coming along well. After having released the trailer and teaser, Pierette debuted a twelve-minute sneak peek of the movie to create buzz about the project and encourage additional investors and sponsors. She plans to have the docufilm done soon. It will then go to the marketing and distribution phase. Pierette hopes it will eventually sell to a cable network to become a TV mini-series, or that someone will buy rights for a feature in time for the sixtieth anniversary of the sinking. Pierette also wrote a novel called, *I Was Shipwrecked on the* Andrea Doria! *The* Titanic *of the 1950s*, a story she hopes will inspire young people to pursue marine sciences to enhance safety at sea.

## The Take-Away

Sometimes we don't fully appreciate the most significant aspects in our lives until time passes and we see them in a new light. Pierette's experience as a survivor was just a part of family history until she chose to dive into it with fresh perspective. That opened up new opportunities for her as an author, speaker, director, producer, and actress and brings a valuable new historical interpretation of the events to the world.

What elements of your life story are gathering dust in the closet of your memories, discounted and overlooked? You are the only person on this planet to have made life's journey in your own unique way. Dare to take a fresh look at your story. You might find a golden opportunity in the past you are taking for granted!

## Q&A with Pierette Simpson

**Q: What did you learn about yourself?**

A: "I learned a lot. Everything about making a movie is more expensive than you think it will be, and more labor-intensive. You have to rely your own resources and be creative about asking for help. In working on this project, I've used my language skills, my writing skills, and my networking skills. As a young girl, I studied music, and I was a professional violinist at one point. That liberal arts background and my teaching experience helped me succeed with Richard's photo exhibit and the documentary about the exhibit. So did my love for art and music. The success of that documentary opened doors for my film project about the *Andrea Doria*. I asked everyone I could think of to help me achieve my goal, and that led to collaborating with my cousin who lives in Turin (Torino), Italy."

"You learn from everything and everyone and carry it on to the next thing, learning and relearning in order to succeed. For me, education and experience are key. I had to learn all the jobs required to produce my movie. Even then, life threw us some curveballs. The costumer for the movie had an aneurysm right before the captain's costume was due. The director's father stepped in and created the costume in one day, just in time for filming."

**Q: How are you a different person than before?**

A: "I learned to be resourceful since I've been self-employed, doing things I had never done before. I've been tough on myself—too tough. I haven't vacationed for more than a week in the last two years."

**Q: What one trait/habit/behavior is critical to your Fresh Start Success?**

A: "I'm motivated and persistent. I can do things I never imagined I could do at this age—I am 'one in a million' according to my friends! I've learned that I'm very creative. I can work with a lot of different people—divers, film crew, naval experts. I'm good at putting people together."

**Q: If you had a superpower, what would it be?**

A: "I wish I had a magic wand. Snap your fingers and whatever you want is magically done. I would have had a more normal life and had a family. I was widowed young."

**Q: What role has marketing and branding played in your success?**

A: "Marketing is essential. Social media is amazing. We released the docufilm trailer on YouTube and Facebook to raise buzz about the project. I'm hoping to use LinkedIn for funding, and I plan on promoting the film on Twitter and Instagram. As for branding, I am the '*Andrea Doria* lady.' I've become the gatekeeper and the go-to expert on the shipwreck. When we were shooting the film, we got international coverage about the project, plus Italian TV and media coverage in the U.S., especially in Detroit. Marketing matters!"

# The Influencer
## Teresa de Grosbois

**WHAT HAPPENS WHEN** you achieve your goals—not once, but twice—and still find that something's missing? Time for a Fresh Start. Teresa had all the right degrees and the career success in corporate life, and then made a shift to fulfill a lifelong dream as an author. She succeeded but found that something was still missing. The really important part is that she was willing to make another shift to live the vision she had for making an impact in the world.

As you think about your Fresh Start Success, remember to evaluate whether you'll be making a living and a life for yourself. Financial success and stability are important, but so is the sense of fulfillment that comes from knowing you are making a difference and leaving a legacy. Realize that it may take a few versions of your Fresh Start to really find a fulfilling path.

## Vision and Influence

With two university degrees, Teresa developed a successful career for herself in Canada's oil and gas industry: first working in environmental, and then becoming an expert in business management systems. At the same time, she distinguished herself by leading large, multi-stakeholder initiatives and large change initiatives to build stronger organizational leadership.

She enjoyed leading change initiatives and influencing corporate and industry culture. At the same time, she didn't really like the oil and gas industry and didn't feel like she was part of building a better world. The shift came in small, gentle increments. She knew she needed to leave corporate work and start her own company. She surrounded herself with people who had done personal transformational work, and they challenged her to put what she had learned to use in the real world.

Teresa had a vivid dream one New Year's Eve and wrote in a journal, "This is the year I leave and create something different." She realized she already had most of the skills and knowledge that she needed for the Fresh Start Success she had in mind. That night, she had a dream that validated her path and helped her recognize that everything she had asked for was in play. The next day, she went to work and asked for a leave of absence. She took three months off. Within two weeks, she realized that she could do what she wanted to do, so she went back to her boss and extended her leave by a year because she needed mental space.

Teresa left a lucrative job in the oil and gas industry to start a charity to build schools in Africa. To fund the charity, she decided to publish some of the children's stories she liked to write for her daughters. She began doing children's programs for an honorarium but quickly discovered she didn't really enjoy speaking in those venues and she wasn't making money. The fulfillment she had hoped to find wasn't present, and the things she was doing weren't really sparking her passion. Even after she had written three best-selling books, she realized she was not enjoying the process and was hungry for something more.

She wanted to leave a legacy by making the world being a better place and didn't feel she was applying what she knew to something with lasting impact. But while Teresa struggled with what to do next, people kept asking her, "Three bestsellers in eight months! How did you do that?" She began mentoring people in how to create influence and word of mouth, which led her to focus on "thought leadership."

"When you find what stokes you up, it's easier to make money," Teresa says, although it took a while before her financial goals were met.

Before Teresa set out on her second Fresh Start Success, she talked "very vulnerably" with friends about living on less money. She was used to a good income, and she needed to cut it in half to accomplish her goal. The support she received overwhelmed her. Making the change became an opportunity to draw a community around her and to enlist her kids in helping her build a dream.

Friends were very supportive, shared resources, and actively stepped in to help. Before she committed to the second round of changes, Teresa talked to her kids and asked if they would be okay with cutting back. They were very excited to help her live her dreams. She was a single mom at the time, so there was real risk, but her family was very supportive at every step. "My kids were my heroes," Teresa says, "and now that they're older, they're stepping out to do cool things on their own. The adventure became one of the coolest opportunities as a family to define who we are. We became a family who were the guardians of each other's dreams."

Of course, there were naysayers. "My mother grieved for two or three years that I had walked away from an indexed government pension," Teresa recalls. "But you have to choose who you want to listen to." She found that the more she stepped into her Fresh Start Success, the more her circle of friends shifted. Some of her old friends were uncomfortable with the new Teresa. "I think they needed the validation of me being the same as them, the way I had been," she says. "Or they were speaking from their own fear. Choose your friends. Staying with naysayers makes it harder. Your truest friends will change with you to support you. But, in reality, some of your friends will change."

It took Teresa between six months and a year for her new business model to become sustainable. She had enough passive income from a rental property and other investments to cover her basic needs, so there was some security. As she honed in on her vision for leadership and creating influence, she had to make choices about how to structure her business. To reduce stress, she chose to forego having a brick and mortar office and kept her cash flow demand low. Over the next two years, her vision continued to evolve and became Teresa's current company, Wildfire Workshops.

Today, Teresa is a sought-after influence expert, international speaker, and the author of the #1 international best-selling book, *Mass Influence*. She is also Chair of the Evolutionary Business Council, an international, invitation-only council of speakers and influencers dedicated to teaching the principles of success. She has lived three very different Fresh Start Success visions of success, with much more ahead of her to accomplish!

## The Take-Away

Somewhere early in our lives, we often get the idea we are cut out to only do one thing in life. The educational system abets this way of thinking as we push children into selecting career paths and declaring specialties at younger and younger ages. It's a very myopic way of looking at life, and a limiting way of looking at ourselves.

Who says you can only do one thing well? And who is to say that you can't do multiple things excellently, either all at once or serially? We live longer now, in better health than ever before. It's time to re-examine the concept of being a "Renaissance" person, good at many things, successful in many venues. If you've made one Fresh Start Success and satisfied your need to accomplish that goal, plan your next reinvention and then take the plunge. We are not limited to a set number of Fresh Start Successes!

## Q&A with Teresa de Grosbois

### Q: What did you learn the hard way?

A: "I learned not to move too far from where you are (not just physically). You don't need to go somewhere radically different to achieve your goal. Just move closer to what you want to do and find ways to make what you're doing more meaningful."

### Q: To what do you attribute your Fresh Start Success?

A: "I am passionate about living my passion. I want to solve a big problem for the world, do something for which there is big demand, something I'm excited about. It is extremely exciting for me to solve a problem that other people perceive as a big hurdle."

### Q: How are you a different person now?

A: "I'm more authentic and confident because I'm aligned with what I love. I'm more savvy—when you're in the weeds making it work, it teaches you true entrepreneurship. I'm also a lot more fun. I laugh more at life and what's coming at me now in a way I couldn't before."

**Q: What did you learn about yourself?**
A: "I learned how significant my own inner dialogue is when events seemed to conspire to stop me. I learned just how much inner dialogue gets in all of our ways. Now, I'm more mindful and aware of inner dialogue in myself and in others."

**Q: What new skills/knowledge did you gain?**
A: "I studied and observed, particularly regarding influence. I focused on understanding and breaking apart what makes influential people tick and how they interact with others to achieve their goals. I observed what they did, broke it down and mapped the steps so they could be repeated and taught."

**Q: How did your prior work prepare you for your Fresh Start Success?**
A: "Everything I did before provided foundational business skills and expertise that I needed to help my new business succeed. Those experiences taught me how to be a change agent, how to create big change, and what a business needs to run efficiently."

**Q: What one trait/habit is critical for your success?**
A: "Love. You've got to love people up in business. Everything is about loving people enough to see their possibilities and give feedback when they're not living into the power of who they have the potential to be."

**Q: If you had a superpower, what would it be?**
A: "Forgiveness. Opening people up to self-forgive. If you can forgive yourself more quickly, you can also forgive others. Judgment is a story in our heads. We need to let go of judgment and create a world of love, acceptance, assistance, and collaboration around ourselves."

**Q: What role did marketing and branding play in your success?**
A: "Marketing has played a pretty big role with my success. But it should always be honest. It's important to be real to who you are. Good branding is

simply a description of who we are in the world that makes it clear enough for other people to understand and remember. When you can bring yourself to your purpose fully, you can clearly state who you are, which is the essence of good branding and marketing."

# Reinvention Without Borders
## Melissa Darnay

**WHEN YOU ENVISION** your Fresh Start Success, where does it take place? Most of us picture ourselves doing something different but in our present location. Sometimes, as Melissa Darnay discovered, opportunity presents itself in a completely new place, where it's necessary to re-define both "career" and "home" at the same time.

If you've got a touch of wanderlust, why restrict your reinvention to your current city, state, or country? You may find that skills that are common where you're currently located are in short supply and in hot demand elsewhere. Or perhaps a passion you've always relegated to being a hobby—like taking tours, skiing, photography, or scuba diving—might be just the ticket to a whole new career where the location becomes part of the payday. Don't rule out options without considering the possibilities. You might find yourself somewhere wholly unexpected—and utterly wonderful—doing exactly what you love.

## Ex-pat Opportunity

Melissa Darnay went to school for journalism and marketing and found jobs after graduation in those fields. "It paid the bills," she says. Melissa spent ten years as a marketing consultant, but the work was missing something, and she lacked fulfillment. "I felt like a mental prostitute, writing copy to support one company or product after another that I really didn't care about, just for the paycheck," she reflects. She was bored professionally, and the death of her husband in a car accident primed her for making a life change.

A friend of Melissa's moved to Panama, and she went down to visit. She fell in love with the country, and the trip opened her eyes to the possibility of relocating. After Melissa came back to the United States, she Skyped with friends in Panama and thought they were living a great lifestyle. Costs were lower, the society was similar enough to the U.S. to make it easy to assimilate, and most Panamanians spoke English. Panama's economy was doing well, and the government welcomed Americans.

"I thought, 'Wow, what if I could do that?' I was living in a McMansion in Dallas, and I wondered if this was just what I needed to change my life and start over," Melissa recalls. She took a second, exploratory trip and asked herself where she could see herself living. When she found the place where she now lives, it was love at first sight. "I thought, 'I could wake up to this every single day for the rest of my life.' So I sold my house and furniture in Dallas, took everything I owned in a twenty-foot shipping container, and I moved to Panama with my two dogs." That was three years ago. Now, Melissa markets real estate to North Americans and is a property manager, and she also takes American ex-pats on tours.

"I had played at real estate back in the U.S., but I had never expected to make my living from it," Melissa says. "I bought a house in Dallas and got a bad deal, so I went to real estate school to avoid a bad experience the next time. I dabbled in the field, but it was never my main focus." She owned a marketing consulting business, so she had been an entrepreneur for ten years before moving to Panama. "I was used to working long hours," she recalls. "I have a lot of drive, and I brought my work ethic with me. Entrepreneurship is not as firmly rooted in Panama as it is in the U.S. If you work your business like a business, it's easy to become successful here," she adds. She targeted other ex-pat Americans because she understands their questions and knows their expectations.

She committed fully to the change. "I was like the conquistador Cortez who burned his ships so his soldiers couldn't count on going home. I sold my house and moved the dogs, so giving up wasn't an option. I wasn't going to run back to Dallas and say it didn't work out when things got tough. Moving the dogs across international borders was complicated —and the move was expensive—so I couldn't easily go back and forth. I had to make it work."

Melissa was successful in one year. She kept her marketing consulting business in the U.S. for a year, and after that, she shifted her entire income generation to her real estate-property management-tour business in Panama.

"I moved to Panama to change my life. I'd been widowed for a while and was opening up to the possibility of falling in love again," Melissa says. "I was tired of feeling stuck, and I was tired of being single. A couple of days after I moved to Panama, I met the man I ended up marrying! We've been married now for a year. I thought I might meet an American ex-pat, and instead I met a Brazilian who didn't speak English, and I didn't speak Portuguese. So we both had to learn new languages!"

## The Take-Away

What's keeping you rooted where you are currently located? You might have strong ties to a particular place, such as family, friends, community involvement, or a love for the climate or local amenities. But if you aren't strongly rooted in a particular place, don't overlook fantastic opportunities for reinvention that allow you to live out your Fresh Start Success in a dream location.

As with any move, an international relocation requires doing your homework. But if you've visited a country in the past that spoke to you on a deep level, maybe you owe it to yourself to figure out whether or not moving there would be a good fit for you and the skills you offer. Don't rule anything out as "impossible" until you've checked out the details!

## Q&A with Melissa Darnay

**Q: What did you learn the hard way?**
A: "I'm a Type A personality, and that had to change. Now I'm an A-. Panama is a Latin American country, and things take longer. Although it's very similar to the United States, it's not just like the U.S. If you're going to live here, you have to adjust. I'm a planner. Everything for me is like a chess game. I'm always thinking twenty moves out. That's hard to do in Panama until you're on the

ground. Not all the information you find on the Internet about the country is correct, so you need to be present to really know what's going on."

**Q: How are you a different person now?**
A: "I've gained an incredible sense of satisfaction to become a success in such a different place. There are a lot of challenges, and it's empowering to overcome them. For example, I'm learning, but I still don't speak Spanish well."

**Q: What did you learn about yourself?**
A: "When I lost my late husband, I thought I was going to break. I hadn't been fragile previously, but I became fragile. I learned a lot about inner strength. Now, I've had to learn about balance, and I'm so much better balancing work and play time. We go to our place in the mountains Thursday through Sunday and come back to work for Monday morning. Moving expanded my sense of play, happiness, quality of life, and ultimately made me more productive."

**Q: What new skills did you gain?**
A: "Real estate in Panama is different than in the U.S. To force myself to learn, I wrote a book about Panama, and so I had to research everything I didn't know. I became an expert on Panama real estate, especially for ex-pats. There is a large American ex-pat community in Panama, and they know that I understand what they're looking for and what their expectations are because we're coming from the same background."

**Q: What is one trait crucial to your Fresh Start Success?**
A: "Being open-minded. People who don't thrive have closed minds. They complain that Panamanians don't speak English; they want to only work with U.S. people. Things aren't just like the U.S.—it's their country!"

**Q: If you had a superpower, what would it be?**
A: "I would like to stop time. I think that right now, Panama is perfect. Twenty years from now, it will be more like the U.S., and it might lose some of the

features I love. Costs here are fifty percent of what they would be in Dallas for a similar lifestyle."

**Q: What role does marketing and branding play in your success?**
A: "Obviously, that's helped a lot. Marketing is huge, and it's an important part of getting new business, getting the word out. I see a need and fill it. When someone says 'I wish we had…' or 'I miss…' it's an opportunity. Marketing lets people know that I've got what they're looking to find."

# Communities Sustain

## Wendy Woodworth

**AS YOU'RE PLANNING** your Fresh Start Success, don't try to go it alone. We all need communities to sustain us, encourage us, and help us gain new skills. Starting, building, and running a business is hard work, no matter how much you love what you're doing. It's essential to be connected to other people who understand where you are coming from and what you're trying to achieve. Ideally, a community should have people at all stages of their growth, from beginners, to rising mid-level performers, to seasoned elders.

Choose your communities carefully to make sure the group is in alignment with your values and that the members are not only supportive but also positioned to be able to teach, encourage, and connect you to help you gain skills and grow your business. A good community is invaluable to your Fresh Start Success because it can mentor you, recommend resources, and help you avoid problems while also reducing your learning curve.

Remember that you get out of a community what you put into it, so commit to being an active participant. Look for ways to give first from your own skills, perspective, and experience so that you build up social capital that you can draw on later, when you are the one who needs support. Communities not only sustain us as entrepreneurs, but they are a wonderful way to give back, pay it forward, and enrich the world around us.

## Strength in Community

Wendy Woodworth has been a court reporter for forty years, dealing with criminal trials, rape cases, civil suits, divorces, and the list goes on. She liked that every day was different and that she was always learning. "I felt like a sponge," she says. "There were always expert witnesses sharing knowledge the average person doesn't get to hear. I was constantly meeting new people." She owns and operates Digi-Tran, a court reporting business.

She liked the variety and insights her work provided, but the "due-yesterday" pace drove her crazy with last-minute demands from lawyers and judges. The frantic pace meant Wendy was spending very little of her time on herself.

Wendy had been married for twenty-five years to a verbally abusive man who was unfaithful to her. When the pain became too much to bear, "I found the strength to say 'enough is enough' and realized that I deserved more out of life. When I asked for a divorce, he became physically abusive. My work took me to a different province, but he tracked me down and threatened me," Wendy recounts.

She put measures in place to protect herself, the divorce was finalized, and Wendy spent the next six years building a new life for herself. "I was holding everyone else up," she says, "my mother, my staff, my four children. I forgot about me completely." Wendy cried herself to sleep many nights and prayed to meet a man with three qualities: a giver not a taker, slow to anger, and someone who could love her as much as she could love him. Although Wendy didn't really believe she would find him, she did. She found the man of her dreams, Carmon, and they married on Valentine's Day 2009 in their home—in front of their combined six children and thirteen grandchildren. Two months after the happiest day of her life, Carmon was diagnosed with late-stage colon cancer. Wendy's world went into a tailspin.

Over the next six years, Carmon and Wendy fought his battle together, and each time they thought they had it beat, the cancer would return. It was when they received the news that the cancer had jumped to his liver that Wendy felt totally devastated. It felt like when she took two steps forward, she went back ten. She was lost and hit bottom. It was only then, when the pain was too great to bear alone, that she reached out and discovered a community of BraveHeart Women that provided her with strength, support, love, and tools to carry her through this journey and onward to her real passion, which she had yet to discover.

By November 2011, Wendy's life had been transformed so much that it created a yearning inside her to give back. She attended BraveHeart Women's international event where the founder asked women to come forward to launch local chapters in their own communities to give back, and Wendy jumped at the opportunity. She wanted to help other women find the peace she had found through BraveHeart Women.

Wendy had to learn how to speak to groups and communicate on a whole new level in order to share the tools that changed her life. She signed on for a three-day workshop to learn how to let go of the negatives that were holding her back. "Until you let go of your past, you can't move forward," Wendy says, a principle of her own Fresh Start Success. She practiced her presentation skills, moving away from using a script to speaking extemporaneously. "I had to move from my head to my heart," Wendy says. "When I did, I discovered who I really was and reached the women I longed to reach."

Wendy trained with the BraveHeart Women's organization and then launched the Calgary chapter. She still runs Digi-Tran, so Wendy had management responsibilities for the company as well as for the new chapter. Meanwhile, her husband's cancer did not respond to treatment, and in December 2014, Carmon transitioned in their home in front of the fireplace, right where they had, six years earlier, exchanged their wedding vows, surrounded by their children and grandchildren.

"I found out that many women who are in a similar situation to what I was going through feel less than whole, almost as if they want to die with their partner," Wendy recalls. She found that by investing in herself and utilizing the tools she learned through the BraveHeart Women community, she could find peace and go on with life in ease.

Before Wendy made her big change, she didn't value herself. She was a perfectionist and was very organized, but she still never felt good enough. "Now I know that everything doesn't have to be perfect. Eighty percent is good enough. I've learned to trust the Universe to provide all that I require. I no longer live a 'what if' life, but an 'I AM' life," Wendy adds.

"I now know that everything in my life happened for a reason and guided me to where I am today. Even my forty years as a court reporter where I have listened, watched, and viscerally felt the pain of women from all walks of life and all ages share their stories, heard their cries of loneliness and feelings of worthlessness. When I look into a woman's eyes, and there is no spark, I know her pain and I want to share with her that I, too, was once where she was, and that if she is open, she can learn to dance with life again, find joy in her heart and friendships that last a lifetime."

Wendy went from being terrified to speak to a group of forty-five people when she first started her chapter to being comfortable speaking to more than a thousand at a gathering in 2013. She developed and held her first Dance with Life retreat in the summer of 2015, and she has now branded herself as "A Guide by Your Side" and is building her community. "I know that community is our strength!" she says.

She has developed her own DANCE4U coaching practice and the 7 Steps to Dancing With Life while working on her first book, *Empty Your Purse*, with techniques to help women let go of the things that are holding them back.

## The Take-Away

As you create your Fresh Start Success, there will be obstacles and times of discouragement. You'll need to find resources and make connections. Being involved in an active and meaningful way to a vibrant community of like-minded entrepreneurs can make all the difference.

The investment of time and self you make in supportive communities can sustain you when the going gets tough. Your fellow members can offer advice based on their own experiences to help you overcome obstacles. A good community increases your personal network exponentially through the connections of all the members. And as you grow and succeed, you'll be able to help others by providing insights and connections, reciprocating the support.

## Q&A with Wendy Woodworth

**Q: What did you learn the hard way?**
A: "Don't wait until the pain is too great to bear. That I am not alone—connect

in community. Be willing to be open and invest in myself and learn from my mentors, then life doesn't have to be so damn hard. Feel into what your passion is and go for it!"

**Q: What did you learn about yourself?**
A: "That Wendy is this amazing soul that is here to share her gift (as we all are here to do) with others, and by holding herself back, she was really doing herself and others harm. I now know that life happens *through* me, not *to* me, and my vision is to create the community that women come to dance with life again."

**Q: If you had a superpower, what would it be?**
A: "To wave a magical wand over you and release what is holding you back and see the fire light up in your eyes as we dance together as ONE in community."

**Q: How important was marketing to your Fresh Start Success?**
A: "Everything! And branding is key so people understand who you really are. Know how the social media sites work and how to use them for specific purposes. Don't have unrealistic expectations. Reach out to others who have expertise—you can't do everything—and learn from them. Marketing is a long process, so commit to it."

# Picking Your Team
## Sheri Fink

MILLIONS OF PEOPLE play fantasy football because of the allure of putting together the perfect team. Great teams are more than just a collection of individuals: the members not only need to have complementary skills, they also need to have the chemistry to support each other and work together for everyone's success.

As you create your own Fresh Start Success, think about who's on your team. Some of those team members may be your family and friends who wish you well and provide encouragement. You may draw on old colleagues and mentors, friends and neighbors, even friends of friends. Remember that the people you choose to be on your reinvention team need to be encouraging yet wise, clear-eyed, but not pessimistic, optimistic, and enthusiastic without being blind to risk or consequence. Perennial doubters and downers need not apply.

Ideally, you want to surround yourself with people whose skills and knowledge fill in your gaps and weaknesses, and for whom you do the same. (A little duplication is good, so people can cover for each other.) Together, you have all the pieces. Most importantly, your team needs to see that working together benefits everyone. Pick your team members with care, and watch your reinvention prosper!

## Embrace Your Destiny

Sheri Fink has been many things. She earned a bachelor's of arts in communications with a minor in psychology and went into marketing because she was intrigued by the consumer thought process. She created an online magazine back when e-zines were in their infancy. Then Sheri earned a master's in telecommunications/eCommerce and taught HTML and marketing as well as web design.

At one time or another throughout her career, Sheri has been a receptionist, waitress, and customer service representative. She worked in retail, where she was responsible for store merchandising, then went back to school to learn web design and spent twelve years in online marketing, where she ran a team and managed strategic partnerships.

Regardless of her role, Sheri liked watching how consumer behavior evolved. "When you're working with the public, there's never any boredom because something is always changing," she says. "I liked serving people, getting them what they needed, supporting big brands. I worked hard and I had a 'sexy job,' one most people would think they wanted, with good pay, travel, and benefits."

Despite her external success and promotions, Sheri was unhappy at work. She was being bullied by a woman in the corporation. "I didn't just want to walk away," Sheri recalls, "but it got so bad that I finally came to a moment of surrender where I thought 'I would do anything to change this.'"

Sheri did a lot of soul searching about what to do next. The image of a rose in a weed bed came to her, clear and strong, and she had an idea about writing a children's book. Sheri created an exit strategy that took her a year from that day to make her escape. "I saw my clients through the end of the business cycle, and the bully was let go," she says. "But even without the bullying, I didn't feel in alignment. So I left on good terms, even though I didn't have anything lined up." She did consulting for small businesses, but didn't enjoy the work. Her clients were happy, but she wasn't. Sheri forgot about her book ideas. Then she went to Jack Canfield's seminar and got into conversations that led her back to the idea of writing a children's book.

"I knew I had to do it fast or else I'd chicken out," she says. She saved as much as possible and lived frugally, which she knew how to do because she had grown up in humble conditions. "My path wasn't logical or planned out. In corporate, I was all in my head, but I couldn't be a robot anymore, and I had to follow my heart. I had so much passion for the book I wanted to write, but I was scared as hell."

Sheri is a natural connector. She had helped a lot of people and had never asked for anything in return, so she started to ask people for their help and connections. "I found the energy, money, and time; got a coach; and after that, everything happened fast," she says. It took six months to get her book into print, and within two weeks she was a #1 Amazon bestseller without running a book launch campaign.

Her first children's book, *The Little Rose*, made back Sheri's investment in twelve months. Her second book earned out in six months; her third book returned its investment in three months. Sheri's books and the world of characters she created have won awards and rave reviews, creating a secondary career as a keynote speaker. Her new novel, *Cake in Bed*, is the first for an adult audience.

It took four years to become self-sustaining. Sheri runs her publishing company like a business, not a hobby. "I'm always investing in the business. I would love to be more fearless—I have lots of good ideas, and I want to bring them to life faster."

Sheri has found deep satisfaction in her new career. "In corporate life, everything was about ego," she says. "That was what I knew—get a big job, make lots of money, land an impressive job title with a big salary, run projects with big-name people. I did those things. But even being successful in that arena led to an emptiness that none of those things could fix," Sheri recalls.

"I've learned that you need to fully embrace your destiny and the magic will unfold," Sheri says. "I feel more inspired now. In the old days, it was all about strategy, and I made millions of dollars for other people. Now, I focus on a more human level. I don't just want people to buy my books; I want them to *love* the books, I want to leave a legacy and change how they feel about themselves, and who they are when they become heart-centered and connected. I love making a difference, inspiring others, and believing in myself."

Not everyone has understood her change of direction. "When you're on any journey, some people won't relate. I have crazy dreams compared to the average person. But you can't spend your time with people who shoot things down. If they're not on the rocket, they need to get out of the way," she says. "Be careful about who is in your inner circle. Not everyone gets what you want to do. You can't give away your power to other people's opinions. For me, readers are the ones who matter."

Sheri measures success differently now. "When a child comes up and looks at you like you are a magical unicorn, all starry-eyed, and gives you a hug, you have made an impact on a life," Sheri says. "I can be my authentic self now. I don't have to hide anymore, and it is so wonderful to have people receive who I am, as I am. I never expected the impact of that."

## The Take-Away

"If they're not on the rocket, they need to get out of the way," Sheri says. Who's on your rocket, and who is in the way? Making a Fresh Start Success requires work and commitment, along with a strong enough belief in yourself to weather the rough spots.

Keep your distance from people who see dangers more clearly than opportunities or who look on the bleak side of everything. If you have no choice about being around people (like family members) who aren't supportive of your vision and reinvention, don't share your concerns or triumphs with them—you don't want to give them ammunition to use against you. Gather your wise supporters and launch your rocket!

## Q&A with Sheri Fink

### Q: What did you learn the hard way?
A: "I learned quickly that if an activity or investment isn't going to sell more books, don't do it. Be strategic in how you invest. Print and illustration quality is imperative; other things are not. You have to let go of ideas, people, and opportunities that aren't a 'hell, yes'."

### Q: How are you a different person?
A: "I'm more me than I've ever been. Be free to be who you are. I no longer

do what everyone wants me to do. Learning that was frickin' hard. I connect more easily with people now because I don't have as many walls built up. I'm happier and healthier."

**Q: What traits are critical to your Fresh Start Success?**
A: "I'm bolder now, and more expressive. I say what I feel, and I put it all out there, even when I'm scared. I'm not afraid to talk about my big goals."

**Q: What new skills did you learn?**
A: "I had no idea how to publish a book. I had business skills and had always been entrepreneurial, even when I was in corporate life, but I had to learn book marketing, budgeting, and public speaking. The topics I spoke on in corporate life hadn't been meaningful to me, so I didn't enjoy speaking. I didn't know how to do events, so I did them my own way, and they worked. 'Be original' is my motto. My vision is bigger than I can currently execute, but what I can do is growing. I trust my inner vision, and I'm always innovating."

**Q: If you had a superpower, what would it be?**
A: "To ignite the spark of possibility and inspiration for each person I meet and eradicate self-doubt."

**Q: What role has marketing and branding played in your success?**
A: "It's huge. I didn't learn social media in school, and I've discovered that social media is not really about marketing: it's about people and relationships. Marketing is just the channel. Social media is a way to connect with people all over the world. I'm very grateful to have thousands of online fans. I invest my time on social media looking to see how I can connect with the most people to make the biggest impact. Social media is all about making a connection to other people."

# What's Your Truth?
## Jo Dibblee

EACH OF US has walked a unique pathway to get to where we are in life. That pathway shaped your perspective, informed your choices, taught you wisdom, and made you who you are today. No one else has walked that exact path, which means you have experienced the world in a way that is all your own. At the same time, many of us walk similar paths, facing obstacles and challenges that share commonalities. We can learn from the people who are ahead of us on a similar path, and we can teach and enable those who come behind us.

The lessons you have learned on your path are your truths. Sharing your truth with others can help them navigate their path with greater ease while acknowledging and validating your own experience. When we share our truths, we all become stronger. Sometimes we are embarrassed, ashamed, or afraid of the experiences that informed us of our truth. But by claiming those experiences and owning the truth that arises from them, we conquer the ghosts of our past and open a door to an empowered future.

As you consider your own Fresh Start Success, look for your own hard-won truths. Probe the areas you may be hiding, where you learned lessons through difficulty, pain, or failure. The seeds to creating a powerful reinvention may have been sown during your greatest trials and can blossom to create value and healing for others when you gather the courage to share your own truth.

## No Longer in Hiding

Jo Dibblee went to school for business administration with a primary focus on marketing and sales. She began her career in hospitality—an easy choice in British Columbia, which has a large tourism trade. Jo felt fortunate to have worked in high-end properties and resorts that attracted people from all over the world.

She loved customer service, helping the guests and seeing them relax into their vacations and be happy. "I believe working in the hospitality industry played a big role in developing my ability to problem-solve and serve clients," Jo says. Yet she felt something was missing.

As much as she enjoyed the hospitality industry, ultimately the work wasn't deep and fulfilling enough. Jo began her career in telecom in 1990 and worked in that industry until 2001. "There was a huge learning curve," she recalls. "This was new technology, and everyone was on a level playing field, learning quickly in a fast and ever-changing industry." During this time Jo had a glimpse of working with entrepreneurs. She was inspired by their drive, tenacity, and persistence.

Jo loved learning, and that passion was validated over and over again when she was recognized as a top performer. Working with entrepreneurs, Jo knew something big was missing from her life. What she loved about the telecom industry was helping others stay connected. She enjoyed helping entrepreneurs run and grow successful, thriving businesses. She excelled and was recognized repeatedly for her work, yet she still felt as though something was lacking.

In 2001, she took a big leap, leaving telecom to follow her entrepreneurial dreams. Jo became a speaker. Her need to serve more people kicked in, and she began to host and run a women's networking organization. She helped thousands of women start and launch their very own businesses while connecting them globally and providing them much-needed access. Yet the pull to do more still tugged at her heart. In 2007, Jo began to move toward her true purpose, acknowledging the missing piece that had been nagging her for years.

Jo had a huge secret—she had been a sexual assault victim when she was younger and a witness in a murder investigation. Law enforcement had sent her into hiding, assigning officers to watch over her case. She feared for her life due to threats by her former foster parent. "Unfortunately, the crime of sexual assault is unique in that the only person guilty is the victim until proven innocent," Jo says. "The weight is on the victim to prove credibility."

Jo grew up in a deeply dysfunctional family. She learned to keep secrets when she was very young, and her assault was something she was conditioned to keep hidden. Jo was fifteen when she was assaulted by her foster parent.

It took her eight months to work up the courage tell the police and social services, and three years would pass before authorities believed her. Jo wasn't the perpetrator's only victim. Children began to go missing from the area and were never found. It was alleged that the perpetrator became a serial killer.

In 1980, the police returned to Jo with news that they now believed her. Jo knew something terrible had to have happened. A murder had occurred. Twelve-year-old Susan Duff had been murdered, and all circumstantial evidence pointed to Jo's abuser, who was the only suspect. Susan was the younger sister of one of Jo's childhood classmates, and the step-niece of the abuser. The police asked Jo if she would stand as a witness against her abuser based on his pattern of behavior, and for Susan's sake, Jo agreed.

Police alleged that the perpetrator had assaulted twenty-six girls. Every three to five years, authorities would tell Jo that her abuser was close to trial. She was afraid that he would find her because he had threatened to kill everyone she loved. More children went missing, and Jo believes that the true death count is far higher than the official count. Police found some evidence linked to one of the killings in the abuser's truck, but he never served any jail time. Jo never had the chance to confront him in court since he was never formally charged, only detained on several occasions.

As a protected witness, Jo was forced into hiding for thirty-five years. She moved fifty-one times, had nineteen different names, and seven different passports. During her many moves, Jo continued to work in telecom. In 2001, she started her own business in customer relations management. Then when she moved to Calgary, a friend told Gail Watson to invite Jo to eWomenNetwork (EWN), a women's professional networking organization. Jo became a managing director for EWN and led several chapters: Calgary, Edmonton, Lethbridge, and Red Deer for seven years.

From 2006 through 2012, Jo was "visibly invisible" running and hosting her networking business with EWN, although she was still in hiding, working with the RCMP, operating under an assumed identity. In 2009 and 2011, Jo was again recognized for the work she was doing with the chapters as well as the philanthropic work she did in her communities. "They wanted to give me an award, and I couldn't tell them that the publicity might get me killed," she recalls. "I was honored with the International Managing Director of the Year award—twice. But I couldn't tell the organization's founder why I didn't want to win. I really didn't want my picture and location broadcast all over Canada because I knew he was still out there, looking for me."

Jo's second divorce became final in 2007. To this day, she attributes the divorce to the many secrets she kept and the shame she felt over the abuse, and over not being able to prevent Susan's death. Keeping secrets greatly impacted all relationships in her life. The authorities told her not to share the details of her case with anyone, including her husband. The secrecy was for Jo's safety and the safety of her friends and family, since the perpetrator had threatened to kill anyone close to her. "I was sick and tired of not having any friends," Jo recalls. She held herself apart because she didn't want to put anyone at risk. Every time she moved, she had to invent a new story. It was hard to reconcile all the lies.

Jo stayed on with EWN in spite of her fear, and in 2011, she knew something had to give. She had to stand up for her life. Jo was tired of being on the outside looking in. So often, people had reached out to her to include her and tried to be friends, but Jo kept her distance out of fear of her abuser. Eventually, she decided that enough was enough.

In 2012, Jo had a pivotal moment. "I was going to release my first book, and even though I was terrified, I knew it was time," Jo recalls. She had written the book without naming her abuser, or Susan. Although it was a memoir, she simply could not speak nor write his name. "Then, I decided that if I was going to do it, I was going to dedicate it to Susan. I didn't know how to contact Susan's parents to get permission. So I went online, and I found information about the case. I had never had the courage to Google it before. I found the abuser's name in the papers and cold case stories about the murders and disappearances."

On Labor Day weekend 2012, Jo found out that her abuser, the alleged serial killer, the man she had been hiding from for thirty-five years, was dead. He had died in 2007. Somehow, Jo fell through the cracks, and the authorities never informed her that the need to hide was over. "I consider that weekend to be my second birthday," Jo says. "It's the day I was finally free at last."

It took her a year to call the police, and the conversation she had with the police was the deciding factor in her decision to tell the story. Thirty-five years in hiding, only to have the police forget to tell her when he died. Once Jo made up her mind, she was not going back to hiding.

"I knew it was time, that my life had been spared for a reason," Jo says. "I realized that I had a bigger, bolder purpose." Originally, she wrote over four hundred pages, and when she could no longer write, she enlisted the help of a developmental editor. There was enough content to make not one book, but two.

Her family didn't want the story coming out, even though she doesn't talk about their part in what happened. She felt so responsible that she didn't manage to save Susan. "We have a responsibility to lift others who have no voice," she says.

Coming forward changed her life and her relationships forever. "At last it was safe to have friends," she says. Jo saw an online news clip of her abuser, and he was old and decrepit. In her mind, he was always young and powerful. At that moment, his mental power over her vanished.

Jo found an award-winning editor and a developmental editor with whom she had good chemistry. The book needed to serve others. "It wasn't about 'take pity on Jo'," she says. "This book was about making change, creating awareness, becoming an inspiration, and providing a powerful message of hope and call to action." Jo donates net proceeds from the book, *Frock Off—Living Undisguised*, to Little Warriors, a camp for children who were sexually assaulted. She also donates to Because I'm a Girl, an organization that works to stop girls from being sold into the sex trade. Through that program, Jo "adopts" and sustains a girl with her contribution of $500/year. She pays for that contribution with book sales and a silent auction. "I want to be the change in the world," Jo says.

Jo also created her "12 for 12" Membership program for change agents who take the books to women's shelters and are part of a powerful community of women business owners who want to make a difference. Because of her experience, Jo is a speaker/expert source and breakthrough expert.

Jo stepped down as a managing director for EWN in 2012. Her book came out in 2013. Now, Jo is a paid speaker, creating live events which she calls "Frock-alicious by Design," in which sustainable transformations are put into place. As a breakthrough expert, she guides others to live the lives they dream of and celebrate success in life and business. Jo remarried, and her husband is also part owner of the business she created—Frock Off, Inc.

"The whole idea of 'frock' comes from costumes, what we use to disguise and cover up," Jo explains. "To 'Frock-off' means to live life undisguised. 'Frock-alicious' means to shed the frocks that don't serve us, to accept and value our scars, to live life deliciously. We need to be accountable for what we do with our lives. Hiding only perpetuates the negative story."

Jo began her business with her life savings. Currently, her business is in the build phase; therefore, she puts most of what she earns back into creating her books and programs. Her book *Frock Off—Living Undisguised* was awarded a bronze medal in excellence for True Crime by the Readers' Favorite International Book Contest in 2014. She recently released the second edition and expanded version, *Frock Off: Living Undisguised—Freedom Edition*. The new edition won a bronze medal of excellence for the Grief/Hardship category in 2015, also from the Readers' Favorites contest, which is the largest such competition in the world.

Now Jo is expanding her live events, moving on with her life and education, developing her business, and teaching people who are over age thirty who want to do more with their lives and are ready to stand up and step into all that awaits them. "My oldest client is eighty, and she is phenomenal," Jo says.

## The Take-Away

Are you in hiding? Maybe your story isn't as dramatic as Jo's, but many people spend years of their lives pretending to be someone they're not on the job, and that takes a toll. Maybe you chose your job for the paycheck, or to please your parents, or impress your friends, but the day-to-day reality of your profession is eating away at your soul.

It's time to come clean and stop the charade. Start asking yourself the tough questions: What have I always wanted to do but was afraid to try? What would I do for a living if I weren't worried about the money? What kind of work makes me happiest? Who do I most enjoy serving? What type of people energize me? In what setting do I produce the best outcomes?

As you reinvent yourself and create your own Fresh Start Success, commit to being the real you, to pursuing your authentic passion, to following your true interests. Once you're honest with yourself about who you are and what you want in your next career, begin to explore career choices that bring out the best of the real, authentic you.

## Q&A with Jo Dibblee

**Q: What did you learn the hard way?**
A: "It's okay to ask for help. I had been so scared of what others would think and how they would react, and I didn't want to have to explain my reasons, so I didn't ask for help. I had to learn how to talk and be vulnerable and let my guard down, to let others in.

"My husband is battling prostate cancer, and I am a twenty-four-year cancer survivor myself, and even with all that, I found it hard to ask for help. But I've learned it's okay to ask and to depend on others. I am stepping out of my need to be in control of everything."

**Q: How are you a different person now than before?**
A: "I'm more open. Along the way, I discovered that freedom is the secret to anti-aging. Everyone tells me I look so much younger now. I have learned how to be vulnerable. It's a choice when you stand up and step into what you want. I get to tell my side now, to be a participant in my life rather than a bystander, to not just listen but be heard. I can be real and show up one hundred percent."

**Q: What did you learn about yourself?**
A: "I gained a deep respect for my younger self. I discovered a resilience that I had no idea I possessed all along. I learned that faith, hope, and optimism

will carry you through almost anything. People who encouraged me without knowing my full story gave me hope. There is so much power in a kind word and gesture. People showed love for me. I am committed to having at least one authentic conversation a day, listening and participating fully to ensure impact and transformation. I want to be the change in the world and share the message of hope and inspiration. It's not about what you do; it's who you are. We are not defined by our pasts, our stories, or by what others think."

**Q: What traits enabled your success?**
A: "I'm driven. All along, I told myself, 'I know what you're saying, but I'm not going to die.' I am driven to be the best I can be in all areas of my life. I am persistent. No matter what happened, I never gave up. I came close to giving up a couple times, but then I snapped back into reality. I have faith. I always had an unwavering faith that things would get better, even in the bleakest moments. Failure was never and will never be an option. To fail is to not try. I help others because I know they have value in the world, and I want to make a difference. My biggest fear now is managing exponential growth with all of our virtual events and online coaching."

**Q: If you had a superpower, what would it be?**
A: "I would beam myself into situations to show up and make a change."

**Q: What role has marketing and branding played in your success?**
A: "Huge. Marketing helps me stay on message. I am one hundred percent in favor of social media, plus live events. I utilize all forms of social media—Facebook, Twitter, LinkedIn—and I make regular daily posts. I blog and write a weekly newsletter. Branding is everything! I didn't have the money for traditional advertising, but now with social media, there are so many vehicles to expand and deliver your message in the marketplace. All you need is a laptop, a fabulous message, consistency, and a desire to serve at the highest level."

# Follow Your Muse
## Debbi Dachinger

CONVENTIONAL WISDOM SAYS that making a living in a creative field is much more difficult than succeeding in business. Maybe that has to do with how we define "success." If we only acknowledge success when someone reaches the pinnacle of celebrity—becoming an A-list movie star or a multi-platinum recording artist—then it's true that a very small number of people reach those heights. And yet, only five hundred people can be CEOs of Fortune 500 companies. Perhaps ten times that many hold C-suite jobs at those companies. But for some reason, we don't consider everyone else in business to have "failed."

Maybe it's time to change our definitions.

As you consider your own Fresh Start Success, look for ways to monetize the things you love doing, the things you do well, and the things that you can do that meet a need in the market. You may find that there are more options available to you to use and monetize your gifts and talents than you initially thought. Look to see what others are doing and how they are utilizing similar abilities. Network and let others know what you can do and what you want to do. Don't worry about fitting into someone else's definition of "success."

## Dare to Dream

Debbi Dachinger loved entertaining. She was involved with acting and dance, and she performed music with voice, guitar, and violin. Debbi loved performing in plays and being on stage. At age seven, Debbi would sing on the bus to a captive audience.

She went to college for acting and waitressed after she graduated. Debbi worked as an actress and a singer for a few decades, performing on commercials, in television shows, and in theater programs worldwide.

"It was wonderful for so long as I loved performing, but eventually it got to be too much," she recalls. "There was no vacation time, no sick time, and no money if I wasn't on a job. The times I was working didn't make up for the hardship and stress when I wasn't. There was no safety net."

Debbi started to do some office work, became very street-smart, and learned a lot on her own. She realized she didn't have marketable skills, so she made it a point to learn as she went and got good at experiential learning. Then, one job she applied for only wanted full-time workers. It was a big decision, but Debbi took the plunge. "I liked having benefits and holidays and consistency, and I did my acting on the side," she says. "Creativity was always on the outside, but I didn't see another way to make it happen."

She got to know a woman in human resources, who heard Debbi speak, and encouraged her to put together a workshop and present it. Debbi then decided to join Toastmasters to hone her speaking skills. "I told the woman that I wanted to be a speaker, and she offered to book me to speak all over Los Angeles. That gave her a reason to work with me, and I got to observe and learn," Debbi says. "That's when I learned that angels show up when you are honest about what you want."

Three months later, Debbi got a call from a director of an animation project who needed a voice-over artist. Someone recommended her. "I had never done voice-over work before, but I auditioned and was cast in the leading voice character. Then, the director found out I could sing, and they wrote me a song," Debbi recalls. "I got an agent and started doing voice-over jobs on my lunch break, then narration and Public Service Announcements." She started thinking about radio as another way to use her voice. This was in the early years of internet radio.

Debbi was still working at her full-time job and doing her acting projects on the side. "My soul just couldn't sustain the job I was doing," Debbi says. "I felt I wasn't doing my best, I had no love for the work, and I had come to resent being taken away from what I loved." She felt shame over not being an entrepreneur and not doing what she wanted. "There was a lot of fear and excruciating doubt, and I wanted safety, but life doesn't always present like that," she says. Two weeks later, she had made the decision and gave her resignation.

"I was so ready for this," she says. "I had honed and honed and honed my skills, I sang at weddings, I gave motivational speeches, I sold jewelry. I graduated from Toastmasters." She had a lot of trust in what feels "light and right." "I like challenges, and I get bored quickly," she says.

Debbi gave herself thirty days to make it as an entrepreneur or get another job. She had already figured out a back-up plan, just in case, but she decided that she was going to make it. That took tremendous trust that she had something people wanted and needed. "Opportunities showed up out of the blue," Debbi says. She continued to use her natural gifts and found that she had more than one area of expertise she could monetize, which opened doors to additional opportunities she had not anticipated.

Things took off fast. With an already-launched radio show, Debbi went from being on four radio stations to being syndicated on sixty-six stations. "I was willing to change and grow," she says. "I believe you have to know yourself, show yourself, and grow yourself. I wasn't afraid to show what I could do, but I was afraid of change. I did it anyway and grew from every move I made. When an idea is given to me, I get excited with the new and unknown, and I have to pursue the idea, which is a very brave thing to do and is the best thing in life. If I don't grab it right then, the opportunity goes to someone else."

Debbi felt pure dread over stepping out into her dream. She had a strong work ethic, but her focus on work meant she was not paying attention to her feelings. Debbi attended a self-development workshop and ended up crying. "I was overwhelmed by my emotions, grieving for not having become an entrepreneur earlier," Debbi says. "But energetically, I knew I was doing the right thing." She was proud and grateful to take a stand and let herself be exactly what she was. "My tears were a way to bridge to my new reality," she says, looking back. "I realized then that I was not alone. People stepped forward to help and gift me with what I needed, and they provided support at crucial times. They let me know that I was loved, and their cheerleading kept me going."

Today, Debbi is a media personality. Her talk radio show *Dare to Dream* is a multi-award-winning program, syndicated on sixty-six stations. Debbi is a keynote speaker at national events and a best-selling author. She runs the *Bestseller Launch Program* ensuring self-published authors reach best-selling book status, and she also provides Radio Mastery Training (private radio interview coaching and workshops) for entrepreneurs, speakers, healers, and authors to parlay radio interviews into publicity for recognition and big business results by being superb on air. Debbi is a certified Dream Coach and is the author of the books *Wisdom to Success: The Surefire Secrets to Accomplish All Your Dreams* and *Dare to Dream: This Life Counts!*

## The Take-Away

Once upon a time, our parents steered us into certain lines of work regardless of what our hearts called us to do because those types of careers were "secure." In our current economy, we now realize that no career path is secure or a guarantee of success. If we are going to live with insecurity no matter what road we choose, why not embrace doing what you love and claim satisfaction, fulfillment, and the knowledge that you are making a difference in the world?

## Q&A with Debbi Dachinger

**Q: What did you learn the hard way?**
A: "I had so much fear about making a move to follow my dream that I lost a lot of time. I wish now that I had left my other job earlier, that I hadn't been so frightened. Change ultimately is a good thing. I was designed to be an entrepreneur, so how did I not live like that for so long? I learned that not being entirely 'safe' is okay. Good enough is ready enough."

**Q: How are you a different person?**
A: "My old job left me feeling stymied and limited. Now I feel solid about who

I am. There is space and bandwidth in my life for me to create what I want. I am mentally available for the things I need to do and the people I need to meet. I feel amazing about myself and my potential. I know that anything is possible. I work long hours, but I also take care of myself. I am learning how to disconnect, meditate, take walks, and spend time with people. I dress up for work, even though I work at home. This is me showing up for me."

**Q: What did you learn about yourself?**
A: "It's a lifelong lesson. I learned that I am always more capable than I initially perceive. I'm very creative, street smart, and scrappy, and I am confident I will figure things out. Business can be super-creative. I knew that I was a maverick. Now, I appreciate doing things in a different way. I trust my inspiration, trust that things will work out well. I believe in authenticity, which means being who I am and expressing myself."

**Q: What trait is critical for your Fresh Start Success?**
A: "Tenacity. Staying on my path. Deciding to do something and making it work. When I become excited about an idea, I fully pursue and develop it into being. I try to remain open. Opportunities have come my way, and when they felt right and light, I shifted into them, and they have created some of the greatest surprises and abundant situations of my life!"

**Q: If you had a superpower, what would it be?**
A: "My superpower would be that whatever I want will come to fruition—travel, money, people I want to experience—I would receive everything positive that I dream of."

**Q: How important is marketing and branding to your success?**
A: "OMG, it's everything! Social media and the internet are the conduits that connect me working from home with the rest of the world. Friends boost the signal. Branding carries over to everything. On social media, it's about me being me. I'm my greatest brand. If I'm a little bit rock and roll, I embody that

and enjoy it. People feel when you're being yourself and are comfortable in your skin. Monetize the things you love doing, the things you do well, and the things that you enjoy doing that also meet a need in the market. Authenticity, genuineness, and having the guts to put yourself and your gifts out there are the keys to marketing, branding, and success."

# When the Sun Opens Up On You
## Sherri Richards

HOW DO YOU know when you're in your sweet spot, when you're doing what you're here on Earth to do? Over and over again in the interviews with these amazing entrepreneurs, when I asked them that question they said something along the lines of, "I found my reason for being here."

When you find your purpose in life, your reason for being on Earth, work ceases to feel like a burden and becomes an energizing mission. Your focus shifts to being about your customer, meeting that need you were born to meet, telling the story only you can tell. You will connect with your ideal customers because your personal approach and story will resonate with them in a way none of your competitors will be able to duplicate. They will "get" you and "click" with you more than they will with others who share your expertise because you are you, and your reason/purpose/mission is a match for what they need.

Sherri Richards is the owner of MyMoneyExperience.com, a one-stop site for entrepreneurs who need help with the financial side of their businesses. But like the other business leaders in this book, it took her a while to separate what she was generally good at doing from what she felt uniquely equipped to offer to the world.

## When a Door Closes, Windows Open

Sherri did her undergraduate work in business with a minor in history, and earned an MBA in finance. She intended to go into the business world from the very start, but clothing and textiles were her first love. Her father insisted that she train for a more general business career instead, and in Business 101 when she first heard about income statements, she fell in love. "It felt like the sun opened up on me," Sherri says. "It was very much a defining moment in my life."

Sherri was one of the first women hired in finance in the early 1980s at what is now Daimler Trucks of North America. At the time, the company was very German in its culture and had a very masculine approach to everything, as well as a largely male management team. She had good bosses and got to do a variety of different things, move around from finance to aftermarket, to IT, to product development and marketing. Her husband also worked for the firm. In 1997, Daimler bought the heavy duty division of Ford, and she and her husband, as part of the start-up team, moved to Ohio where the new company headquarters was located.

In 2005, the headquarters moved to Michigan, and in 2009, Sherri's division moved to South Carolina. She was only two years short of retirement and did not want to relocate from their beloved Michigan. That was when Sherri started to look for a way to turn a closed door into an open window and find a way to create her own Fresh Start Success.

Sherri loved working with small businesses and bringing order around how business was done. She enjoyed setting a goal and making it happen. Sherri was especially excited about bringing clarity and skill sets to small business. She decided to create a company that combined those interests and areas of expertise to make her corporate-level financial skills available for entrepreneurs.

Everyone around Sherri supported her shift. There was a lot to learn. "I fell flat on my face all the time," Sherri admits. But she recouped and recovered—and continued. One big epiphany was how much entrepreneurs are on their own. "In corporate teams and structures, there are people to do everything to support for you, but in a small business, you do it all yourself," Sherri realized. It was an important insight not only for her own business, but for the needs of her customers. Sherri dug in to make her dream happen. She has a strong work ethic, wakes up early, works all day, and brings lots of self-discipline to the equation. Finding a support team that could match her focus and energy level was the first hurdle. To find clients, she went with what she knew—contacting truck dealers and people in the automotive field. She called people she knew to see if they knew anyone who needed what she did. Dealer principals hired her for campaigns, and word of mouth spread.

"It's been a journey," Sherri says of the path she traveled between her time in corporate and now. There were starts and stops, but it took about seven years for her company to truly become successful. It took years before she was no longer in debt. One partnership fell apart, and she had to start over, so progress was not always linear. "You don't know what you don't know," she warns. Through it all, her husband was supportive, and his income provided a safety net. Now, MyMoneyExperience.com is profitable and paying its bills, and her firm has supported two additional start-ups, one non-profit and one for-profit. Sherri teaches creativity and innovation at a local university, which is a dream come true for her. She also started the Holistic Chamber of Commerce.

"What didn't I learn the hard way?" Sherri muses, looking back on the journey. "Being on your own is a very different world than being in corporate," she says. "A lot of skills that worked in the corporate world required a change of mindset once I was on my own. I learned to rely on myself, find my own voice, and find my own way to do things."

For Sherri and her husband, it was crucial that their Fresh Start Success enable them to stay in Michigan, which they loved. Sherri didn't want to move. She had a desire in her soul to build something from scratch. Working with dealers and other small business customers was an opportunity to create something for herself. Her approach was "try, tweak, then try again."

## The Take-Away

The idea of "try, tweak, then try again" is at the heart of every success. Even our best ideas often need refinement to take off. We may need to adjust our target audience or the story we tell about ourselves or our business, our products, and services. We might need to shift the branding or change up the packaging. The important thing is to realize that no one's bright idea works perfectly right out of the gate. Refinement and continual tweaking is part of the process it takes to achieve your Fresh Start Success.

The other thing that made an impression in Sherri's story, and in so many of the other entrepreneurs' stories, is that they used skills and contacts from their old careers to launch their reinvention, even when they were making significant changes in the type of work they set out to do. Don't assume that because your Fresh Start Success is a career change that your old skills or former colleagues won't be valuable. Inventory your skills and see which ones translate to your new vision. No life experience is ever wasted! Then use personal branding and marketing to educate your existing contacts about what you're doing now and enlist their help. You'll be amazed how many contacts, resources, referrals, ideas, and connections may come out of your old network. The trust you have built up with your network and their knowledge of you and faith in your skills are valuable assets. Put them to use as you create your own Fresh Start Success!

## Q&A with Sherri Richards

**Q: To what do you attribute your Fresh Start Success?**
A: "Tenacity—a willingness to get up every day. I met amazing people with big ideas who wanted to make things happen but needed help with structure. I keep showing up, even when things don't go as planned. I also credit meditation, a huge amount of curiosity, and a driven desire to understand how things really work."

**Q: How are you a different person than before? What did you learn about yourself?**
A: "I'm much more comfortable with risk now. I have more faith than I used to. If there is a desire in your heart and you're doing the important things, a way will show up to move forward. I'm also more comfortable now talking to people instead of making decisions for people. Every day is so exciting because of the possibilities!"

**Q: What new skills/knowledge did you gain?**
A: "Self-trust. In corporate, I had the whole power of the company behind me, but on my own it was just me, and I had to be okay with it being 'just me.' Finding genuine confidence took a while, and so did learning skills to make things happen. I'm better now with technology and computers, time management, self-management, and energy management than I used to be. I'm still grateful for what I learned in corporate, and I recognize that I couldn't do what I do now without the skills I gained from my corporate days."

**Q: What is one trait critical to your Fresh Start Success?**
A: "I'd say creativity and tenacity, as well as being able to step back and take setbacks as part of the process and not see them as a personal failure. I understand the role of failure now and the part it plays in the bigger picture process. I also really appreciate the value of creating daily rituals to stay focused and grounded."

**Q: If you had a superpower, what would it be?**
A: "Like in the old TV show *Bewitched*, I wish I could wiggle my nose and make everything okay."

**Q: What role has marketing and branding played in your success?**
A: "Social media was a huge hurdle. It was hard to wrap my head around it, so I had to study and hire resources to get it down to steps I could manage. But it was important to learn how to use social media because that's the way the world is. I've created five different income streams and some are dependent on social media."

# Dying to Succeed
## Sheevaun Moran

CHRONIC STRESS KILLS. We know that from study after study. Not only does chronic stress factor in heart attacks, cancer, and other diseases, it also produces illness and physical discomfort to reduce quality of life. We are, literally, dying to succeed.

Step back and realize that the dog-eat-dog, forced ranking, hyper-competitive corporate world is an artificial construct. It is the way it is because we made it so—and it continues because we permit it. The unpleasant and unhealthy aspects of a toxic corporate culture are entirely man-made and could be changed if those in authority were suitably motivated to do so.

Once you realize that, it becomes harder and harder to acquiesce to the demands of an arbitrary, soul-sucking environment. Perhaps you've decided to leave because you realize the impact corporate life is having on your health and relationships. Or maybe you've already had a health crisis and found that the organization for which you sacrificed your well-being does not return your loyalty. Maybe you've become the caregiver for a loved one, only to discover that the corporate world was not accommodating or flexible. Whatever the reason, you are here, now. And it's time to make a decision.

As you consider your Fresh Start Success, you have a choice to perpetuate the familiar but toxic hard-charging, take-no-prisoners corporate environment you left, or create a new, productive, and humane business model that provides the flexibility you and your employees need to remain well, become healthy, and care for others. Models exist, if you are motivated to look for them. It's your reinvention. How will you re-imagine your life and work?


## Mental and Physical Well-Being

Sheevaun Moran finished high school early, at age fifteen. Her mother wanted her to go into computer programming, which looked like a stable, well-paying career. Sheevaun did as her mother recommended, studying computer science and math in college, but also taking classes in art, marketing, and sales.

After college, Sheevaun worked for a computer accessory company that went from a start-up to having hundreds of employees. She helped the company grow and get sold to Rubbermaid. Sheevaun liked the creativity and freedom of her job, as well as the computer work. "The intensity of the experience was satisfying, and I loved feeling like I could create something—my computer programs and marketing—from nothing—a blank computer screen," Sheevaun says. "I enjoyed finding ways to do what needed to be done. I felt like I got a chance to use all my skills in systems, sales, marketing, and leadership."

In her corporate positions, Sheevaun was very good at building teams and always put the customers first. She had a knack for getting to the heart of the issue and resolving problems quickly, as well as for streamlining processes. Sheevaun was successful but increasingly felt out of step.

"The last company I worked for felt very rigid," Sheevaun recalls. "It lacked creativity. I also saw a lack of ethics in corporate life. I became disillusioned with the leadership training and the focus on all the problems. The products were excellent, but the people weren't in it for the right reasons once the company grew from five employees to dozens."

Then she got sick, and her company was not supportive of her during her illness. "That was the last straw," Sheevaun says. "I was misdiagnosed, and I learned how to heal myself. After that, I wanted to help others never be in pain or at the mercy of another's mistake."

Sheevaun had sampled being an entrepreneur a couple of times before she left the corporate world. She started her first business at age eleven when her parents wouldn't buy her something she felt she needed. Sheevaun started her first "real" company while working for a pharmaceutical company when she created a sideline of packaging travel-sized necessities in kits for frequent travelers, a convenience which did not exist before.

"I saw that people who had their own businesses had more time, fun, and freedom," Sheevaun says. "I wanted the freedom to do what worked for me. I really wanted to make an impact because I knew I had gifts I wanted to use." Her husband told her, "Don't let anything stop you. You're here to do something big."

Sheevaun founded Energetic Solutions, Inc. She is a business advisor, master coach, and energy thought leader, providing one-on-one coaching as well as hosting events and masterminds. "By the end of my first year, I was making the same six-figure salary I had in the company I left," Sheevaun says.

## The Take-Away

If you still see the work world through the paradigm of "no pain, no gain," it's time to change your perspective. Your Fresh Start Success should suit you in every aspect of your life. That means creating and sustaining physical health, healthy relationships, mental and spiritual health, and building a healthy community—as well as creating a healthy cash flow.

Take this opportunity to examine your beliefs about how a business "should" or "must" be run, how people should be managed, and how you manage your own time and energy. Now is a good time to get rid of outdated and toxic ideas and search out more enlightened, holistic, and humane approaches.

Instead of focusing on the "cost" of accommodating the health and life crises of your employees, think about avoiding the very real costs associated with absenteeism, on-the-job accidents, and decreased productivity/morale due to a stressed-out, burned-out, sick, and tired workforce. Create the company you've always wanted to work for!

## Q&A with Sheevaun Moran

**Q: What did you learn the hard way?**
A: "I learned that there is a price for not taking care of my physical body. I also learned how important it is to engage in clear expectations from vendors and to be wary about believing that others have a similar core value to over-deliver, since some people do not."

**Q: To what do you attribute your Fresh Start Success?**

A: "Getting back to basics. Listening and acting on what I knew was right. Communicating with my team daily. Creating really good systems and lines of communications. Nobody has the same drive/passion/focus for your mission that you do. Nobody understands the 'why' behind what I'm doing until I communicate clearly. I've also learned how to create detailed communications so that others can put what I teach into their own context and make it work for them."

**Q: How are you a different person?**

A: "I was pretty tolerant before; now I'm extremely tolerant. I've learned how to get to the core of the matter without slicing people out of my life. I have softer edges, and I can pull back more to allow others to do what is delegated to them. I take regular time away from my business, I practice compassionate communication, and I shares resources quickly."

**Q: What did you learn about yourself?**

A: "I learned to say something if my body is tired and I need to pause and rest. I have recognized that others don't have the same level of urgency that I do. I've also learned that most people want to be kind, to do well, to get to the next level, but they have internal traumas and issues that get in the way. If I can help them address those issues, I'm in my happiest place."

**Q: What new skills did you learn?**

A: "Something new every day! I learned to meditate, to give people latitude to succeed or not as they need to do, and I learned to build multiple streams of income."

**Q: How did your prior work prepare you for what you do now?**

A: "Every company I worked with gave me something that helps my current team and clients, from new product launches, to sales and strategy, to venture capital, to overseas manufacturing, to regulation, to how to be a really good traveler, to ethical marketing."

**Q: What traits are critical to your Fresh Start Success?**
A: "Making connections and making sure they are nurtured. Taking something into the world that leaves a meaningful imprint to make people more prosperous, more capable, and less reactive, something that helps them understand their gifts, especially those gifts that are disregarded in a corporate setting."

**Q: If you had a superpower, what would it be?**
A: "To solve suffering instantly."

**Q: What role has marketing and branding played in your success?**
A: "I understand the importance of good internet marketing and of being a good steward of words and message. Social media is a tool and not just a personal outreach. I've also learned the importance of the image, video, and pictures you put into the world."

# Creating Champions
## Lauren Brett Randolph

**ATHLETES DON'T MAKE** it to the national level without good coaches. Coaches advise, develop training plans, assess the competition, refine performance, and encourage athletes to get past performance plateaus, personal challenges, and life's rough spots. We wouldn't expect a top athlete to succeed without a coach, so why do entrepreneurs believe we can do it alone?

Coaching can take all kinds of forms for entrepreneurs. Life coaches help us figure out what we want to do for our Fresh Start Success. Success coaches help us get over limiting beliefs and behaviors. Media coaches help us look good in front of the cameras. Financial and systems coaches help us put together accounting and back office practices that work. Human resource and management coaches teach entrepreneurs—who are usually subject-matter experts—how to be a good boss and manage a company. As marketing consultants/coaches, we help entrepreneurs see and seize opportunities to gain visibility and translate that into a stream of new clients. The bottom line is, regardless of our individual competencies, there is always more to learn—we all need coaching of one kind or another.

When you're making your Fresh Start Success, don't try to go it alone. If Olympic athletes need coaches, despite the fact that they're the best in the world at what they do, then maybe you could benefit from experienced counsel, too. Don't let your ego get in the way of finding the help you need to reach peak performance.

## Coaching for Results

Lauren Brett Randolph wanted to be a teacher. She went to university to study teaching and discovered that she hated being in the classroom. "That was a huge eye-opener," Lauren says. "I really gained respect for the teachers in university." From the time she was seven years old until she was nineteen, Lauren was a competitive rhythmic gymnast, competing for Canada internationally in events that included World Championships. She was a member of the Canadian National Team for rhythmic gymnastics and eventually became National Team Coach.

Falling back on her experience as an athlete, Lauren refocused her teaching background and trained to be a coach. After university, she joined a dance company, but it didn't satisfy her love of gymnastics, so at age twenty-three, she began coaching full-time, then became one of Canada's national coaches. "It hasn't been about the job; it's been about the higher purpose," Lauren says.

As much as Lauren loved coaching and rhythmic gymnastics, she became disillusioned with the sport in 1991. Behind-the-scenes changes she saw at the World Championships were not aligned with her core values, and Lauren quit the sport again in 1997. Her first Fresh Start Success began when she went to work for her husband, a former New York City professional dancer, who ran a post-secondary college for musical theater students. For sixteen years, Lauren was the managing director of Randolph Academy for the Performing Arts. She taught herself how to use a computer and poured her passion into the business, which grew from $300,000 in revenue to $1.5 million in ten years with new programs that she created. She was a catalyst for infrastructure changes that supported such rapid growth and honed her skills on the job even without a formal degree in business.

Lauren realized she needed to reinvent herself again because it became clear that although she was doing amazing work and putting in a lot of hours, she was supporting her husband's dream, not her own dream. She had tried to make the school her dream, but it wasn't where her true passion lay. Lauren realized that she needed to make a change for herself.

"I was caught up in the cult of being the 'ideal worker,' working insanely hard to prove that I was smart and accomplished, and the 'ideal mother'—trying to prove that I was a supermom," Lauren recalls. "So I 'demoted' myself to a smaller role. But I was still super goal-oriented and a perfectionist, and pretty soon, I realized I was building myself another new, huge role with the school even though it wasn't my passion." Lauren did some soul searching and looked inward to listen to herself. She paid attention to her conversations with people, looking for direction.

As Lauren listened to what themes kept coming up in conversation, she heard people asking for a life coach. Coaching was in Lauren's blood, and she had a track record working with gymnasts, students, and the faculty at the school. Still, it took her four years to decide to go back into coaching—this time, as a life and leadership coach. Lauren did her research, hired a coach for herself, and went back to school. As an athlete and now as an adult, Lauren recognized that her inner dialogue was holding her back. "I had to silence the negative mind chatter and my doubts about being too old to start over, since I was already forty-nine," she says.

"I realized that the gremlins in my head are full of shit," Lauren adds. "Getting to the point where I could acknowledge that was a profound way to step into awareness. I was in my own way with disempowering thoughts, doubts about my ability, and crippling perfectionism. It was holding me back." She also learned to give herself permission to reinvent her career. "It was my turn," Lauren recalls. "For sixteen years, I had supported my husband's dream, and now he was supportive of me." Her family was very supportive of Lauren's reinvention, even though it meant a shift away from the family business. Some people were judgmental and made her second guess herself. Prevailing against the naysayers helped Lauren become more determined and grounded.

Immersing herself in learning went well. Lauren felt like she was starting late, and that sense of catching up from behind was a motivator to keep her focused and driven. She was still working full-time while she trained to be a coach but quit her job at the school when her coaching client roster grew to where it was too much to handle both.

Lauren attended The Coaches Training Institute and found their programs to have great synergy with her vision for the future. Then she dreamed up a new life that could provide her with autonomy, allow her to set her own hours, and work at a less compulsive pace. She started providing life and leadership coaching programs of her own in 2013 as The Cartwheel Coach. "Sometimes, I regret that it took me four years to decide what to do," Lauren says. "But then I realized I needed that time to gain the wisdom to make the shift successfully."

Championship-level gymnastics—as an athlete and a coach—required visualization, goal-setting, forward-thinking, visioning—all skills that Lauren brings into her work now. "I'm curious about the person in front of me, and I am passionate about supporting them to reach a greater purpose and be their best."

Two years into coaching, Lauren is still early in her new career. She considers herself successful, since she is making a living from her coaching practice and earning as much money as when she was at the school. "I'm always setting my goals for something bigger and greater," Lauren says. "But the real success for me was in taking the risk to jump without a net and trusting that I was going to be fine. I've learned that success is waking up and feeling fulfilled, having less stress-filled days (and nights), and knowing that I have the resilience to live through change."

Before the self-discovery work she did as part of her preparation for coaching, Lauren would have said she was a Type A personality. "I was driven and controlling, and hiding a lot, distanced from my emotions. I knew people were depending on me, and I covered up my fear with arrogance. I had also been a huge people-pleaser, and I needed to deal with that." Lauren had not finished her university degree because she got an offer from a dance company and always felt "not enough" because she hadn't graduated. Going back to school and getting certified as a coach let her lay that concern to rest. "I know now, though, that I don't need a degree to define me," Lauren says. She furthered her education by attending Leadership Development Training, learning how to have an impact in the world at large.

"My goal now is to learn to slow down, center myself, and find a new way of being present in the moment. I used to be stuck in fear and regret. Now, I'm mindful of how I show up," Lauren adds.

## The Take-Away

When you look at your career, can you see a central theme that has transcended your individual jobs? Lauren was a teacher, and then a gymnastics coach, and then part of the management team at a performing arts school, and finally a life coach—roles that all centered around educating and mentoring. As different periods in her life unfolded, her central theme was reimagined, but it always remained a part of what gave her purpose and satisfaction.

As you're planning your own Fresh Start Success, realize that the answer to the question of what to do next might be closer than you think. Look for the central themes in your work history, and then look for other jobs that emphasize those same aspects. Don't get hung up on titles—pay attention to what the meat of the actual job entails. You might find that a new career that seems radically different from your past on the surface shares essential common threads at its heart.

## Q&A with Lauren Brett Randolph

**Q: What did you learn the hard way?**
A: "A lot. There's no easy way to get to where you want to go—in your career or in life. You can't take shortcuts; you have to go through it and sit with the discomfort of being where you don't want to be. I have learned to be able to sit with my feeling of being uncomfortable because that is where the learning and growth lies. Sometimes you're in a good place with lots to discover and sometimes you're not, but you have to go through it all to get to the other side. I had been looking outside myself for answers, and I had to learn to find the answers inside.

"I also know that I'm not 'there' yet. One-on-one coaching is fulfilling, but there's more I want to do, so this is a step, but not the end. I like working with groups of people to help them flourish. I learned that I feel most compelling and most alive when I'm with other people and see the 'aha' moment, when I get feedback about changed lives, when I see and hear people tell their stories. And I've discovered that other people just want to be seen and heard."

**Q: To what do you attribute your Fresh Start Success?**
A: "Courage and curiosity. I was not okay with the status quo or sleepwalking through life. My coach taught me about courage. Before that, I had faked being okay through the distraction of busyness. I have the support of people around me, including my husband and our children, and that provides a sense of comfort and acknowledgment that I'm okay, right where I am."

**Q: What one trait is critical to your Fresh Start Success?**
A: "Perseverance in the face of adversity. Doing it anyway, even if you don't know how, learning on the fly. There are beautiful gems of knowledge waiting for us to discover if we allow ourselves to be present in our fear or in the unknown and to lean into the fear instead of running away from it."

**Q: If you had a superpower, what would it be?**
A: "To go into people's brains and remove the 'itty bitty shitty committee'— gremlins, bad mental roommates, mental saboteurs."

**Q: What role has marketing and branding played in your Fresh Start Success?**
A: "Marketing taught me that it is not okay to hide. I put off launching a website, which was another form of hiding. Creating my website has kept me accountable to my business. By showing my true self on the website and in my blogs, I am attracting my ideal clients. Clients want to be seen and heard, so there needs to be a high trust level. What works best in social media is sharing your true, authentic self, saying what others think but don't say. I chronicled my travel across Canada speaking to schools, and I intentionally included things that were funny and mistakes I made. So many people connected to me through that, and it led to gaining new clients and getting invitations to speak. My goal is to make every interaction a way to give my clients an experience or take them on a journey."

# Perspective
## Loriann Oberlin

MARCEL PROUST SAID, "The real voyage of discovery consists not in seeking new landscapes but in having new eyes." Many of the people interviewed in this book found their Fresh Start Success by finding a way to view their experience, education, inclinations, and talents through "new eyes."

Opportunities for reinvention often involve trading places. For example, a student might be so moved and changed by a great teacher that he or she decides to go into teaching. That role reversal can also involve seeing the impact of outcomes first-hand. So someone who experiences a life-changing outcome from working with a talented coach, massage therapist, doctor, Reiki practitioner, etc. might decide to "pay it forward" by going into that profession to help someone else.

Trading places and changing roles requires a shift in perspective. When you're the student, you see the world differently than when you're the teacher. Becoming a good guide requires subject knowledge, but even more importantly, it requires self-knowledge. The best guides, teachers, healers, and coaches understand the inner struggle involved in making a change as much as they understand the details of the subject matter. Reinvention comes from a changed perspective that provides a wider, deeper, more inclusive view. When you have learned to see the world in a different way and it has changed your life for the better, don't be surprised if you discover a new zeal to help others make their own shifts.

What can you see differently in your reinvention journey that you did not see before you made a change? How can shifting your perspective open your eyes to new possibilities for Fresh Start Success?

## Learning to Listen

Loriann Oberlin went to college to become a journalist. She spent the 1980s and 1990s working as a writer for a variety of magazines and publications. "I loved being a journalist," she says. "It was a great fit for someone with lots of natural curiosity. I loved to write, and I enjoyed educating people on how to make better consumer decisions. Interviewing people in the community also had an educational component."

Loriann branched out into public relations work and taught life-long learning classes for local community colleges. Her portfolio landed her a publisher, and her first book equipped freelance writers with the basics of how to earn money from their writing, whether for professional or personal goals. Writing for major national magazines sent Loriann on location to report about honeymoon options and family-friendly vacations and led to the chance to write a travel guide. Freelance writing enabled her to work from home, something she prized with two young sons, one of whom had significant challenges as a preemie. She wrote more books, including a child-friendly guide to American history and a guide to working from home while raising children.

Following divorce and single parenthood, Loriann wrote the book she would have wanted to have while facing those experiences in *Surviving Separation and Divorce*. Also during this time, she struck up a collaboration with a local psychologist who also wanted to publish. They wrote *The Angry Child*, which was released in 2001.

Loriann remarried and moved to the Maryland suburbs later that year. Writing was the mainstay of her income even during this transition, but a lot was about happen in the world and economy. Post 9/11 realities changed everything. With no one traveling and advertisers pulling back commitments, editors sat on large stockpiles of freelance contributions, so they had little need to commission more. In addition, the rise of the internet squeezed publication budgets even further.

Loriann kept her hand in various projects. She edited an already-published travel guide, revised her separation/divorce book, and penned another idea guide for freelancers on how to earn a paycheck more quickly in a post-9/11 world. At the same time, Loriann was open to new possibilities.

Several of her books fell into the psycho/social realm. With new economic realities and her children a bit older, she began to consider the idea of graduate school. "I had always been interested in psychology," Loriann says, "and now Johns Hopkins University was just minutes from my home—with a great master's program. It was attuned to adult learners and made it possible to earn credits in a very streamlined way." She excelled, combining her long-time love of learning with her new focus on clinical counseling.

"Originally, I expected to add knowledge that would help with the book projects. I didn't intend to become a counselor," she admits. "But I saw a new skill set emerge. A career change, or call it a 'career addition,' took place."

Loriann graduated with a master's of science in counseling in 2006 and completed post-master's work to further her path toward state licensure as an LCPC. "It was difficult to find a paid position in which I could earn the large number of clinical hours mandated, but I wasn't deterred. Fortunately, I knew how to market myself, and I made it happen," Loriann says. Right after she finished one internship with degree in hand, she created an advanced internship in her post-master's program, and then also worked at a hospital with the second busiest emergency room in Maryland.

For Loriann, it was a perfect merging of the two careers, though as with any change, there were challenges. "When you introduce yourself as a writer and author while obtaining your higher degree," Loriann recalls, "it meets with very interesting feedback. Sometimes people would ask questions and be intrigued; on a few occasions, you could just see a negative reaction."

She put her personal challenges into context using new concepts she learned. "When anyone in a family system makes a shift, the system has to reorient," Loriann explains. "A change like the one I made requires an adjustment from everyone. My husband and sons, who are now glad I went back to school, weren't used to me being gone. Financially, it was a very positive move given the decline in magazines and newspaper income. It certainly helped me put my sons through college."

Loriann graduated in 2008 as the market plunged into recession. "It simply meant I wasn't able to do everything on my bucket list right away. On the other hand, the market needed counselors, so I found my new skills in demand."

Making the change paid off in satisfaction, as well. "I'm able to wake up and go to work where I make an impact," Loriann says. "I learned a lot, and I keep on learning. I usually take more continuing education credits than required, but I learn the most from clients, from the fascinating lives they lead, and from different cultures. I really do love my work."

From 2005 to 2014, while she was working on her degree, Loriann put her publishing aspirations aside. "I didn't write anything except school assignments and possibly a few minor freelance pieces in almost ten years," she says. "For someone whose goal was to combine the two fields, it was a catalyst to get back to the keyboard."

Loriann had not yet fulfilled one long-time dream: to write fiction. "When we moved to the Eastern Shore, I went to a writer's conference and joined a supportive writer's group," Loriann says. "I was inspired by others who met with success in e-books. That revived dreams from the 1990s. Having already gone through one reinvention, I decided to add another facet to my career." Loriann decided to maintain a separation between her fiction and non-fiction writing and created a pen name for her fiction.

Loriann now writes a contemporary women's fiction series as Lauren Monroe (her pseudonym). Her series, *The Maryland Shores,* features strong female characters who deal with personal struggles as they navigate professional challenges that steer their course to love in the end.

"After so many years of traditionally-published non-fiction, self-publishing these novels has given me a renewed appreciation for the behind-the-scenes work required," she says. "I've learned a lot through very kinesthetic growth, a few mistakes, and things I just learned from the ground up. Overall, it's made me a more polished writer and so much more proficient with different software."

Journalism requires good listening skills, but Loriann believes that her counseling training further honed those abilities. "My friends and family say I'm a better listener now," Loriann says. "Whether it's age, my training, or simply the human condition itself, I go with the flow more, too. In my twenties and early thirties, I had a schedule for what I wanted to accomplish. Now, I live a lot more in the moment, and I'm better able to deal with suddenly changing plans. I've also learned that everyone has a struggle hidden somewhere. It really makes you more accepting and more patient."

## The Take-Away

As you look back at your own career, where have you made the shift from student to teacher? Where has your outlook changed because of life experiences? When you create your own reinvention, hone in on the times when you've experienced a new perspective as fertile ground for your own Fresh Start Success.

## Q&A with Loriann Oberlin

**Q: What did you learn about yourself in the process of making your own Fresh Start Success?**
A: "I learned I can do a lot of different things. If I put my mind to it, I can do it. I continue to set goals. I'm always reinventing and tweaking what I want to do."

**Q: What is one trait that has been critical to your Fresh Start Success?**
A: "Perseverance. You're always going to have people who dissuade and question you, or who don't understand why you want to do what you're doing. There will always be someone who is better than you. Some people give up because of those factors. I've made a lot of my goals come true. I've initiated that success. I didn't just make a to-do list; for example, I made the fiction writing happen even though my life is very busy and complete as it is. That's something great about being in my fifties—I have a lot more confidence—or maybe a sense of 'who gives a darn.'"

**Q: If you had a superpower, what would it be?**
A: "I would be able to wave a magic wand and people would be happier, less angry, and less resentful. In my daily work, I see the damage anger does. I wish

I could make that anger and destruction disappear."

**Q: What role has marketing played in your Fresh Start Success?**
A: "Social media is a necessary evil. It can be a creative way to market yourself, but it's easy to get hooked on it. It can be a time drain if you're not careful. You have to manage your schedule. Marketing is essential, not always easy to measure, and it's hard sometimes to know what's really effective. My marketing skills helped me to establish my private practice. They enabled me to pitch articles and book proposals. It's all about being able to sell your expertise and outcomes. Marketing takes time away from other things, but it's something you have to do when you have a business. But because it can zap your time, it's very important to have boundaries."

# Be the Change
## Faith Monson

**WHAT WOULD YOU** change about the companies where you've worked, if you could wave a magic wand? Would you root out a toxic culture? Eliminate a glass ceiling? Seek a fairer pay scale? Confront ageism, sexism, racism, or any other –ism that holds back talented people and protects the status quo?

As you consider your own Fresh Start Success, seize the opportunity to be the change you want to see happen. Maybe you can't go back and fix the problems at your former company, but you can fix the little corner of the universe under your control. Whether you build a company that is just one person or one hundred people, refuse to accept "same old, same old" as the default. It's your life, your reinvention—your power to make a difference.

If your reinvention takes you into another organization, look for ways you can bring about positive changes. Even shifts that may seem small to you might make a world of difference to those around you.

## Change Agent

"I've always been a change agent." Faith Monson trained to be a salesperson. She moved up through the ranks, from salesperson to sales manager, then to regional manager, always changing how things were done. She stayed at each job longer because she reinvented the job while she was doing it. That helped keep her interested and let her take advantage of potential opportunities.

As one of the first women in a full sales position in the companies where she worked, Faith had a major role in changing company culture as to how the corporations treated women. "Early on, women were only allowed to be in customer service, not in sales," Faith recalls. "The outside sales people were male, and even when a woman in a showroom sold something, it wasn't considered to be 'sales'." In fact, while male salespeople won awards, there were no awards for women in the showroom, no matter how many sales they closed. Yet the showroom saw many more clients each day, meaning that the women actually had more client contact than the men."

Faith created a corporate recognition program for the showroom sales staff and got the customer service workers reclassified as "inside sales people" by pointing out the volume of sales they generated. She fought and won approval to promote female inside sales people to outside sales people, pioneering a program that was later replicated across the country. "These women were great sales people," Faith says. "They just hadn't been recognized."

"I've always been a catalyst. I like to mentor and empower women and watch them grow," Faith says. But the leadership's micro-management culture drove her crazy. "I was all about opportunity and looking for new ideas," Faith adds. "The management preserved the status quo and limited opportunities and innovation. Ultimately, running into a brick wall took its toll." She felt that the company's leadership was unsupportive and unresponsive to the needs of the sales force. "That did it for me."

"I had always wanted to have my own business with bright, talented, and enthusiastic people. I knew how to run a business, and I had ideas on how to make it grow. In my corporate experience, my clients were primarily small business owners. I listened and learned about their challenges and concerns, strategized with them, made suggestions, and had creative brainstorming sessions on how they could best promote themselves," Faith recalls. "I met so many clients with unique and creative abilities that weren't promoting their businesses, and I wanted to help them be successful. I found working with them stimulating and challenging, and a part of my job that I really enjoyed. Now, I see that it was a training ground for my next job."

It was time to move on. Faith was ready to be her own boss. She had proven herself and believed in herself. The turning point came when she was sitting in a train station reading *You Are a Brand* by Catherine Kaputa. Faith devoured the book and decided to go out on her own and help businesses be more successful by using the skills she had honed in her corporate job to establish their brands and promote their success. Faith partnered with the best website designers, professional writers, and marketing and promoting gurus she could find. Her first clients were people who knew her from her corporate experience, accepted her in her new role, and hired her to coach them to success, which was very validating.

Throughout her career, Faith created books of quotations and inspirational photos to motivate herself and stay pumped up. "Those quotes inspired me to go for it," Faith says. "They encouraged me to take risks. They taught me to be my own biggest cheerleader." Sales turned out to be a great training ground. "I sold myself to myself, and I sold myself to potential clients," Faith said. Her contacts believed in the "new" Faith and referred her.

Being her own boss was freeing. "The sky was the limit," Faith says. "I could try things, take risks, and learn on my own. There was endless opportunity, and I was uncovering my untapped talents and skills." There were some downsides to being on her own. "I'm not an IT person," Faith confesses. "I had to hire people to do those things, and I would have liked to have been able to do more social media and internet work myself."

Faith's new venture was successful immediately. "I was my own boss, I used my ideas and stuck myself out there, out of my comfort zone, and stretched myself at every opportunity," Faith says.

Faith came from a competitive, goal-driven environment, and while she had excelled in that situation, she wanted to shift gears and make her vision all about her clients' success. "In my corporate world, I mentored peers and subordinates. Now, I wanted to mentor my clients, help them to fly, come out of their shells, burst out of their insecurities," Faith says. "I wanted to be in their corner. Often, that's all they need. I'm there, cheering them on, being their Sherpa. Everyone is different in what inspires them. I empower them so they can go for it."

## The Take-Away

Everyone has the power to be a change agent and a catalyst; you just have to acknowledge your own ability to make a difference. Start by becoming mindful about how the organizations you've worked for actually functioned. Where were the inefficiencies and redundancies? Who was doing a great job without acknowledgement? What could have been done better, and how could it have been improved? Take those lessons with you to the next role you play— whether it's within another organization or in a company you start.

Make a conscious decision to build an ethical company—not just by observing the letter of the law, but by maximizing the human potential of your employees, customers, and industry through recognizing and rewarding actions that mentor, empower, and implement new ideas. Resist the comfort zone of default thinking and challenge "the way it's always been done." Make your reinvention a Fresh Start Success for everyone involved.

## Q&A with Faith Monson

**Q: What did you learn the hard way?**
A: "Everything that I learned the hard way, I learned in my corporate life. In my own business, I learned the value of establishing an LLC and having a lawyer draw up a client contract. I've also discovered that a lot of clients don't want their success as much as I want it for them, which is disappointing for a coach."

**Q: To what do you attribute your Fresh Start Success?**
A: "My daughter calls me an 'idea machine.' I have unending curiosity, high energy, lots of creativity, and I love life's possibilities. Inside, I'm twenty years old. Every place I visit, I see possibilities. Every business that I step into that interests me stimulates my imagination. I talk to the managers of businesses and give them input to expand their opportunities."

**Q: How are you a different person now?**
A: "I'm more confident, empowered, assured, and rooted than before. The buck stops here and it's a nice feeling. When I stand up and say 'yes,' no one is in my way."

**Q: What did you learn about yourself?**
A: "I'm as good as I thought I was. Before, I was successful on paper, but corporate culture is not validating, and there was sexism. In my own company, I learned to appreciate my creativity, my willingness to take risks, my idea generation, and my flexibility. I enjoy helping my clients recognize their own unique skills and talents, which are integral to their business success."

**Q: What is one trait critical to your Fresh Start Success?**
A: "Self-confidence. I believe in myself, and I'm highly motivated, and indefatigable. Show me a wall, and I'll find my way around, through, or over it. There's no stopping me. I have searing determination."

**Q: If you had a superpower, what would it be?**
A: "I would have a magic wand and use it to change things for the better, right the wrongs, bring justice, and help people reach their full potential and enjoy their success."

**Q: What role has marketing played in your success?**
A: "Enormous. I get really good people to help me. When you're with the best, you learn a lot. I partner with people who bring creative synergy. Personal branding is essential, and a professional and carefully constructed website equals credibility."

# Left Brain / Right Brain
Oksana Gritsenko

YOU CAN BE good at a job and not be required to do that job for the rest of your life. Unfortunately, we often pick our careers based on what we're good at, instead of what we're both good at *and* passionate about doing. Early in life, we may only know our natural aptitudes and, therefore, choose a career doing something that comes easily for us. It's what our teachers, parents, and advisors recommend, and the direction in which they guide—or push—us. That's especially true if those aptitudes align with a lucrative career like medicine, engineering, or information technology.

Our culture stereotypes people according to their aptitudes. We tend to think that people with natural abilities for math and science are completely analytical, while people whose talents run toward language and art are not. Yet individual human beings are complex and contradictory. It is entirely possible to have left-brain (analytical) and right-brain (creative) talents of equal strength and worth. You don't have to choose one or the other, and the greatest satisfaction seems to come when a person blends his or her talents, rather than emphasizing one and denying another.

Later in life, many people realize that they are good at more things than they originally thought. Not only that, but they begin to long for a level of satisfaction, a feeling of purpose that isn't completely filled by a paycheck or title. Perhaps the stress that goes with a career outweighs the natural aptitude for the work itself. Or maybe they've just lost interest, ready to move on to a new challenge.

When you're ready to make your own Fresh Start Success, don't assume that the skills you use in your current job are the only skills you have. Be aware of your hobbies and the interests that fascinate you outside of work, especially if you have gained proficiency in your spare time. You may be able to create a viable career out of interests you considered to be hobbies, or you might find a way to marry those interests to the skills gained in your current and past jobs to create a brand new opportunity.

## Free Your Mind

Oksana Gritsenko came from the former Soviet Union, where she went to a fine arts college and then studied economics and marketing. She moved to the U.S. in 1998, working in information technology and business analysis.

Oksana spent fourteen years working for two Top 100 Fortune Companies, mostly in project management and business analysis. Her last job was as a business analysis manager at a top international consulting company. For many years, Oksana really enjoyed what she was doing in the corporate world. She was good at what she did and was successful.

Yet, at the same time that Oksana's job was very analytical and hard data-oriented, she discovered a passion for metaphysics, which she studied as a hobby for years. Oksana liked the idea of helping people on a deeper level, enabling them to embrace who they were and guiding them through difficult times in life. Her metaphysical studies fed that passion, and she increasingly felt disconnected from her data-driven job in information technology. Oksana chafed at the hierarchy and sense of entitlement she saw in the corporate world and disliked politics and the "old boys club" network. She was earning six figures but feeling unfulfilled. Her stress rose as the dissonance increased between her interests and her career. Even though she was earning great reviews and winning kudos from clients, Oksana knew something big was missing from her life.

Oksana considered her options. She knew she could find a similar job, but she wasn't convinced that would solve the problem. Oksana decided to start her own company and co-founded Solful Gifts with her younger sister, Lucy, and became a mind transformation coach. The goal was to help clients see themselves and their possibilities in a new light. Oksana wanted more flexibility and creativity in her work than she had found at the consulting company, and she wanted to focus on people in a meaningful way. Her plan was to begin part-time, but a month after she started the company, she was laid off from her corporate position.

"Most people think a layoff is scary, but when it happened, I felt like I was getting out of prison," Oksana says. "People started calling and offering me jobs like the one I had before, but I just couldn't force myself to go back into that kind of environment, doing a similar job. So at age forty, I chose to invest one hundred percent of my time and energy into my own company and reinvent myself."

Oksana's parents were supportive, but the move surprised them. As immigrants, Oksana's well-paying corporate job seemed like a dream come true for her parents. Many of Oksana's friends and former co-workers were also surprised, since they didn't know about her passion for metaphysics. Her sister Lucy was one of Oksana's biggest supporters.

"Now, we help people become self-realized, aware, and happy," Oksana says. "We show them how to navigate through stress, anxiety, and dissatisfaction with life. I enjoy helping people transform their lives and careers, to love and accept themselves unconditionally, often for the first time in their lives, and to become aware of who they are as spiritual beings. I want to help them manifest true miracles in their lives." Oksana now helps clients overcome stress, anxiety, and a lack of purpose in order to feel peaceful and happy within, no matter what the outside world is bringing.

It took some time to build the business. For the first six months, Oksana worked on administrative aspects, building the entire concept from scratch, as well as earning the necessary certifications for coaching. She had no paying customers, no office, and a very few leads. She invested her time to build a foundation. Then, word of mouth started filling her programs, and Oksana began to collaborate with other businesses that shared her vision and principles. She was the founder of the Serendipity Expo, and her company expanded, offering new services, classes, and related products, all with a focus on mindfulness and wellness.

"Now, we're self-sustaining, and I'm earning money doing what I love and helping other small businesses be successful. New clients come in nearly every week. I've learned to measure success in how I can help others and in the results I see in how I can touch people's lives," Oksana says. "I have an opportunity to help shape the future of this planet one person at a time, by helping these bright, beautiful souls embrace who they are without waiting for midlife crises to occur." While Oksana's original client base tended to be people over forty, her base has grown both younger and older, ranging now from seventeen to seventy.

"It always pays forward. Happy people make others around them happier," Oksana says. "I'm successful because I do what I love, I'm passionate about my business, and I bring smiles to people's faces and love to their hearts. I joke that I'm on vacation now every day because I enjoy what I do so much that I can hardly call it work."

## The Take-Away

Oksana left a heavily left-brain oriented, analytical field for a very right-brain oriented, metaphysical role. Yet so often, we have been trained to think that we are only good at one type of thinking or a single kind of work. We have more talents and possibilities than we are usually encouraged to explore in a society that constantly exhorts us to focus, "stick to the knitting," and repeat past successes.

It requires courage to make a one-hundred-eighty-degree turn professionally. But doing so is not only possible, it can be profitable and fulfilling if that is where your passion lies. As you're planning your own Fresh Start Success, don't automatically limit yourself to the skills you used in prior jobs or offshoots of your current career. Explore your hobbies, investigate the areas of study that fascinate you, and pay close attention to the elements that have attracted you again and again over a long period of time. You may be able to reinvent yourself in a way that not only provides fulfillment from those elements, but earns a living as well.

## Q&A with Oksana Gritsenko

### Q: What did you learn the hard way?

A: "Life has given me many lessons, and I cherish every single one of them. Without those lessons, I wouldn't be the person I am today, and I'm very happy with who I am now. One of the hardest lessons was working so hard and taking things at work so personally that it ended up affecting my health in a pretty severe way. I spent almost five months on disability while I was still in a corporate world. That was a wonderful learning opportunity, and it changed the way I saw the world and myself forever. I realized that true peace and happiness were unconditional and can only be found within. It was a definite pivotal point in my life."

**Q: To what do you attribute your Fresh Start Success?**
A: "I love what I do. I am so passionate about it, and I feel in alignment with my life's purpose. I'm authentic. I am surrounded by incredible people, including my sister. I learn something new from everyone I meet. I've also discovered that evolving and changing keeps me open to new opportunities, so I can take risks and grow quickly. It's also important to have clarity about what you want to accomplish and where your strengths are so you can stay focused and disciplined."

**Q: How are you a different person now that before your reinvention?**
A: "I am changing every day. I've learned to be comfortable with discomfort. Things are evolving, and so are we. Change and transformation are necessary for progress and growth. I didn't understand that before, but I do now. You have to be willing to allow for shifts to occur. My biggest challenge when I started my business was the fear of failure. I didn't realize that I had that fear my whole life. Even though I wasn't aware of the fear, it kept me from starting my own company at an earlier point in my life. When I became aware and went ahead and started my company, I realized that the only way to overcome the fear was to face it and move right through it. Fear is an illusion. I knew that in theory, but sometimes illusions seem real. I took a risk and embraced my strong desire to inspire others, and it paid off."

**Q: What new skills did you gain? How did your former career prepare you for your reinvention?**
A: "I gained skills throughout my entire life that I am using now. From my fine art background, I gained understanding of creativity, how to create a compelling story through visuals, and the nuances of how colors affect us on a subconscious level. That knowledge has served me well, from the way I dress to what colors we use in our marketing materials and physical environment. I designed all my

marketing materials, including our logo and website. I learned leadership from the corporate world: how to work with people of all backgrounds; how to deal with stress; how to be disciplined and very organized; how to create a successful marketing campaign; and how to understand the end users, my customers. My corporate background also taught me how to stay neutral in a conflict situation. I learned how to prioritize, when to let go, how to schedule time to allow myself balance. Other jobs and activities enabled me to appreciate multiple points of view and what everyone has to offer, as well as how to work successfully with other people, organize successful events, and make presentations with clarity and ease. I also learned how to embrace differences and diversity. All of those skills serve me well now with my own company."

**Q: What is one trait is critical to your Fresh Start Success?**
A: "Integrity—not just what you do for others, but also being honest with yourself. For me, that means follow through, speaking the truth, treating others the way you want to be treated. It includes being kind and compassionate, and keeping promises to yourself and others. When you are true to yourself, everything else just works out. And when you maintain a positive attitude with that integrity, the world is your oyster."

**Q: If you had a superpower, what would it be?**
A: "At first, I wanted to say to fly. I love flying in my dreams because it means freedom. But my most desired superpower would be to grant people the awareness to know their true selves and what is truly valuable in life, seeing it now rather than on a death bed. I want to shatter the illusions people have to show them who they really are, so they won't accept less than their best. That was the reason I have created a twenty-five-week 'Know Your True Self' Program."

**Q: What role does marketing and branding play in your success?**
A: "Quite a bit. I'm very active on social media, I collaborate with social marketing companies, and I coach people on sales and marketing. It's important to reach people at their level. To do that, people need to find out about you, and sometimes you can reach people faster and easier through social media channels."

# Structure Matters
## Lisa Mininni

WHEN YOU LEAVE corporate life and strike out as an entrepreneur, you quickly notice that you miss the lovely support that was always just a few steps away.

Computer problems? There's no IT department, so you either fix it yourself or find someone who can. Ditto accounting, marketing, sales—you get the picture.

As a business owner, you're the CEO—and the one who empties the garbage cans. It's a real adjustment to make.

Setting up systems is crucial to your Fresh Start Success. Your systems need to be suited to your personality so that you use them without constant friction.

Creating systems isn't always intuitive, but having them is essential. As you consider your reinvention, think about how you want to structure your new business, as well as the impact you want to have in the world.

If systems and structure aren't your strong point, find a mentor who can help you avoid pitfalls. Getting the structure and systems in place at the beginning can be a real factor in creating your Fresh Start Success!

## Building Systems

Lisa Mininni knows entrepreneurship firsthand. She studied business in college and went on to earn a master's of science in administration. She became a vice president of human resources for a large healthcare system early in her career and enjoyed a lot of success. A number of mergers and acquisitions gave her the opportunity to gain plenty of experience in organizational change.

While she was the catalyst for successful union negotiations, had high employee engagement scores, and was good at turning chaos into order, when the decision was made to dismantle the division she was working in, she laid everyone off, including herself.

Lisa wanted to find a similar position, but in 2001, she was in her mid-30s and there were few vice president of human resources positions open. People said she looked "too young" for the job.

Then one day, Lisa was driving down the highway, and something popped up from the freeway. She covered her face with her hands, and a tire iron flew into the front seat, shattering the windshield. Lisa shook off the glass and realized she had no injuries, but the tire iron had only missed her by four inches, and it left a six-inch gash in her hood. When the cops came to the scene of the accident, all three of them said, "Geez, you're on this Earth for a reason," because she survived without injury.

"All I had known my entire career was working for someone else," Lisa said. "I had been asking God whether I should start a business and write a book, and then the accident happened, and I knew I was here to do something important."

The first two years striking out on her own were hard. Thanks to her background in quality improvement, Lisa was very good at streamlining and found that coaching was intuitive for her. She was good at helping people control costs and save money. Her mentor asked her what her conversion rate was and she reported eighty percent, thinking that wasn't very good, but that success rate stunned her mentor.

That's when Lisa realized her system was working well. She intuitively assessed how people wanted to receive their information, then validated those prospects through her pre-qualification systems, and that led to them becoming very successful clients.

At that point, Lisa decided she was onto something. She created her own signature program and started attracting people who wanted to know how to build systems to show their uniqueness and work in alignment with who they were. Lisa created Excellerate Associates, an entrepreneurial and leadership institute, to share her vision.

After Lisa began coaching, she realized she needed to make a mental shift to focus on what she wanted to contribute to the world, instead of what she wanted out of coaching. "I wanted to make an impact. I didn't want someone who was making the transformation from corporate employee to success to struggle as long as I did. Gradually, I developed systems to make that transformation easier. If I'd had my own system right from the start, I believe I could have cut two years off my three-year learning curve," she says.

Lisa also wanted to make a contribution based on her unique self and to work in alignment with who she was, rather than trying to fit someone else's mold. "Being in alignment makes it much easier to triage priorities," she says. "And I needed to figure it out quickly because I did not want to keep working a ninety-hour week."

So she worked with a coach for over a year to shift from a self-serving point of view to a vision of contributing to the world. "I learned that it's not all about me, me, me," she said. "People are put in your path for a reason," Lisa says. "That proved itself again and again as I was networking while I developed my program. You just don't know who you're going to meet."

With her hardwiring, she empowered business owners to transform their contribution in the world.

Lisa discovered that she had always connected disparate ideas, and her skills were honed by working in chaotic organizations without good infrastructure. "In successful businesses, you create accountabilities and strong systems. When that is missing, there is chaos. Now, I've married both hardwiring and systems to create a powerful shift, and it is something we teach through my business."

The third year of business was the tipping point for Lisa, when she hit "critical mass" and revenue went way up. Now, Lisa and her team of Profitability Lab Leaders educate small business owners, entrepreneurs, and business leaders on biological hardwiring. Mental "wiring" is biological and dictates the type of environment in which a person is best equipped to thrive and succeed, and the kind of environment in which people prefer to live and work. She is also the best-selling author of *Me, Myself, and Why? Get More Clients Now!* and the co-author of *Leading Women*.

## The Take-Away

What kind of environment makes you the happiest and most productive? Don't automatically replicate the standard office or repeat what you're used to if that was part of what made you unhappy or less fulfilled in prior jobs. Start with understanding your natural wiring. Think outside the cubicle!

When you work in alignment with who you are innately, it's not work.

Maybe you thrive working around other people. Consider planning to spend some of your day working from a coffee shop, library, or fast food venue, rent a keyman office in a shared office building, and do a lot of networking events.

If solitude helps you focus, find a quiet place where you can gather your thoughts. Reinvent your approach to filing, document storage, and other key aspects. As long as you meet legal requirements, create systems that work well for the way you think and work. Make creating the right environment part of your Fresh Start Success!

## Q&A with Lisa Mininni

**Q: What did you learn the hard way?**
A: "If you're going to expand your business, you can't do it alone. I had to let go of perfectionism."

**Q: How are you a different person than before?**
A: "I've softened. Now, I know how to go with the flow."

**Q: What have you learned about yourself?**
A: "I'm a bold leader. A colleague told me, 'You not only had your own business, you kept at it.' Tenacity, keeping at something, is a strength."

**Q: What new skills did you gain?**
A: "I had to get in touch with how I can contribute to the world. That opened up a whole new ballgame of what is possible in life.

"I believe that when business owners are successful, they give back to non-profits and causes. Those non-profits and causes go out and they help their communities. Those communities then pay it forward. Through that ripple effect, we will achieve global peace.

"It is that global peace that I take action inside of each and every day. When business owners get in touch with and take action inside of their contribution, whole worlds open up."

**Q: What is one trait critical to your Fresh Start Success?**
A: "Open-mindedness. Really listening to what's important to other people, being open to different ways of thinking, to things changing at rapid pace. The notion of permanency and perfection needed to go away. What I learned yesterday is obsolete today. I had to learn to be agile and open-minded."

**Q: If you had a superpower, what would it be?**
A: "I would have a magic wand and use it so that the people I meet can instantly see their innate uniqueness and how they can contribute to the greater good. I wish they could see that in themselves immediately, rather than having to discover it. So many people have the potential to make a great contribution, but they never act on it. I would want them to see their greatness instantly and to instill confidence."

**Q: What advice would you give to others?**
A: "When you've got a choice to make, make a commitment yes or no, but don't be on the fence. Get outside help. Look for ways to create a contribution rather than just making a living. Then, live in and take action consistent with your contribution, not your circumstances.

"Entrepreneurs get up in the morning because they know they can help and make a contribution. When you work in alignment with that contribution, you're inspired and inspiring. When others are inspired, you will attract your ideal clients and make a contribution in their lives."

**Q: What key marketing tools have you used?**

A: "While I use many of the tools that others do to generate and attract my ideal clients, like LinkedIn and YouTube, I take the same systems approach I teach at my Wake Up Profitable Boot Camp.

"We put the systems in an order that generates leads, pre-qualifies those leads, and adds consistent value. That is the key for any business in today's marketplace. And, when you marry your online and offline marketing as well as systematize your business, you provide consistency. That consistency creates trust. And people do business with people they know, like, and trust."

# Taking Control
## Wendy Ida

TODAY, WENDY IDA is a best-selling author, a motivational speaker, life transformation coach, and fitness expert. She is an eight-time national award-winning bodybuilding champion and holds two fitness-related records in the *Guinness Book of World Records*. Most of those achievements occurred when Wendy was in her late fifties and beyond. She didn't even become a trainer until she was over forty.

As you consider your Fresh Start Success, are you holding back from something you want to do because you're afraid you're too old to try? Have you convinced yourself that certain achievements just aren't possible after you're past a certain milestone birthday? Many of the people interviewed in this book made huge, successful life changes in their fifties and sixties and are enjoying their reinvention with a whole new lease on life. Don't allow your inner critic to talk you out of following your passion just because you're not the "typical" age. Fresh Start Success isn't limited by the calendar. Start working on your reinvention today!

## Taking Back Her Life

In high school, Wendy Ida took her cues from her older sister, who she admired. Her sister took business courses, so Wendy did, too. But when her sister took up stenography classes, Wendy realized that wasn't for her, so she switched gears to take advanced math and statistics classes instead. Her math grades were very high, and she soon realized that she was good with money and good with numbers. At that point, Wendy researched careers and decided to be an accountant.

She went to junior college and took accounting courses for two years. Wendy earned an associate's degree, and while finishing her coursework, she received honors in her major, was voted campus queen, and got married. She planned to continue on to earn a bachelor's degree, but her marriage began to deteriorate, and her abusive husband physically stopped her from doing anything that might challenge his control, although he did allow her to continue working full-time in accounting. At one point, he chased her through the streets and stole her shoes to keep her from attending an event her aunt was hosting. Wendy began to feel like she was a character in a horror movie with no way out.

Finally, Wendy got up the courage to take her children and flee her husband with nothing but the clothes they were wearing. She left New Jersey and made it safely to California, where her sister lived. Once they got settled, Wendy finished her bachelor's degree and landed a better job than she had before, earning good raises.

Although she had successfully fled her husband and was getting a divorce, there was a lot of damage to repair. Wendy's primary goal was safety. At the same time that she was grieving the loss of her marriage and trying to deal with her own emotions, she had to get her children settled and help them feel safe. Her ex-husband had not allowed her to discipline the children, so there were behavior problems to address, and Wendy knew she had to get those issues resolved as soon as possible to minimize problems for her children. The challenges were overwhelming. Wendy put everyone else's needs first, with no time to focus on herself.

"I felt broken down all the time, scared of shadows," Wendy recalls. "I was going through the motions of getting things worked out, but I didn't feel loved or confident, and I didn't know how my life had gotten to this point." She gained weight, eventually putting on eighty extra pounds. That led to health problems and more stress. Wendy soldiered on, trying to cover up her problems when she was at work. But life was taking its toll.

Wendy didn't know how to lose weight and reshape her body. Because she was over forty, she thought she had lost her chance for a better life. Then a friend encouraged her to work out regularly at a local gym. Wendy decided to work out with a trainer. Gradually, Wendy realized that her body was changing. She started to get compliments. She hadn't noticed the change herself, but when she started to see what a difference her workouts were making, she began paying more attention to results. She started to ask her trainer more questions and continued to see results. Her body felt better, she had more energy, and her head cleared. "Working out changed me entirely as a person," Wendy says. "It gave me more confidence and helped me take back my life."

Working out also kept Wendy from dwelling on the past. Her gym routine gave her purpose and awakened her body and mind. Her only goal when she came to California was escaping her past. She didn't have a plan for the future. But as her training continued, Wendy began to feel at home in the gym. She watched how her trainer did his work and promoted his training practice, and her spirit felt at home.

Wendy was still working in accounting and earned raises despite bias she encountered against women and minorities. Wendy loved her work and the stability it created. She liked accounting because she enjoyed reaching goals and finishing projects, which she found rewarding. She enjoyed balancing the numbers on her spreadsheets and getting the right answers. Accounting gave her all those things, but it wasn't creative, and Wendy wanted more.

"I realized that I became a different person at the gym, and that was the 'real' me," Wendy says. She also realized that her office personality was a façade. "I wanted to do something more creative when I was younger, but my mother steered me toward a safer choice," Wendy recalls. "I was a good little girl and did what I was told to do. But eventually, I needed something that I couldn't find in accounting." She researched how to get certified as a trainer.

By then, she had remarried. Her new husband encouraged her to make the change and supported her financially as she made the switch. He wanted her to be on her own and independent. It took five years for her to let go of her accounting career, but once she made the choice, she never looked back and never felt happier.

Wendy built a practice as a personal trainer based on her own approach to diet and exercise. She got results for her clients, but what the media really noticed was Wendy's excellent level of fitness, which enabled her to win bodybuilding championships throughout her fifties and sixties. Wendy decided to share her vision in her book, *Take Back Your Life! My No-Nonsense Approach to Health, Fitness and Looking Good Naked.* The book became a bestseller and award-winner and landed Wendy on TV and in commercials, exercise videos, and magazines. "It's never too late to take back your life!" Wendy says.

## The Take-Away

Wendy discovered the strength and power within herself when the life she planned was completely disrupted. Something as simple as saying "yes" to a friend's invitation to go to the gym changed her health, her career, and her future.

Your Fresh Start Success isn't limited to how you earn your living. As you consider your options, make sure you also consider how best to build a future that reduces stress, encourages healthy habits, and enhances your overall well-being. If you now realize that you pursued your former career to make someone else happy, invest the time to discover your real passion and purpose, and make sure to weave those into your reinvention. What you discover and what you're capable of achieving may go beyond your wildest dreams!

## Q&A with Wendy Ida

**Q: What did you learn the hard way?**
A: "I learned to listen to my gut and intuition. I didn't do that for too long. I'm stubborn, I can be too analytical, and I was always afraid to take risks or make a mistake. I've gotten better about being afraid to be wrong or fail. I used to put off things that I knew I should be doing. That's another area where I've made improvements."

**Q: To what do you attribute your Fresh Start Success?**
A: "The single biggest factor is that I found my home, root, joy, purpose, and reason I was born, which is to be of service and help people change their lives.

I am a people person: people feed me energy. When you find your purpose, that's when success comes."

**Q: What did you learn about yourself?**
A: "I've learned that I can look back and see some talents I had when I was young that got suppressed and stomped out because life happens, and sometimes life spoils your hopes and ruins your dreams. When you know better, you do better. I speak my mind better now, and I've learned not to limit myself in any capacity. I just put myself out there, which brings great rewards."

**Q: How are you a different person than before?**
A: "I used to be naïve and fickle. I didn't know enough about how the world worked, so I was too trusting. I had strengths, but I couldn't recognize them because I was too caught up in daily life, and what others wanted. I was a people-pleaser. Now, I accept my strengths and vulnerabilities, and I know it's okay to just be me."

**Q: What is critical to your Fresh Start Success?**
A: "Integrity is really, really important. Be true to yourself, treat others as you want to be treated. But always keep one eye open to protect yourself because some people do not have integrity. Have faith. Love what you do; drive to push through whatever gets in your way. I used to stress out when someone did me wrong because I always tried to do the right thing, and others didn't seem to care about doing the right thing. I used to try to analyze and understand their behavior. Now, I've learned to just let it go."

**Q: If you had a superpower, what would it be?**
A: "Dancing. I love to dance. It makes my heart happy. I would be a star dancer on *Dancing with the Stars*. I would also like to wave a wand with a star on it and dance into people's lives, tapping them with my wand and getting them to dance with me and feel my joy."

**Q: What role did marketing and social media play in your success?**
A: "Wow, wow, wow. OMG! Marketing and social media are the core of my whole outreach. Social media and blog posts help me get more done. I hired help, and now I ask fans to help me spread the word. My content goes viral and leads to new connections, traffic, inquiries. I always ask, 'How did you find out about me?' and it's because of social media, word of mouth, people sharing content.

"I'm on Facebook, Instagram, LinkedIn, Pinterest, blogs, online magazines, and YouTube. I'm doing YouTube videos and getting requests from fans to do more. That's how *Essence Magazine, CNN, Inside Edition* and the *Dr. Oz* TV show found me and invited me to be on the show. Marketing works!"

# Fear or Feast?
### Lisa Manyon

SCIENTISTS TELL US that the primitive part of our brains, the amygdala, governs fear, greed, and lust. It's the fight-or-flight center, often referred to as the "lizard brain" because it covers the most basic survival instincts. The amygdala is the brute force, take-no-prisoners, grab-all-the-cookies-for-yourself part of the brain, and while it may be successful under extreme conditions, it doesn't make for civilized society.

If you've worked for a fast-paced corporation that stoked unhealthy competition between colleagues with the constant fear of bad reviews or job loss, you know how miserable such an approach can be.

Marketers, politicians, and the media poke our lizard brain over and over again, using fear and scarcity to push our buttons and manipulate our actions. If you've ever seen an advertisement that held out the product as salvation from a terrible fate, you've seen lizard-brain thinking at work. Buy the product or service, or suffer the consequences, we're told.

You don't have to become one of the fear-mongers. When you're creating your Fresh Start Success, question the status quo—especially if the established norm is based on fear and scarcity. Alternative approaches always exist. Ask yourself whether you could make a compelling case based on positive outcomes, tangible benefits, and creating "results envy"—the desire to replicate for oneself the success a happy customer has achieved using a product or service. More importantly, examine your own worldview and become aware of the places where you may be acting or making decisions based on fear/scarcity instead of confidence/abundance.

## Accentuate the Positive

Lisa Manyon went to college to major in journalism but did not complete her degree. Instead, she worked in a variety of jobs in the for-profit and nonprofit world. She worked for advertising agencies, radio stations, and non-profit organizations, becoming a certified radio marketing master through the Radio Advertising Bureau. Lisa was drawn to social service work and marketing, and she taught pre-employment skills for at-risk youth in a Job Training Partnership Act Program. Lisa also managed a Community Action Partnership, overseeing millions of dollars in grant funding to programs combating poverty in a six-county area. As a certified family development specialist for this nonprofit, Lisa oversaw life skills classes to people coming from a history of generational poverty.

The clients of these organizations made big advancements on an individual level, but the scope of the problem was overwhelming. The benchmarks and measurements required to keep funding often seemed divorced from the real-life situations and problems confronting the people Lisa served every day. Budgets were always tight. Lisa felt rushed, frustrated, and discouraged that she and her staff couldn't spend the time she felt was necessary with each client.

While at Community Action Partnership, she was offered a position with an advertising agency and decided to accept. Lisa loved the work, and for many years handled large accounts, including Lewis-Clark State College, where she managed their campaigns for college enrollment and retention. The work was fun, and Lisa enjoyed being an account manager and working with media. But eventually, Lisa grew tired of seventy-hour weeks and not being free to choose her clients. As much as she liked aspects of the work, overall she wanted to make a difference in a bigger way. It was also clear to her that the company was seeing more profit from her skills and hard work than she was. It was time for a change.

Lisa knew she wanted to focus on writing, but she had a non-compete contract in the local market that prohibited her from using her marketing and advertising skills. That forced her to take a different approach and go global. She turned to the internet for clients and new skill sets. She jumped into online marketing and direct response copywriting, training in long copy and direct response techniques. Lisa took a part-time job at a call center to make ends meet while she got her new business, Write On Creative, off the ground.

"I focused more on evolution rather than considering it to be a complete reinvention," Lisa says, pointing out that she refined and extended the writing skills she had used in prior jobs, rather than going in a completely different direction. As she built the foundation for her Fresh Start Success, Lisa learned all about the online marketing world, studied how to leverage technology, and honed her direct-response copy skills. She earned certification by Glazer-Kennedy in copywriting and worked with many high-level coaches.

It took almost four years for Lisa's business to reach the point where she didn't need to supplement her income. "When the time was right, I did the free-fall into full-time freelancing," Lisa recalls. "I just made it happen because I didn't have a choice. I committed to making the business work."

It didn't take long before she had made a national name for herself. Colleagues pushed her to create her own advertising agency, but Lisa wanted to find low-cost and no-cost solutions for clients instead of traditional, big-budget advertising campaigns. Her passion is strategy and positioning clients as leaders in their field by leveraging publicity and creating marketing messages with integrity.

Lisa noticed that the norm for online marketing and direct response was to gain new clients through a problem/agitate/solve approach. In this model, the marketer identifies a painful problem for the client, ratchets up the anxiety about the problem and its potential consequences, and then presents a solution. While this was a tried-and-true approach that had long been used successfully by marketers, Lisa felt it was manipulative. "I think the traditional approach does a disservice to clients," Lisa says. "Poking at pain points and agitating the problem actually perpetuates buyer's remorse. I knew there was a friendly and effective way to encourage a client to take action without manipulation."

Lisa created the challenge/solution/invitation model. "I wanted to shift the energy to a more positive place," she explains, "instead of putting people into fear and anxiety. This model is especially suited to mission-driven clients." Lisa's model and results have won her major awards, earned national press coverage including *Inc. Magazine*, and led to her being featured in several books.

"When I first developed the model, I had a bit of the 'who-am-I' syndrome about questioning the status quo," Lisa admits. "All the other 'gurus' were using the traditional, manipulative methods. I'm driven by service—I want to make a difference and see transformation." Lisa's approach to engage critical thinking and break the "trance" to move away from fear-based marketing helped her work take on a life of its own.

"The response has been very good," Lisa says. "Everyone feels the power of a shift from negative energy to positive. I'm so excited about the amazing results we're seeing when we create marketing messages with integrity." The one push-back Lisa has gotten is that the new positive approach requires critical thinking; it isn't just a "paint-by-numbers" system like many of the fear-based models. "The positive approach feels right and solid to me," Lisa says. "It brings relationships back to marketing and gets results."

## The Take-Away

When you shift your marketing and business model from the negative/fear/scarcity approach to a positive/results/abundance perspective, you create a change beyond the tone of your advertising copy—you influence all of your decision-making and priorities. Greed, ruthless behavior, and unfair practices come out of scarcity thinking. A commitment to a worldview of abundance leads to collaboration, ethical practices, and fair win-win solutions.

Creating your own Fresh Start Success includes leaving behind the outdated, counterproductive, and toxic aspects of your former experiences. Commit to approaching your evolution with an abundance mindset, and you'll be amazed at the people you attract, the opportunities that unfold, and the outcomes that result.

## Q&A with Lisa Manyon

### Q: What did you learn the hard way?
A: "What didn't I learn the hard way? The biggest thing I learned was the importance of doing due diligence. Early on, I signed up to attend an event in Las Vegas that featured a lot of big-name speakers I wanted to hear. I paid

for the event ticket, flew to Las Vegas, and found out that the event had been cancelled without notice. It turned out that the whole thing was a fraud, and the big-name speakers had never agreed to be part of the event. I reached out to the speakers who had been listed on the site and got so much support from them—people like Jay Conrad Levinson, who extended an offer for me to attend any of his events and gave me a testimonial about my writing skills based on article I wrote about the experience. After that, I learned not to take things at face value."

**Q: What did you learn about yourself?**
A: "It's really important to ask for help, get the right help, and outsource tasks that aren't your magic."

**Q: What trait is critical to your Fresh Start Success?**
A: "Determination and an absolute belief in what I'm doing. Service comes first. Even though things have been done a certain way, it's important to challenge the status quo."

**Q: If you had a superpower, what would it be?**
A: "I always come from a place of high intuition and high integrity. I think intuition is a superpower."

**Q: What advice would you give to someone making their own Fresh Start Success?**
A: "Follow your heart and passion, but have a plan. I did part-time work while I set up the business and took time to build a solid foundation. You can't just ditch the day job. Be dedicated, determined, and open to self-discovery. Focus on evolving and being the best YOU that you can be."

**Q: What role has marketing and branding played in your success?**
A: "Branding and image are key, which I knew from my ad agency background. I keep up a visible, consistent presence on social media, not necessarily to pitch,

but to talk about what I'm doing. I have an engaged and active following. They know me and trust me, and that's given me international reach. I keep my strategy consistent, focus on value, and remain true to myself."

# Optimized Luck

## Debbie Peterson

**I LOVE THE** phrase "optimized luck." It recognizes two important things. First, that circumstances come our way that we don't completely control (luck). Second—and most important—is that while we may not be able to control when luck strikes, what we do with that lucky break is up to us. That's the "optimized" part.

If you think of life like a board game, working hard and being prepared is like rolling the dice to keep chugging along the track. Luck is drawing the card that cuts off a corner or jumps you ahead of everyone else. You may not be able to control luck's timing, but you can put yourself in its path by being ready to make the most of it when the breaks fall your way.

Here's Debbie Peterson's story about taking optimum advantage of lucky breaks. Watch for how she made the most of all the unexpected opportunities life handed her as they came up—opportunities others around her failed to recognize.

## The Power of "Yes"

"I really didn't 'train' to do anything," Debbie says, looking back. She went with the flow. Debbie got married at age seventeen, and she was going to go to school to be a guidance counselor because she wanted to help other students. She had kids of her own instead, managed an apartment building, and then helped to manage the construction company her husband's family owned. After some time, she went back to college but didn't end up getting a degree. Although she took classes in accounting, business management, and corporate structure, she did so without a clear plan of where she wanted to go with that knowledge.

Debbie applied for a job that only required typing and became the "office person" for a brokerage firm. She didn't want to be a stockbroker on commission, but her boss sent her to do portfolio analytics and she ended up doing software design specifications and testing that were really business analyst work (although she didn't get paid like a business analyst). This was in the late 1970s when computers were very new and their potential wasn't yet completely understood.

She moved to the trust department of a bank that she had helped with portfolio analysis, and in 1980, Debbie was the first woman in the trust department who made $200/week. She notes that the men thought that was an ungodly amount to pay a woman. The bank created a job for her in the investment side of the business working with money market funds, fixed income, and common trust funds (mutual funds), all of which was done by hand on ledgers.

Three months later, the department was told it needed to computerize manual tasks. The head of operations had no idea how to do a computer conversion. Debbie knew about computers, so they gave her the job. She was thirty years old.

To do the conversion, she had to learn every job in the trust department and figure out how a computer could help. The hardware was very glitchy, and there was a lot of internal politics that slowed down the process. To make matters worse, her boss wasn't honest with his superiors about the difficulties facing them as they implemented the conversion. His evasions caught up with him, and he got in trouble for lying about the progress when they finally had to ask for more time. When the cut-over date came, the boss went away for three weeks in a camper without any way to contact him (remember, no cell phones) the day after the department switched over, leaving Debbie to handle everything, then came back and took credit for the successful implementation.

Debbie might not have gotten credit with the higher-ups at her own company, but the software firm that helped handle the conversion knew who had done the work. That company told Debbie that she had managed its smoothest conversion ever and put her on their national software development committee. Debbie confronted her boss and told him she couldn't work with a liar. Senior management gave her half of the operations department to manage (although the operations manager was making far more money than she was, even so). When some of her contacts from that bank moved to the rival bank across the street in 1983, she eventually followed and went to their small trust department.

That November, Debbie's husband had a bad accident. He was in construction and fell off a roof and broke his neck. He wasn't paralyzed, but he would require a long recovery in a hospital an hour away from where Debbie was working. Debbie took care of him and her school-age children and recalls that the bank was very accommodating of her need for flexibility during a time of crisis.

During her husband's recovery, Debbie saw a job for a trust officer advertised in the paper, and it turned out to be a sister bank to her prior firm. Debbie was living in Syracuse, NY, and the job was in Rochester, which was about ninety miles away. As it turned out, Debbie had also helped out with the Rochester bank's computer conversation, so she had contacts there. When she interviewed for the position, Debbie met with the head of the division and asked for more money than was originally offered because she would have to move her family. She ended up getting a fifty percent salary increase over the original offer plus paid relocation.

By 1984, Debbie was the head of operations and technology for the Rochester Bank's trust department. She continued doing the same kind of job for bigger and bigger banks, and she survived the buy-outs and mergers because she had such good knowledge of the processes and the technology. By this time, she was designing specifications for the trust tax, investment management, and accounting systems.

Debbie was able to capitalize on the cutting edge of the technology revolution and introduced the first PCs into the bank as well as email, local area networks, Wi-Fi, portfolio modeling, and performance management systems. But she ran into a glass ceiling and realized her opportunities to rise beyond her present role were very limited. Debbie's personal situation was also changing. Her sons were grown, and she was newly divorced. In 1999, two of her adult sons moved to Charlotte, NC, to start their own business, and Debbie moved to Charlotte to be closer to them.

Debbie didn't know anyone in Charlotte, but she was determined to find opportunities in her new city. She went to a career counselor, who told her to write up an ad for her dream job. She wrote down exactly what she wanted in a new job, in detail, turning off any internal judgment about what was likely or possible. The next day an ad for someone to do process re-engineering for a Charlotte based insurance company showed up in the newspaper that was almost identical to her dream. Debbie was hired.

Three weeks into the job, the head of human resources asked Debbie to meet her in the president's office. The company had a problem with a Kansas City insurance processor they owned which was not yet Y2K compliant. Debbie had never worked with insurance and had only been in Charlotte for a month. She agreed to go help out, thinking the project would only take two to four weeks in Kansas City. It actually took ten months to resolve. While she was in Kansas City, Debbie worked with three different processing areas and several different types of insurance programs and market segments. After analysis, Debbie advised the company to sell off the segments to a Y2K compliant insurance company. Instead of the company needing to invest millions bringing that Kansas City firm up to speed, the sale netted eight million dollars. Debbie got a bonus for her work but no credit that she had turned what would have been a huge financial loss into a multi-million-dollar win.

Debbie decided to look for a new opportunity and started her career as an investment advisor with a local firm, which required getting her broker licenses and taking a lot of training to work in insurance, planning, and cash-flow management. She also did a lot of networking. Most of the other advisors were men, and there was a strong "old boys" network with an emphasis on traditional (mostly male) clientele. Debbie worked hard to bring in female clients. At that point, the company was restructuring its advisors into teams and spinning them off into independent affiliates. Debbie found a team she worked well with, incorporated, and created her business under the name "Money Counts" in 2002.

Debbie took a novel approach, turning the relationship between affiliate and corporation on its head. She used the investment firm as her back office, with the idea that they were working for her, not the other way around. Debbie also worked hard to create a brand and image for Money Counts as its own company, instead of trading on its relationship with the larger company's image and branding.

Money Counts took a different approach by counseling clients on how to adjust their current financial portfolio and cash flow to be able to afford their personal priorities, instead of offering one-size-fits-all advice. It was a model Debbie believed in and her clients loved.

The broker-dealer was a subsidiary of AIG, and in 2008, right at the start of the financial crash, AIG was in trouble. Debbie was savvy about watching market trends, and she didn't want to be sucked into problems she anticipated if AIG got bought. Then a competing broker-dealer company called her, and she switched over to their back office. It was a good transition, and she enjoyed working with them. But her vision for where opportunity lay was in doing more training and workshops to help bring in and educate female clients.

In 2011, Debbie was looking for a new broker-dealer that would support her vision and switched over to her current broker one month before she got married and was temporarily sidelined by health issues. At this point, Money Counts was totally independent, no sales quotas required. Her broker-dealer does the due diligence and back office work, and Debbie and her team began doing workshops training the general public and corporate employees on financial literacy, which is a first step to helping them become savvier managers of their own money.

## The Take-Away

Doors opened for Debbie because she wasn't afraid to say "yes" to new opportunities, even if saying "yes" meant learning whole new areas of expertise. Debbie trusted in her own abilities to be a quick study and a good organizer, and she also recognized her own value, which meant she either negotiated for better pay or was willing to change jobs for better compensation.

Even when doors shut, like the boss who didn't give her credit for the huge job of a successful conversion, Debbie seized the opportunity of working with the software company behind the conversion, which broadened her network. Because Debbie knew how to optimize luck, she managed to find a way to move forward even when setbacks appeared. That challenge you say "yes" to might just be your lucky break!

## Q&A with Debbie Peterson

**Q: What did you learn the hard way?**
A: "I don't fit in to big corporations because I'm good at getting things done quickly. Senior management tends to talk more than act, and they were put off when I got my work done so quickly. I also discovered that people became suspicious when I offered to help them because they were afraid I was trying to take their jobs. I really was just trying to be helpful. I was very lucky to have worked for small banks where I reported to the head of the division who reported to the CEO, so I had the freedom to do my job. It's also been a hard lesson to learn that some people are intentionally dishonest."

**Q: To what do you attribute your Fresh Start Success?**
A: "I look at prospects as if they are interviewing me, not the other way around. People gravitate to me because I'm direct and honest. I'm authentic and I'm good at simplifying complex concepts. They can tell I have their best interests at heart. I present options to them instead of just telling them what I think they should do. I love giving them choices—I'm the 'what else can you do' person in terms of getting people to see new alternatives."

**Q: How are you a different person now?**
A: "I'm not as naïve as I used to be. I don't feel like I have to prove anything to anyone. I'm tough on myself, but I have nothing to prove. Experience has shown me that volatile markets are a temporary situation, so I don't get rattled. I can relate to all kinds of people because of my varied experience. That means

I can talk to people in their own language—big business, small business, entrepreneur."

**Q: What did you learn about yourself?**
A: "I learned I have a deep faith in God, who has supported me through all my trials and tribulations, and I have never questioned that."

**Q: If you had a superpower, what would it be?**
A: "My superpower would be the ability to hyper-focus. I might already have it! I'm very good at figuring out what needs to be done, getting things in the right order, getting the job done. I don't get distracted. I usually have a clear vision for my company, my clients, and myself. Our process is all about focus and priority."

**Q: What role has marketing and branding played in your success?**
A: "Marketing has played a huge part in our success. We're somewhat restricted right now in the financial services industry in terms of using social media, but that is changing. We're studying social media, and I think it will be very useful when we finally get the go-ahead to use it more broadly. In terms of branding, I put my picture on everything, including videos. I want to look different from other financial planners, let people know I am very down-to-Earth. I've bought print ads, but I've also done public speaking and made plenty of presentations to get out in the community and be known. You can't build a client base without marketing. I put about ten percent of revenue into marketing. I'm not afraid to try something new, and if it doesn't work, then I change tactics."

*Opinions expressed are that of either the author or the interviewee and are not endorsed by Summit Brokerage Services, Inc. or its affiliates. Money Counts, Inc. is an independent company with securities offered through Summit Brokerage Services, Inc., Member FINRA, SIPC.*

# Healing Hands

Tamara Green

WE HAVE A deep need to know our work provides value to the world and that it is valued by other people. Work that is profitable without also being psychologically rewarding can drain our energy even as it pads our bank account. Most of us look beyond the bottom line to find meaning, purpose, and long-term impact in our work. When those elements are missing, we become restless, unhappy, and depressed.

As you plan your Fresh Start Success, think about the times you have felt most fulfilled and valuable. What services were you providing? What problem did you solve? Who was your audience? Many people who embark on a mid-life career change intentionally choose a healing or helping profession such as coaching, counseling, clergy, therapist, or wellness practitioner because they have benefitted from those services themselves and want to give back, or because they see those roles as a direct way to be the change they want to see in the world.

## Helping Profession

Tamara Green knew in college that she wanted to be in a helping profession. Her parents were psychologists, and she wanted to follow in their footsteps, but they opposed that career path. So Tamara worked in financial printing, in sales and reception, moving into customer service for eighteen years.

The money was satisfying, but the corporate culture was toxic. Coworkers who were dishonest or who were substance abusers made her crazy. The last straw was being moved to sales, and because she did not believe in the product, she did not do well and got fired. She was still trying to please her parents, so she tried to stay in the business world, selling insurance, then taking a job in marketing, but none of the jobs resonated. "I did a lot of crazy things back then because I loathed myself," Tamara recalls.

Tamara was miserable. She finally went into therapy. Seeing a therapist made such a difference in her life that she decided she wanted to become a therapist herself. "I was called the 'dorm shrink' in college by the other girls because I was the person everyone came to talk to when they had problems," she says. "After I got fired from my corporate sales job, I worked in restaurants to get my head together. I took a year and a half off, then decided to get a master's degree in social work."

Tamara grew up in Los Angeles. She moved to New York City and went back to work in the financial printing industry to pay for her master's degree. "My therapist suggested that I estrange myself from my family to make the shift from people pleasing to focusing on my own dreams—not theirs," she says.

She earned her master's in social work and took classes in public administration. Tamara landed a job at a hospital as a social worker on psychiatric units, and earned her LCSW designation. At the same time, she started a part-time practice and created a niche for herself. After she added enough private clients to her roster, Tamara went into her business full-time.

Tamara trained as a Love Mentor®, individual and couples psychotherapist, meditation facilitator, and hypnotherapist, and found her niche as a loving relationship expert. She is the author of *Transform Your Life Using The 7 Sacred Flames: Daily Guided Meditations*. Now Tamara is an author, speaker, and trainer. "My specialty lies in helping single people to meet and marry their soul mates and couples to heal their relationships—all while falling madly in love with themselves in the process," she says.

It took her eight years for the business to become self-sufficient. "Now, my target audience is ninety-five percent women, and I hear them doing the same things that I used to do, the same self-loathing and limiting behaviors," Tamara says. "I grew out of those behaviors, and I know now that I can help others grow out of theirs."

## The Take-Away

Whether or not you choose to reinvent yourself as a "healer" in the traditional sense, you may well be providing a healing role in the services you offer. Do you help people solve a problem, overcome an obstacle, realign their thinking or their finances, or rid themselves of a roadblock? If so, you are providing "healing" in the broadest sense of the term because you are removing disease.

When you are choosing among your options for creating a Fresh Start Success, look at the times in your life where you have faced a setback, failure, or difficulty and think about who helped you move forward. What did you learn? How can you turn that experience and wisdom into a new career so that you "pay it forward" by lifting others up and helping them to succeed? Regardless of the industry in which you provide that service, you are providing a healing presence. Factor that in as you consider your path!

## Q&A with Tamara Green

**Q: What did you learn the hard way?**
A: "I knew what I wanted to do early on, but I shut down my own vision and dreams to please my parents and fulfill the wishes of other people."

**Q: To what do you attribute your Fresh Start Success?**
A: "I'm passionate about my vision, and I'm successful at what I do because I'm doing what I love. I love my career and working with clients. I love waking up every day because I have a wonderful life."

**Q: How are you a different person?**
A: "Dramatically! When I look in the mirror, I see someone I like. I'm happier, I have fun, I laugh all the time, and I have more confidence. Eventually, I bridged the thirteen-year estrangement with my family. Years back, I took my therapist's advice to pull back from them to find myself. I know now that was

not necessary. My refusing to connect with my parents and siblings caused them tremendous pain and heartbreak. I reconnected with my family when my daughter was born, and I'm happy to report that we are now all very close. They are proud of me and support me one hundred percent."

**Q: What did you learn about yourself?**
A: "I learned that all the challenges I faced have turned out to my benefit. All my wounds turned out to be gifts. Anything is possible. Life should be fun and filled with joy. Work is fun."

**Q: What new knowledge did you gain?**
A: "I learned that I can do anything. I used to question and doubt myself, even when I worked two full-time jobs plus taking a full load of college courses. Now, once I make a decision, nothing can stop me; I can create anything I put my mind to."

**Q: What trait is critical to your Fresh Start Success?**
A: "Love. Loving yourself is the most critical thing ever. Everything else blossoms when you love yourself. You can hear what to do next, honor the guidance, and tune into your highest self."

**Q: If you had a superpower, what would it be?**
A: "I would want to take all fear-based thinking and feeling out of the world. Fear is the opposite of love and is the cause of most problems."

**Q: What role has marketing and social media played in your success?**
A: "Marketing helps me stay focused and keeps me targeted. Otherwise, I would be all over the board. It helps me hone in on who the audience is and what they need."

# Making an Impact
## Barbara Edie

AS YOU THINK about your next step, do you have a deep desire to make an impact, change the world, or leave a legacy? Many people who reinvent themselves are driven by a desire to feel part of something meaningful and lasting, to contribute to society beyond a paycheck, to make the world a better place. Often, we have a limited view of what kind of work has that kind of impact, believing it to only apply to people like doctors, teachers, artists, and visionaries who can make a difference.

The truth is, every kind of work has the potential to leave the world a better place and touch lives. When you use your gifts and talents to help others learn, thrive, and succeed, you are changing their world—and the world as a whole.

As you consider your Fresh Start Success, consider how your unique talents, perspective, and personal journey make a positive impact on your clients through providing your services. How will their lives be better because of the work you do? How is the world a little bit happier, more whole, or healthier because you do what you are uniquely able to do? Don't short-change yourself believing that making a difference is only possible for people in certain professions. Each of us leaves the world a little different than we found it every day. Make your difference part of your Fresh Start Success plan.

## A Shift in Perspective

Barbara Edie wanted to be a nurse. She earned her nursing degree and enjoyed her work. Barbara liked helping people and believed that what we do for others, we do for ourselves and the world. She was proud to be in a profession that did good work in the world, and she liked the fact that nursing was something she could do anywhere, which allowed her to travel.

After seven years, Barbara decided to change careers. She went back to school for a year, earning a master of arts in journalism. Even in her undergraduate degree, she loved the liberal arts classes and loved writing. Prior to pursuing journalism, Barbara took writing courses at the Universities of Manitoba and Winnipeg, and joined a writers' guild.

After completing her MA, Barbara worked for several companies' communications/PR departments as a writer. She freelanced for magazines, wrote feature articles, and became the editor of two lifestyle magazines. It took about two years for her to replace her nursing income when she was working for other companies and organizations. Longing for more freedom, Barbara decided to start her own company. After three years, she had again replaced her nursing income.

Making the change from secure positions with other companies to owning her own freelance business worried some family members who thought Barbara should have a "real job" with more security and benefits. Her friends and mom were supportive and believed she could do anything she wanted to do.

Barbara went on to coauthor *The Manitoba Book of Everything*, an insider's guide about her home province. In 2013, she published a best-selling e-book, *Sparking Change Around the Globe: Five Ways to Make Your Difference in the World*, where she interviewed leaders from around the world. She also worked with entrepreneurs, other writers, and non-profit organizations to tell their stories in a way that promotes their work, businesses, or services.

"My old life as a nurse gave me perspective," Barbara says. "I can handle stressful situations and deadlines more calmly than most people because of it. I worked as a critical care nurse with premature and sick babies—in an Intermediate Care Nursery, not an NICU—and as a pediatric resuscitation nurse, so I was prepared to handle difficult situations." She also worked with terminally ill children and teens. "It taught me what is and isn't a crisis," Barbara adds. "I know the difference between 'urgent' and 'important' and what it truly means to live in the present moment. I also know how to prepare for the unforeseen, manage deadlines, and stick with things to completion."

Barbara discovered the power of following your passion. "When you do what you love, something that matters to you, you don't give up. You find a way to make it sustainable," she says. "I had a talent that came naturally, and other people encouraged me and gave me positive feedback on my writing and editing. Telling powerful stories, my own or my clients', is important because stories are what connect us and help us make sense of the world. It's my way of making an impact and showing others what's possible. I believe it's what my soul came here to do."

## The Take-Away

Is your Fresh Start Success enabling you to put your passion into practice? Your work will be even more meaningful and satisfying if you look for and celebrate the positive impact you make on those around you—family, friends, customers, and community. There are many ways of giving back and paying forward, lots of opportunities to inspire and mentor others, plenty of chances to make the world just a little bit better because of what you do.

## Q&A with Barbara Edie

**Q: What did you learn the hard way?**
A: "You can't do it all yourself. Ask for help. You need a team to grow. Hire coaches, virtual assistants, online managers, get your systems in place."

**Q: To what do you attribute your Fresh Start Success?**
A: "Following my own 'GPS of the soul,' perseverance, learning from mistakes, and learning to make changes quickly if not getting the desired results. I don't believe in 'failure' as it is commonly defined; I believe you simply get what you're looking for—or you don't—and then you just keep going until you do."

**Q: How are you a different person now?**
A: "I feel more empowered, knowing it's always possible to change course and

follow your heart, and create a life that expresses what your soul came here to do. I like to write about visionary people who make a difference, but I believe everyone has the capacity have an impact. So, helping my clients tell stories of their unique talents, gifts, and contributions to the world is an important part of my purpose. I believe when we set out to do what we really want to do in the world, we find out we can create what we love, and everyone benefits. I also believe reinvention is possible and change is a good thing; we are here to evolve. Life is one opportunity to reinvent yourself after another."

**Q: What did you learn about yourself, and what new skills have you gained?**
A: "I learned to stretch and do things I didn't think I could do. That included embracing new technology, which is a continuing learning curve, and to create projects and programs that scared me a little. I continue to hone my abilities as a writer and editor, and I'm also learning to work with mentors and partners so I'm not doing it all alone."

**Q: If you had a superpower, what would it be?**
A: "I would want to have a never-ending, instant energy source."

**Q: What role has marketing and branding played with your success?**
A: "Marketing plays a big part in continuing to build connections and helping me get my message out. You never know who will hear your story or discover your work and what your impact will be."

# The Spirit Surives
## Poonam Gupta-Krishnan

FROM THE TIME children are small, we give them the pretend tools of various jobs to play professions. Toy power tools, doctor sets, and chef's pans abound, along with costumes for pretending to be police officers, fire fighters, pilots, soldiers, and many other jobs. We nudge children toward jobs we think they might be good at doing that pay well and discourage them from career paths that might not be lucrative. But we say very little to our children about the pervasive climate in certain professions that makes talented people who don't quite fit the mold feel uncomfortable and unwelcome.

As you make your own Fresh Start Success, look beyond your title and salary to decide what's missing in your current job from a personal satisfaction and balance standpoint. Does your employer appreciate your contributions and effort? Are your ideas heard with respect? Do you feel like you make a difference, not just to the bottom line, but in a meaningful way in the wider world? Does success at work mean compromising your health or family life, or having no time left to recharge? As you build your reinvention, take care not to perpetuate the same elements that made you unhappy in your prior work. Seize the chance to do this your way at every level, including creating meaning, satisfaction, and balance.

## More Than a Paycheck

Poonam went to school to be a chemist. She earned degrees in chemistry and education, and later taught math, physics, and chemistry. She moved into research and was very successful, working for two multinational chemical manufacturing corporations. She liked her work and the corporations gave her experience in both chemistry and manufacturing. Poonam also understood the technology challenges facing manufacturers.

As a research scientist, she handled all aspects, from lab research to the production process, which meant that she also knew where the processes faced problems or had room for improvement. She did well in the corporate environment and liked her work but realized after a while that there were no growth opportunities for women of color. When Poonam moved into information technology, she gained a different understanding of problems from the user's perspective. So Poonam developed software for manufacturing focused on fixing the end-user's problems.

Poonam was in a well-paying job heading a research group when her daughter was born, but the position required long hours and did not have flexibility. That was difficult now that she had a small child. It also bothered her that she did not see promotion opportunities for herself. "I did not want to kill my spirit by completely leaving the workplace or feel humiliated by staying in a ninety-nine percent male dominated company that did not understand the need for flexibility," she recalls. Getting a PhD might have led to some additional internal opportunities, but Poonam wanted more independence without the pressure to perform to other people's standards. "I looked for options and considered my skills, talents, and experience," she said. "I thought about what kind of fulfillment I wanted, and what kind of flexibility I was looking for. I wanted to fix IT processes and help businesses that hadn't been helped by large IT vendors. I'm very analytical, a good problem solver, and I knew the technology and process challenges of manufacturers. I wanted to help manufacturing companies thrive."

Poonam became an entrepreneur. She started a company that provided software services to small and medium-sized manufacturers. Over the years, it grew into providing a range of data and information management products and services. Today, her company has evolved to become one of the most sophisticated technology services companies in big data analytics. Her firm provides IT consulting and data analytics services to the private and public sectors in manufacturing, education, healthcare, and finance.

Poonam built her company facing limited resources, as well as social, financial, and health challenges. She is a first-generation immigrant, who came to the U.S. as a student. When she resigned from her last corporate job, she had a two-week pay cushion and started her IT services company with no money. "I didn't worry about money, even when I didn't have much, because I knew that if you have quality offerings, the money will come," Poonam says.

It took two years to build her company, and Poonam put everything into the business with no financial support or equity. "Having no money and making no money even after long hours of work was not fun," she recalls. But she kept at it, honing her skills, getting out to network, and learning to be "a little bit shameless" about promotion and asking for what she needed. She went back to her last employer and talked to the head of the MIS department, since she had parted ways on good terms. "I found that the fear is less when you focus on the job," Poonam says of venturing beyond her comfort zone. "Frustrations are often deep and long, but if you do something enough times and you appreciate what you bring to the table, you will succeed." Poonam found that her self-confidence and her belief in the value of what she had to offer grew as she got out and talked to people. "Stay with it, have faith, keep expenses low, and be humble," she advises.

For Poonam, the social part of growing a business was more difficult than the technical aspects. She was very aware that she was different—as a woman, and an immigrant, and a person of color—and that sometimes presented a hurdle. "People subconsciously like people who are like themselves," she says. "That can be difficult when you're an intelligent woman trying to get into a male-dominated industry, and I was often the only woman present in chemistry and IT circles. Men were used to a boy's club. I looked different and was a woman, and I had family responsibilities, where men were free to just hang out in the bar and talk," she recalls.

Poonam networked with professional women in a variety of organizations and found them to be kind and supportive. She learned to accept their help, mentorship, and guidance. That led to an important discovery. "If you have something of value, the differences don't matter," Poonam realized. To get the word out, she gave free speeches on technology, innovation, and best practices, which also helped people get to know her and helped her become more comfortable with networking. As she demonstrated her experience and showed what she knew, people asked to learn more.

In Poonam's journey, she found opportunities to improve IT innovation in the government sector. "There's a disconnect," she explains, "because they lack a collaborative platform that brings private sector, public sector, entrepreneurs, small businesses, universities, and special interest groups together." Poonam founded a not-for-profit organization, Government Technology Foundation, Inc. (GTF) to address that need. "The reason entrepreneurs take the route of 'path least traveled' is so they can fulfill their heart's desire," Poonam says.

Along the way, Poonam faced health challenges with no extended family nearby. A serious infection caused problems that meant she couldn't drive for over a year, and she was faced with large medical bills. During that time, she had to delegate, and her employees, at that point, were not as skilled as she was. They made some bad financial decisions, which undid more than three years of what had been built. When Poonam returned to work, she knew she needed to turn things around, so she decided to lower prices and pick up small jobs to build cash. That got the business back on its feet, and she kept improving processes. As her children got older, she could put more time into the company, and she is still constantly gaining new skills.

"Persistence is the key!" Poonam says. Despite a later health problem and surgery, which led to more setbacks, Poonam's persistence kept her and her company on track. She credits meditation for helping her overcome obstacles and improve her physical and emotional health.

Poonam's reinvention in starting her company was successful, and the firm is still growing. But despite her success, Poonam believes that she and other female entrepreneurs still struggle more than their male counterparts. Regardless, she is determined to succeed. "Success is a journey for me, and I have been on that journey now for fifteen years," Poonam says of the ups and downs along the way.

## The Take-Away

Our current business culture wastes a huge amount of human potential. We underutilize older workers who have valuable experience and perspective. We still fail to promote and incentivize talented women and people of color who could make essential contributions, due to unconscious bias in hiring, evaluation, and promotion systems. And we cling to outdated, short-term thinking and to business structures that burn out employees and demand they sacrifice work-life balance while providing no loyalty in return. Is it any surprise that our best and brightest flee the corporate life to strike out on their own, accepting risk in exchange for the reward of meaningful work as well as challenging opportunities and income without a glass ceiling?

When you're crafting your own Fresh Start Success, design your reinvention to include balance for yourself and your employees. Resolve not to make the same human resource mistakes made by the big corporations, which overlook proven talent because of old stereotypes. Make sure your work provides both a livelihood and meaning. Use your reinvention to create a life, not just a living.

## Q&A with Poonam Gupta-Krishnan

**Q: How are you a different person now?**
A: "I'm not concerned about as many things. If I know something, I share it. I'm more comfortable in my skin. It used to be that I was bothered when I ran into negative feedback, even from people I didn't respect. Now, I've grown to have more inner peace."

**Q: What new skills/knowledge did you gain?**
A: "Technology is very fast-moving, so I took a lot of business classes, took all kinds of training, earned a business school MBA, and took specialized classes. I read journals, and keep up with industry news, and I pay attention to emerging technology. Most of all I learned to be comfortable in *not* knowing *everything*."

**Q: If you had a superpower, what would it be?**
A: "I have a superpower already—I am a human! I would have the power of technology collaboration to bring more of society onboard with innovation and encourage people to live to their highest potential. I want to create a culture of innovation. That's what I did by forming the Government Technology Foundation. It's helping innovation to thrive in our society."

**Q: What role did marketing play for you in your Fresh Start Success?**
A: "It played a big role! I didn't realize earlier just how important marketing is, and now I regret that because I lost opportunities. You can be the greatest expert or have the greatest product, but unless others know about it, nothing happens. I realized that I didn't sufficiently value the impact of sales and marketing to get the message out to people who needed it, so I changed that. Marketing is extremely important for success, and today social media is more essential than radio and TV."

# Risk and Reward
## Dawn Fleming

OUR CULTURE HAS a love/hate relationship with security and risk. On one hand, we are encouraged from childhood to choose a profession that offers a steady paycheck, good benefits, and some semblance of job stability. On the other hand, we're constantly told "no risk, no reward." Which is it? The truth is, it's some of both, and the balance shifts depending on the goal.

The kind of job security our parents and grandparents had, where you could remain with one company until retirement, is long gone. While that represents risk, it has also opened the way for us to reinvent ourselves, explore several career paths, and find the right job for us at different stages of life. In other words, there is a trade-off between risk and reward.

Where are your priorities at your current stage of life? Are you ready and able to take a risk, or do you long to create stability and security? As you imagine your Fresh Start Success, consider what is most important to you from a financial, health, and stage-of-life perspective. Then design your reinvention with that goal in mind.

## Peace and Security

Dawn Fleming went to college for music, but along the way, she decided that she didn't want to teach music if she couldn't get into an orchestra. Instead, she earned a degree in business administration management and was open to all possibilities except one: her family was poor, and she was determined not to be poor.

Dawn worked at the Social Security Administration as a benefits authorizer for a few months, and hated it. She got an offer to work for the Department of Defense, tested to see if the work would be a good career fit, and became an intelligence analyst. Getting clearance took time. Dawn found that the work was very interesting and she liked her co-workers. She did well and was promoted to senior intelligence analyst.

Then in 1989, Dawn began working on energy balancing, and in 1993, she took a Reiki class. She connected deeply with Reiki and felt strongly that she should become a Reiki practitioner but didn't know how to leave a well-paying job to start up her practice. At the time, Dawn was a single mom with young kids, and she made good money, with corporate health benefits. She owned her own home. Dawn knew she couldn't quit just then. Instead, she started to build a part-time practice, growing her clientele, and getting a lot of clients from her co-workers who also felt stressed by their work as analysts.

Dawn married a man who was in the military but expected to leave the armed forces in 2001. He encouraged her to quit her job and do what she wanted to do. The attacks of September 11, 2001, made Dawn re-evaluate the potential impact of her work on her family life, and she decided to quit at the end of the year.

Her family and coworkers thought she was crazy because she had a very secure job making good money. "No one resigns from the kind of job I was in," Dawn says. "They retire after thirty years. But my soul was not there." By the time she left her government job, she was already earning $40,000 on a part-time basis from her Reiki practice. She was profitable from day one. "Because I had built the business up part-time, it only took eighteen months to surpass my salary working for the government," she says. "I worked my butt off."

Dawn looked for alignment with what she was passionate about when she decided to leave her government job. She took time to heal and release blocks to her energy and creativity. She also loved the idea that no one else would be her boss. Now, she feels freer. "With a government job and clearance, there were so many rules," she says. "When I was attached to a job, I was tied to a location. I recently moved from Maryland to Arizona because I can work anywhere now, and I set my own schedule."

She had a lot of determination to make it work and networked to connect with groups that she couldn't access when she worked full-time. "I liked to write articles, so I was featured in local health magazines, women's magazines. This was before the internet," Dawn says. "I was picked up by professional magazines for social workers, physical therapists, massage therapists, and nurses. Then I got my workshops approved for continuing education hours, and I would offer workshops and write an article for the organization's newsletter."

Now, Dawn runs her company, Energy Transformations, LLC, and is the author of five books: *Creating a Successful Holistic Health Practice, Teaching Workshops Effectively, Navigating the Continuing Education Approval Process, Chakra Empowerment: 24 Days of Transformation, and Heat Rising: Survive and Thrive through Menopause.*

Seven years as a senior policy officer taught Dawn to talk to people in other departments within the federal government, so she gained the ability to speak to all different kinds of people. "That's so valuable as an entrepreneur. It also gave me the confidence to speak to groups and taught me a lot about coordination and scheduling," she recalls.

"Nobody explains how to become an entrepreneur," Dawn says. "No one teaches you, even with a degree in business, what you really need to know, things like how to set up your company from a legal perspective, how to budget, how to create boundaries. Everyone wants a piece of you. That's a real danger in a healing profession. Teaching and healing bring you into contact with a lot of people without healthy boundaries. I consider myself a work-in-progress."

## The Take-Away

Once a job has met our basic needs for paying our bills, satisfaction and fulfillment become paramount. As you consider your own Fresh Start Success, think about your tolerance for risk and reward, as well as your need for security versus satisfaction. Most mid-career reinventors look to balance those elements, providing a way to make a living that enables them to experience financial stability and still pursue interests, while being happy and fulfilled doing the work itself. You don't have to settle for one or the other. Build in both satisfaction and security to your Fresh Start Success and thrive!

## Q&A with Dawn Fleming

**Q: What did you learn the hard way?**
A: "Learning how to spend time and money well on marketing and advertising."

**Q: To what do you attribute your Fresh Start Success?**
A: "Determination, drive, and a positive state of mind. I never thought that I could fail. I wasn't unrealistic; I just had an inner knowing that this would work out. Don't waste time on naysayers. Focus on the positive."

**Q: What did you learn about yourself?**
A: "I discovered that I was really brave and gutsy. I didn't have a role model for leaving a government job early instead of retiring at age fifty-five with great benefits. I didn't allow that to stop me."

**Q: What one trait is critical for your Fresh Start Success?**
A: "Having a positive attitude. A negative attitude won't get you off home plate. I am passionate about what I do, which gets me up in the morning and keeps me going."

**Q: If you had a superpower, what would it be?**
A: "Knowing the future, so I could be prepared."

**Q: What role has marketing and branding played in your success?**
A: "I think marketing has been a lot of my success. I began my company before social media, but now social media helps me expand on what I do making it possible for my articles to reach a broader audience. I work with clients from around the world. You've got to be on social media if you want to grow more quickly."

# Learning to Fly on the Way
## Grace Kelly

INCREMENTAL CHANGE CAN be prudent, but sometimes life doesn't give you that option. You find yourself pushed into reinventing yourself because of a sudden life change, like a layoff or illness, or you finally reach the point where anything seems better than where you are at the moment.

If you can lay the groundwork for a Fresh Start Success before you give up your day job, it can help you lessen your stress about the transition. On the other hand, unbearable pressure in your job can make it almost impossible to focus your thoughts and energy until you leave it behind you. Look before you leap, consider your resources, and have a fallback plan and alternatives in mind in case your new venture takes longer than expected to blast off.

As you consider your Fresh Start Success, think about how timing and location factor in to your plans. What would be the best time to make a break? The worst? How much control do you have over the timing? If the timing is being imposed from outside your control (like an upcoming layoff), what can you do to prepare your resources so that you can get your reinvention up and running as quickly as possible? Also, consider location. If you're in an area with a very high cost of living, you'll need to bring in more money with your new venture than if you live in an area with more moderate costs. Many people forget to think about timing and location as they plan for the future, but both items impact your path to success, and elements of both are always within your control.

## Jump Feet First

Grace Kelly wanted to be a teacher. As a child, she loved playing school. When she went to college, she studied languages and trained to be a language teacher. Grace taught French for six years in London. But she didn't enjoy being part of a bureaucratic system and dealing with school politics. She hit a career plateau and realized that she was bored, burned out, and exhausted, and she was spending a lot of money to regain her health. That's when Grace read a book by Dr. John DiMartini about finding purpose in what you love. She decided that it was time for her to leave teaching regardless of the money, time, and energy she had invested in the career.

"I just knew that I had to get out of my day job," Grace says. "I didn't care what I did next." She saw other entrepreneurs becoming successful, so her initial drive was to find purpose in life and to do what she loved, although she didn't know for certain what that would be. "The real turning point was when I had a mild anxiety attack on the train heading to school one day. I had to get off the train. Right then and there, I decided that I didn't want to live like this anymore," Grace says. "There had to be a better way."

Grace and her partner decided to leave London and go to Italy. She had been organizing events in London, but she left that behind when they moved. She spent a year trying to figure out the next step and recover from exhaustion through relaxation and meditation. "I'll never forget, there was one day that I sat on the beach, staring at the ocean, sobbing because I didn't know what I wanted to do with my life except for the fact that I didn't want to keep doing what I'd been doing," she recalls. The cost of living in Italy was a quarter of what it had been in London, and that made one part of the transition easier by reducing income pressure as Grace considered her options.

New opportunities arose forming retreats and hosting speakers, and by the end of the year, Grace knew what she wanted to do. She realized that she was a "born teacher" and was happy with a student audience. So she began to look at coaching and trained with a woman she met at a conference, even attending an event in London the coach hosted. Grace gained the knowledge to package her expertise and sell it. Then, she got her first high-end VIP client and found herself easily slipping back into teacher-mode, feeling that her coaching and teaching served a purpose.

It took six months to make six figures, not just a client here and there. She gained a consistent base of income less than a year after the day she had spent on the beach crying because she had no idea what to do with her life.

"It took a while to learn how to gather my 'tribe' because building your own global community takes time," Grace says. "I also had to learn how to do business in a sustainable way. Now I understand that you have to have structures and systems in place, and I can appreciate the value of contracts, processes, and safeguards."

Grace believes that she needed to get out of the "masculine" mode of teaching she had done in London. Now she feels more feminine and more relaxed. "No more heart palpitations!" she says. "My energy feels more integrated, and I'm more inspired, energetic, and aware. I travel a lot and I think I've matured as a person, with a deeper sense of self-trust," she adds.

"I discovered that I am really capable of doing more and bigger things than I gave myself credit for," Grace says. "I've learned that exhaustion and burnout is your body saying that you are not in alignment. You learn that you are stronger than you think you are."

## The Take-Away

Timing and location are factors that can make your reinvention easier or harder. Look at your options for place and time in order to maximize your range of choices.

Style is also important. What Grace refers to as a "masculine" mode is a style that is generally authoritarian, hierarchical, and punitive, with rewards going to those who can out-fight, out-yell, and out-intimidate competitors. Don't accept this familiar model as the only path. Collaborative, team-based, incentive-motivated (aka "feminine") styles that emphasize listening, cooperation, and empowerment draw on the strengths of the leader and the group and lend themselves to higher long-term satisfaction. Don't let arbitrary gender labels keep you from embracing the approach that is best for you. Style is a choice; be conscious of the ramifications of the style you choose to embrace.

## Q&A with Grace Kelly

### Q: What new skills did you gain?

A: "I learned how to coach more effectively, and I learned about marketing and how to set up a business, how to sell my own services as opposed to selling someone else's, how to speak effectively in public, how to write, and a lot about self-management."

### Q: What one trait/habit/behavior is crucial to your Fresh Start Success?

A: "Spiritual practice. I start every day with meditation. That habit is the foundation of connection to everything, to hear my own answers and my own truth. I learned to leap and allow the invisible safety net to appear."

### Q: If you had a superpower, what would it be?

A: "I would love to never experience tiredness or weakness and have all the energy in the world."

### Q: What role has marketing played in your success?

A: "My brand is inspiring and enticing to those who are interested in my message. I get constant feedback, and I apply it. Marketing is very important because it's essential to communicate regularly with your audience. I'm experimenting with social media to create brand buzz."

# Opening New Channels
## Marla Goldberg

PEOPLE TAKE MANY different paths to make a Fresh Start Success for themselves. Some find success in a field but feel unfulfilled. Others pursue a life course to gain stability, please someone else, or be "secure," only to realize that their passion lies elsewhere. For many, a door closes on one path due to job loss, health issues, or personal problems, requiring them to reinvent themselves and develop a new path forward.

The exciting—and scary—thing about reinvention is that you never know where your Fresh Start Success may take you. You may rediscover talents long forgotten and find that you're in a stage of life to let those abilities blossom. An inventory of your skills may show you that you have been mentored by life circumstances to step into a new role that opens up for you. Perhaps your network of colleagues and friends sees potential in you for success of a completely different sort than you previously pursued. Or maybe dreams long denied come to the fore, and you discover a way to meld personal satisfaction and financial success.

The door that opens for you might take you somewhere you never imagined, even in your wildest dreams. Yet when you step through that door and embrace the opportunity, you discover you are where you need to be, in the role your entire life has prepared you to play. Seize the moment and experience your own Fresh Start Success.

## Following the Heart

When Marla Goldberg was fifteen years old, she toured The Quaker Oats Co. test kitchens in downtown Chicago. "Light bulbs went off for me that I could be 'paid to play' using my baking and art skills," Marla recalls. She loved making cream puff towers, intricate pies, and decorated birthday cakes for fun, and she had started collecting cookbooks at age twelve. As a teen, Marla would go out to eat with her parents and be able to recreate the meal intuitively at home.

Marla learned about color and design from her mother, Ileane Tatar, a national award-winning Sumi-e artist. Both of Marla's grandmothers entertained with flair and taught her about preparing delicious and beautiful food. Her mother was happy to hand her apron over as Marla developed her cooking skills since Ileane preferred to paint rather than cook.

Marla decided to take her love for cooking and food beyond making meals at home. She majored in "Foods in Business" with a minor in business and took additional courses in food science at the University of Illinois Champaign-Urbana. The Foods in Business program trained her for a position in a corporate test kitchen developing consumer recipes, creating package preparation directions, and styling food for photography. Marla spent her life savings to spend ten weeks in ten European countries to experience authentic local foods and learn local recipes towards her goal of becoming a food expert.

Marla's dream was to someday work for Kraft/Quaker Oats. In 1976, Marla graduated and started her food career working for The Jewel Foods Company. For one year she worked as an in-store home economist in Jewel's Highland Park grocery store, demonstrating recipes and conducting store tours. Marla's skills blossomed in unique areas. She was quickly known as the Jewish foods guru and microwave cooking expert, which was very new at the time. She was one of the first to demonstrate how to use the new Cuisinart food processor and was trained by the inventor. Then, her big break occurred. Marla physically bumped into the head of The Quaker Oats test kitchens at a networking event and was told they had an immediate opening and that her resume had been read just hours before. She was interviewed on the spot. Two weeks later, she was working for The Quaker Oats Company in her dream job with a twenty-five percent increase in salary.

Marla worked for Quaker Oats for five years and was a successful food stylist who was promoted to manager and became responsible for planning and executing all food photography and managing food stylists for national TV ads. She developed hundreds of recipes for newspapers, cookbooks, brochures, and packaging, and she worked closely with marketing and with food scientists to develop new products.

Marla got married in 1977, and in 1982, she left Quaker after having a daughter. She wanted a more flexible, part-time schedule and became a freelance food consultant. Over the next twenty-five years as a consultant, Marla handled high-level corporate events for companies like Kraft Foods and Philip Morris. She orchestrated the displays of international food products for Kraft's IPO on Wall Street along with masterminding many high-profile meal events. She worked for the CEO of Kraft and flew on the corporate jet. She supervised Tombstone and DiGiorno pizza commercials in New York and Hollywood, and her photo was featured for four years on the back of the Minute Rice box.

Gradually, the things that used to be fun about Marla's dream job held less appeal. She perceived a shift from more creative opportunities to re-developing recipes. During these years, she had two more children and found that the stress, tight deadlines, and demand for perfect execution was causing burnout. In 1991, she was diagnosed with an "incurable" disease of the bladder, called interstitial cystitis. She experienced chronic debilitating bladder pain and had to hire live-in help.

Everything began to change in 1999 when, on the recommendation of a best friend, she attended a personal development seminar called Pathways to Successful Living Seminars. At this point, Marla had lived with chronic pain for eight years. She was disillusioned with her career and desired a more fulfilling marriage. Then, she participated in an experiential, five-day retreat seminar. She set intentions for change.

During the retreat, Marla did an automatic regression during group guided meditation to a traumatic moment in time when she was two or three years old. She realized that she had decided at a very young age never to advocate for her own needs out of fear of confrontation. Instead, she repressed her feelings and became convinced that this was the root of her chronic pain. She was guided to release decades of pent-up frustration, forgive herself and others, and learn to love and accept herself for the very first time. This completely erased the condition causing the chronic pain and also healed a pattern of anorexia, which had been a problem since high school.

She became very aware of the stress levels in her life as a food consultant and mother of three. Six weeks after the seminar, Marla sat up in bed early one morning and saw her room filled with bright sunlight. Then, something happened that changed Marla's life.

"I looked up at the ceiling and thanked God for getting me through these challenging times," Marla says. "I felt an instantaneous shift in the room. As my gaze drifted down towards the top of my nightstand, it was like I was seeing a holographic movie image. It just appeared to me, and I could see my beloved grandfather, Frank. I felt like I had died and gone to Heaven," Marla remembers.

"I was enveloped in a cocoon of unconditional love. I'm certain that the image I saw was not a memory. It was very much like a holographic movie. I saw my grandfather as a man in his mid-thirties, all dressed up in a suit, smoking his cigar, smiling from ear to ear as he puffed. And I saw myself as a little girl, maybe five years old, dancing in a circle around his feet, absolutely happy and carefree." Then, she heard the words that would make all the difference.

"He said, 'Marla, the reason why I was in your life was to teach you unconditional love,'" Marla recalls. "Immediately, I saw a white beam of light that arced from his heart-center to mine. The light gently pushed me backwards, intensifying the sense of unconditional love. It was as though time had melted away."

Marla had three more visions from dead grandparents, each telling her what gifts they had given her in this lifetime. From that morning on, she felt like a wide-open radio receiver to 'the other side' and became a 'blown open' psychic medium. Marla received messages from departed loved ones for her co-workers on her consulting projects. That's when she knew it was time to leave her lucrative, flexible freelance career to open a private practice, first as a psychic medium and then as a facilitator of guided meditation workshops on developing intuition.

In 2005, Marla earned certification as a consulting hypnotist, training in multiple modalities to facilitate change. "I know that I am meant to help others succeed," she says. "I help my clients access and reframe the triggers and deeply-rooted memories that lead to overeating, chronic pain, and fears that hold them back." She has helped world-class gymnasts, CEOs of major corporations, professional performers, and students, and she has worked with clients of all ages and walks of life. As a medium, Marla has helped clients around the world connect with departed loved ones. She is an expert on guided meditation and weight loss with hypnosis, and she developed a powerful, yet gentle, program called "Weight Release through Inner Peace."

Making such a huge change was challenging. Marla experienced harsh judgment and anger from certain relatives because she had quit her previous line of work. Her husband was skeptical at first, but later supported her choice. Marla pushed deeper into developing her guided meditation skills while helping one of her best friends successfully navigate breast cancer. Friends and former coworkers were extremely supportive of Marla's new career, as were her parents, sister, and children. "It helped that I had learned to communicate my needs and feelings clearly," Marla says, "something I couldn't do before."

Marla became a certified consulting hypnotist in 2005, traveling the U.S. to attend cutting-edge conferences in neuroscience, guided meditation, and personal development. She also revived a deep passion for music. Marla has an operatic-quality singing voice and began to perform professionally at age forty-seven. Desiring to take her voice further, Marla followed her inspiration and researched making guided meditations. Best-selling author and co-creator of Chicken Soup for the Soul®, Jack Canfield, urged her to follow her ideas of recording professional-quality guided meditations. Marla took this encouragement straight to the recording studio upon arrival back home.

## The Take-Away

Have you ever considered the idea of "serial success"? So many of the people interviewed for this book have been successful at more than one career—in sometimes wildly divergent types of business. Our culture does us a disservice when it suggests that we need to find the "one thing" we're good at and stick to it. That's fine up to a point, but that kind of thinking tends to ingrain the idea that we might only be good at one thing or excel in one kind of environment. As you see through these interviews, Fresh Start Success occurs in all kinds of different ways! When you're considering your own reinvention and reimagining your life, don't let yourself get locked into thinking there is only one right path, or that you are only good at one type of thing. Reexamine your dreams and passions and discover your unique road to Fresh Start Success!

## Q&A with Marla Goldberg

**Q: How long did it take to become successful?**
A: "It took three or four years to replicate my corporate income and go from part-time to full-time."

**Q: What did you learn the hard way?**
A: "I was trying to do too many things on my own. I didn't have someone else help me develop my business plan until I had been in business for ten years. When I turned my guided meditations into recordings and wanted to develop an online business, I realized that I needed a financial analyst to help with budgeting and cash flow. I needed more tech support. I had been doing my own marketing and PR. I taught weight release workshops at Whole Foods to reach the public and did other workshops for charity. I had to learn to ask for help and not try to do it all myself."

**Q: How are you a different person?**
A: "Now, I'm living an authentic life. I'm more peaceful and joyful. I manage stress better. I always believed in doing what I loved. Now, I feel more fulfilled, and I'm able to give back to people. I'm using my inborn gifts in a new way. I think all those things have made me a better mother now—more present, a better teacher—better at experiential learning and less fearful."

**Q: What did you learn about yourself?**
A: "I learned that I am a courageous, highly intuitive, compassionate person with an ability to help others create their best lives. I have a gift for adapting what I learn from all of the training and educational programs I attend and

using those new insights in my own style of experiential facilitation. I trained in guided meditation, multiple modalities of hypnosis, and took lessons to learn to use my voice. I discovered how to listen to myself and check-in with my feelings to see how things were resonating with me. I invested in myself, attended many amazing trainings and workshops, learned to facilitate programs and learned motivational speaking skills. I graduated from Jack Canfield's Train-the-Trainer program.

"Now, I want to work with fellow trainers, providing my guided meditations and utilizing tools like inspirational singing and group hypnosis expertise. I want to continue to get out of my comfort zone and take risks, even if it scares me to death. That has brought me incredible personal growth. Having an 'I can do it' positive attitude is critical. And being a 'recovering perfectionist,' I have learned to move forward with a 'beginner mind' willing to make mistakes and 'fail' my way to success, rather than waiting until I think the project is 'perfect.'"

**Q: How did what you did in your prior work prepare you for your Fresh Start Success?**
A: "I learned a lot about marketing in my corporate roles, including PR, graphic design, messaging, and advertising. I learned good organization skills and business skills, the importance of keeping my word and being on time, how to network, and I gained computer skills. I also discovered the secret of being an efficient traveler."

**Q: What traits are critical to your Fresh Start Success?**
A: "Resilience and perseverance. There is no such thing as failure if you keep taking action. Success is based on multiple failures. My first speech in front of sixty business owners was a miserable failure. It was mortifying! But moving forward required courage and risk-taking, as well as positive beliefs and releasing negative beliefs. I am the ultimate optimist."

**Q: If you had a superpower, what would it be?**

A: "I feel like I already have one. I am psychic. I have served as a conduit for delivering supportive messages from people's past loved ones. What I see is a movie in my mind's eye. I hear words and phrases that are meant for others. Similar to the movie *Ghost*, I have experiences like Whoopi Goldberg's character, where spirits have spoken through me to connect with their loved ones. It is considerably less dramatic than Hollywood's version, but it is very exhausting. I have learned to trust my intuitive abilities and have discovered that everyone knows their own truth."

**Q: What role does marketing and branding play in your success?**

A: "Marketing is everything. How we leave people feeling is our brand. Marketing is the most important element because it informs the prospective clients of our existence. So many people are talented, but no one knows about them because they aren't marketing effectively. It's crucial to get the message out there. There is power in extreme word of mouth, but I've also invested in advertising and bartering. I've hired top marketers and designers. In each case, I found the right person at the right time. I'm not shy about tapping my network of 'superstar' former colleagues at Kraft and Quaker to barter/exchange/partner."

# Finding Your Fulcrum

## Katana Abbott

WHEN YOU USE leverage, you maximize your strength while minimizing your effort. If you've ever used a crowbar to pry up a heavy object, you've seen the physical results for yourself. We use the term "leverage" in finance, business, and elsewhere to indicate utilizing resources for maximum impact. Leverage gets you more bang for the buck—and it all happens because of the fulcrum, the base you push against to multiply your strength. Learning to leverage is an essential part of creating your Fresh Start Success. Your "fulcrum" is what you do best, your unique ability. The leverage comes when you take what you do best and do it in a new or different way or in service of a new audience, in a way that meets an unmet need.

Many of the successful people profiled in this book created their Fresh Start Success by leveraging old skills, connections, or interests into something entirely new. They may have stayed within a particular industry or specialty, but they took their skills and unique abilities and made a strategic shift to serve a different type of client with a product or service that no one else was offering. Leverage can create a whole new way of applying your expertise and providing an outcome without having to start completely from scratch. Sometimes, leverage involves using new technology, while in other cases, it lies in doing something in a way no one else has done it. When you create leverage for yourself, you reap the first-mover advantage because you're benefitting from your unique previous experiences and hard-earned perspectives.

As you consider your Fresh Start Success options, look for ways to leverage your experience, perspective, and unique gifts. You might create a whole new industry!

## From Abuse to Abundance

Katana decided to study business administration because a friend was taking secretarial classes, so Katana did, too. She took classes in shorthand

and typing and landed a job as a clerk/typist at a big company with forty thousand employees. Eventually, Katana ended up in the advertising/marketing department. It wasn't sexy: the company made hydraulic products. But when Katana found a bunch of surveys stuck in a drawer that no one had ever even compiled, she took them to the art director, who graphed the results. Katana then showed the department how to use the survey as a forecasting tool. She wanted to do more research and sales but was told that she would never advance in this company without an engineering degree. This prompted Katana to leave a good paying job in advertising and move into sales, where she discovered that selling was her unique ability.

Katana came from a dysfunctional family. Her father died when she was six years old. Her mother soon remarried, and Katana's stepfather was physically and financially abusive. Katana believes that when there is adversity, there is always a gift. Even though her mother didn't protect her from the abuse, she gave Katana the gift of learning sales skills and making a difference at a young age by encouraging her to go door-to-door selling flowers and fruitcakes, and gathering donations for the poor through her church and the parochial school she attended. As a teenager, Katana staffed the phones on tele-fundraisers for charity. She honed her sales skills, and her success gave her recognition that she wasn't getting at home.

Because she was a war orphan, Katana qualified for free college tuition, health insurance, social security, and VA benefits. However, when she got married at age nineteen, she lost her scholarship and was forced to leave college. Katana's husband was abusive, so the marriage ended. That was when Katana went into commission sales, a field she felt comfortable in, thanks to her early door-to-door sales experience. She discovered that passion for a cause helped her fully invest herself in whatever she was selling. Katana was very successful in sales for several companies, becoming the top Honda salesperson by age twenty-five. This is when she met her second husband, to whom she has been happily married for thirty years.

By 1983, Katana was making great money in car sales and wanted to learn how to invest and grow that money. She went looking for information on financial planning and ended up working for a financial services firm that offered good training.

Katana went from earning big money and having a company car when she worked at the car dealership to earning a lot less when she started out in financial services. She was ready to give up. Then she found a mentor who was an attorney, and when he learned about all the great contacts Katana had from her years of working with business owners, he offered to take her under his wing and teach her how to work with affluent clients.

Her practice transformed in the next year. Katana started working with affluent individuals. When she saw what she was capable of doing, her mindset shifted from selling financial products to becoming a trusted advisor. It took almost four years to earn her Certified Financial Planner ™ designation at a time when she had two young children at home. Katana worked all day, took care of kids in the evening, and then studied late into the night. Earning the CFP® designation totally transformed the way she worked.

Years later, Katana helped her mentor retire by purchasing her practice, and Katana was able to double her number of clients.

As her practice grew, Katana faced the need for another reinvention. She realized that she needed to focus on what she was good at and delegate the rest. "I'm not a details person," Katana admits. "So I created teams and systems so the business could run without me having to be involved at every step. I also hired an intern who was my opposite—he liked the backstage details, while I took the front stage. We became one of the top teams at Ameriprise. I couldn't have been as successful without John to mind the details, and he would have had a lot of potential but fewer clients without me up front bringing people in." John and Katana worked together for fifteen years. Then, after nearly twenty years in the financial services business, Katana was ready for a change.

One incident sparked Katana's passion to create her next reinvention. "I was speaking at a Smart Women Finish Rich seminar about building up financial security from scratch. The audience was very poor—they didn't even have bank accounts. There I was in my expensive suit and jewelry, and I tried to figure out how I could make myself relatable to the people in the audience," Katana recalls. "I had never told my personal story because I was embarrassed by it. But that day, I told these women where I came from, and that if I could get from where I started to where I was today, they could too, and today I would show them how." Seventy-five women wanted an appointment after that, but Katana had no way to help them. That was when she decided to start Smart Women's Coaching®. It took her four more years to leave her financial services business and dive in to creating her vision.

Thanks to the business systems and passive ongoing income Katana had created in her financial services practice, she was able to sell her business to John, and he had the revenue to pay her one million dollars over seven years. This gave Katana the revenue she needed to start Smart Women's Empowerment, a 501(c)(3) where she and a team of contributing experts teach financial literacy and entrepreneurship through live and online events, blogs, and resources. She also founded Smart Women's Coaching® and Midlife Millionaires® where she offers private wealth coaching and transformational retreats to Costa Rica and Panama.

Katana is the host of Smart Women Talk Radio ™ and has contributed to three books. She is currently working on her new book, *Midlife Reinvention: The 6 Step System for Retiring Happy, Healthy & Wealthy*.

## The Take-Away

Katana leveraged her life experience and her sales ability, plus her financial savvy to create something bigger: her nonprofit to support financial literacy and her wealth-building company for women in midlife. While both programs draw on her gift for communicating—a key to success in sales—they also draw from her financial services expertise. She builds on what she does best but also provides a different type of service than before, which is delivered in a very different way. Doing this fills an unmet need in the market and creates satisfaction for Katana—a big win-win.

As you create your own Fresh Start Success, look for opportunities to leverage what you know and what you do best in a whole new way.

## Q&A with Katana Abbott

**Q: What did you learn the hard way?**
A: "A lot of it. It was all very difficult, but I didn't give up. Like many entrepreneurs, I have big ideas and never give up. In addition, I'm not a detail person, so creating something from the ground up is not my unique ability. I tried to create a for-profit organization to help women with financial literacy and later realized that it should have been a nonprofit. That became my nonprofit, Smart Women's Empowerment. I don't see that as a failure because I believe that things happen for a reason. Mistakes are often our greatest teachers. Always ask 'what did I learn from this, and how can I grow?' Part of my coaching now helps others decide whether to create their company as a for-profit or nonprofit and how to help nonprofits get funding, grants, and sponsorships."

**Q: To what do you attribute your Fresh Start Success?**
A: "Finding a mentor and getting a coach. It's essential to surround yourself with supportive people. Never give up—even when you feel like you failed. Learn from it, change course, and believe that you are here for a purpose. Learn to focus on your key strengths and passions, understand your weaknesses, and then create systems and a team so you can delegate and outsource things that drain your energy. Focus on your strengths."

**Q: How are you a different person than before?**
A: "I feel much happier now than I have in years. I've found my own inner peace, and that means learning to be very present in the moment. I now have a lot of free time for my family and time for self-care and fun. I'm working for the total pleasure of it instead of striving to get somewhere. At midlife, it's time to master the art of 'arrival.'"

**Q: What did you learn about yourself?**
A: "I see myself very differently than others see me. I wish that I knew years ago how powerful I really was. So often, we don't see how beautiful and powerful we are; it keeps us from shining our light and being brilliant."

**Q: What one trait is crucial to your Fresh Start Success?'**

A: "Curiosity. I am a student of life."

**Q: If you had a superpower, what would it be?**

A: "I wish I could stop the clock and just study. Or fly. No limitations, total freedom."

**Q: What role did marketing play in your success?**

A: "I'm grateful for good marketing leaders who made a huge impact and enabled me to reach and help so many people. The internet makes it possible for me to create a global business with radio, e-zines, and tele-summits, and it's only going to get better!"

# Trust Your Intuition
## Cha~zay Sandhriel, PhD

DO YOU TRUST your intuition, or work strictly by the numbers? Most entrepreneurs are data-driven to a point but admit to taking a cue from gut feelings when data alone is inconclusive.

Science has shown that intuition isn't as mystical as we may have thought. Experts in micro-expressions—small facial movements—have studied the way those movements signal truthfulness, avoidance, and intentions. We're told that the vast majority of communication happens, not through spoken language, but through our body language. Some people are naturally gifted in picking up on those nonverbal cues and seem to have an uncanny ability to "read" people accurately. To the extent that these elements factor into what we consider "intuition," there's a scientific validation for those on-target "hunches."

Some of what we chalk up to intuition also comes from experience. For example, if you've had a bad experience with someone, the next time you encounter a similar situation, you'll probably hear mental warning bells. That's the benefit of graduating from the school of hard knocks. Are there other unexplained, perhaps unexplainable, aspects involved in intuition? Who knows? What matters is whether your gut feelings and hunches are right more often than they're wrong.

As you're creating your Fresh Start Success, trust your intuition and your due diligence. Numbers alone may steer you toward a career path that just doesn't sit right with something inside you. Go with your gut. If you're uneasy with a course of action, that's a signal to step back and re-evaluate. On some level, you've realized there is a problem. Don't allow people or circumstances to force your hand until you've figured out why you felt uneasy. Charting a new course for yourself is full of risks. Consider your intuition to be a form of internal radar to help you watch for hidden dangers and find a safe path.

## Mogul to Mentor

When Cha-zay was little, she knew she wanted to work with animals. She loved horses and thought about becoming a veterinarian, then became a horseback riding teacher. Health issues got in the way. Cha-zay got very sick and realized she could not meet the physical demands of the job.

So Cha-zay changed direction. "I was very good at languages," she says. "My mother had been one of ten children in a family with no money, became a nanny, and taught herself to speak other languages. Her experience inspired me."

Cha-zay traveled and studied languages. She completed an apprenticeship in Zurich in customer service working for the Swiss Government, and then worked for a Swiss private bank. Then Cha-zay landed a job with an American company in Switzerland, which required her to speak English. She intended to be in the U.S. for nine months and then go back to Switzerland and work as a translator, but she ended up staying in the States. "I had skills, but no degree that was recognized in the U.S., so I had to reinvent myself again," Cha-zay recalls.

Her first job in the United States was making $8.75 an hour as a receptionist. "That was a lot less than I'd made in Switzerland, which was hard on my ego," she says. Cha-zay was ambitious, and she made a connection with a German CEO who wanted to start a headquarters in the U.S.

The CEO offered Cha-zay the choice between working for accounting or human resources. She picked accounting but discovered it was a lonely job, even though she loves numbers. So she did a u-turn into HR and discovered she had a talent for selecting the right employees when starting new businesses. Cha-zay went back to school to get her GED and eventually her BS in business management. By this time, she was in her mid-thirties and realized that her real talent was in seeing possibilities.

Cha-zay put together teams and HR budgets for Silicon Valley start-up companies. She set up operations, payroll, and insurance; wrote employee handbooks; and set up 401K plans. "I was completely in my element," she says. "And what I was doing worked. Our turnover rate was less than one percent while the industry average was ten to twenty percent. I used my intuition when hiring people and realized that I love working with people."

She came to a point where she had reached an income ceiling. Then, Cha-zay thought about going out on her own and specializing in working with German and European companies relocating to California, but she got bored with the repetition. "I felt like I was living on the edge, not sure whether I would make it or not," she recalls. "There was constant risk." By this point, Cha-zay was making a six-figure income and knew she had an entrepreneurial spirit.

The big shift came when she saw a magazine headline about millionaires creating ten new jobs each year. "I realized that if I had a company that earned a million dollars a year, I could provide ten jobs. I was questioning whether or not I had what it took to succeed at that level," Cha-zay says. "I asked myself, 'Who am I to do this'? Then I realized, 'Who am I not to?' I felt responsible for creating those ten jobs."

Cha-zay asked her husband for his support and made a list of all the things she believed were holding her back. "I sorted through my fears," she recalls. "My top fear was public speaking. I hated to present at meetings, and I was very shy at that time." Her second top fear was flying. She decided to tackle both fears because they were holding her back financially and keeping her from promoting her new business. "I came to see those two fears as a drain on my pocketbook and debilitating to my confidence," she says. "There was a woman on the other end of this fear who was going to emerge. This woman scared the crap out of me."

She gave herself two years to overcome the fears. Cha-zay signed up for Toastmasters, took workshops, and pushed out of her comfort zone. She moved past the physical symptoms of fear. When it was over, she couldn't believe who she had become. Unfortunately, during this process she also grew apart from her husband. She wanted to make an impact and live a big life, and he wanted to keep things simple. They divorced as best friends.

She approached the CEO of Mindjet, where she worked, and asked to reduce her hours. At this point, Cha-zay was a full-time student, in the middle of a divorce, and running her own business. She was also sixteen units short of a degree and was working part-time while running a part-time business. She was also a single mom. The CEO gave her more flexibility, and Cha-zay reduced her hours to four days a week and spent three days a week on her own business. The CEO of Mindjet was also on her company's advisory board.

Cha-zay bought and rented real estate to create a passive income stream. Then, she built several houses. She also became a Learning Annex instructor and spoke on stage with the author of *Rich Dad/Poor Dad* in front of thousands of people.

"That's when I made my mistake," she recalls. "I lost sight of my intuition and took too many risks. I had a ten-year plan, but I didn't stick to it. I got into bad partnerships and lost money and clients." Cha-zay lost six million dollars and all her assets, plus the time and money spent on lawyers. "I lost faith in humanity," she says. "I was devastated."

So she went back to the drawing board. Cha-zay had visionary experiences, but her mother and ex-husband didn't believe in the unseen world or intuition. So she left the U.S. and took a few years to turn inward. She went back to the Swiss and Italian Alps and earned a living as a consultant for several years. Building a life for her daughter kept her going. During that time, Cha-zay completed two PhDs in metaphysical science and holistic life coaching. Then she came back to the U.S. and trained in Reiki, becoming a certified hypnotist and an ordained minister. "I'm not religious, but I wanted people to be able to make their confessions and provide a minister's non-disclosure protections," Cha-zay says.

Cha-zay started her Core Freedom community to provide a "home away from home" for others and to share what she learned about the unseen world. She volunteered as a suicide prevention hotline counselor for several years and draws on that experience as she helps others discover their purpose in life. She is also the host of *The Core Freedom Show*, a podcast dedicated to the evolution of the soul.

"Today, I have new opinions about money and what I want out of life," Cha-zay says. "I'm authentic with myself and with others, and I don't hide behind my business. My new project is helping low-income people create start-up companies. It's my passion to bring out their gifts."

For Cha-zay, it's no longer about having that big company to hire ten people. She has hired those ten and more. It's no longer about making one million dollars a year; it's about reaching one million people per year with her message.

## The Take-Away

Due diligence plus finely-honed intuition make for a powerful combination. Run the numbers, do your research, and then listen to your gut. How do you hone your intuition? Test it on less consequential decisions. Your intuition has always been with you; what's been missing is your mindfulness. As you begin to practice being aware of your intuition, you'll notice it speaking to you more often.

Don't make the mistake of confusing your intuition with your own desires. Your intuition is the still, small voice that wakes you up in the middle of the night with insight, or that makes you hesitate about rushing in to a bad idea. In contrast, our desires shout so loudly we can't hear ourselves think, let alone hear that whisper of intuition. Knowing the difference takes practice and mindfulness, but it's well worth the effort as you craft your own Fresh Start Success.

## Q&A with Cha~zay Sandhriel

**Q: What did you learn the hard way?**
A: "I learned that teaching is my passion. I also learned how important it is to be honest and ethical, especially with ourselves. Don't sell out."

**Q: How long did it take for you to become successful?**
A: "With my new holistic community, it took about four months before I was at break-even, switching from a donation basis to paid memberships and a fee-based level. I provide content, tele-seminars, mentorship, products, and online workshops, and I've written several books. Added to my real estate and consulting, it took about six months to become totally self-sustaining. I'm not earning as much as I did before, but that's not my goal. Now, I want to make an impact on as many people as I can."

**Q: If you had a superpower, what would it be?**
A: "I am working at subliminally photographing information and placing that information directly into the subconscious."

**Q: How has marketing played a role in your success?**

A: "It's my least favorite part, but the most important. Ninety-five percent of my community members come from YouTube. My channel has over 20,000 subscribers and over 2.8 million views. Videos and audios are the key to building audience. I also have my own podcast show called *The Core Freedom Show*. I consider myself poor at tending to marketing; I could do better at it. Fortunately, people resonate with my message and refer me to their friends and in doing so, word-of-mouth referrals are great."

# The Power of Intention
## Mike Jaffe

WE'VE ALL HEARD Lao Tzu's quote, "A journey of a thousand miles begins with a single step." Maybe you've even quoted that to yourself as you set out on a new diet, a new job, a new workout routine, or some other big change. But we often fail to realize the power in all the other "single steps" we take throughout our day—things like the time we allot for family, our work schedule, our exercise habits, time set aside for recreation, etc.— most of which we don't even think about because they have become routine.

As you engineer your own Fresh Start Success, be mindful of your routines and all the "steps" you are taking in your life. Are those "steps" taking you on a journey you want to make? Or have you changed your route and destination, but forgotten to update your inner navigation system—the routines that get you through the day? You will make the best progress toward your reinvention when you are mindful of all your "steps" and bring them into harmony.

Every new beginning is also a good time to take stock. Make a Fresh Start Success of your whole life, not just your work life. Does that mean prioritizing relationships, healthy eating, exercise, and other good-for-you habits and routines? If so, this is a good time to make tweaks or major adjustments. While we know that investing in our work satisfaction, our relationships, and our health is good for us, we often have no idea just what impact even seemingly minor changes can make in our lives and the lives of those around us. Tune up your inner nav system and set your destination for Fresh Start Success!

## The Difference a Day Makes

Mike Jaffe had no idea of what he wanted to do in school. "I didn't have any real clarity," he says. "I was just floating down the river. I was good at a lot of things, but there wasn't any passion. I envied people who had a clear vision."

Mike majored in business administration as an undergraduate, with a technology minor. After graduation, he got a job on Wall Street, went into management training, and earned his MBA in marketing and management. Mike was involved with new product rollouts and gravitated toward developing loyalty retention programs and being an internal consultant. His work took him to live in the UK for a year, and Mike came to realize that relationship management was his strength.

As a summer intern at American Express in 1994, Mike led the team that created the corporate platinum card for small business, and he really liked that experience. He became director of ecommerce in 1999. "The Internet was exploding," Mike recalls. "I left AmEx and went into a small start-up that eventually became several other start-ups. We were all working in a loft in TriBeCa, raising angel funds, and everything was unknown and unscripted. Even back then, I knew I had a tendency to take risks. I needed adventure."

Then the dot com bubble burst, and the money dried up. Mike was married and had a young daughter, so he had to find something soon. Mike tapped into his network and landed a position at Marsh & McClennon, which he started in July 2001. He needed the money, and the work was fine, though it didn't provide the passion or adventure he was seeking.

Mike worked long hours, and he had a two-hour commute each way. That meant that his daughter was asleep when he left in the morning and asleep when he got back in the evening. "I felt like I was only alive on weekends," Mike remembers. "And even then, I wasn't being the kind of parent I wanted to be." He knew he had to make a change and decided to start making small steps in service to creating a larger shift, even though he had no idea yet just where his reinvention would take him.

So, one Monday, Mike decided to make a small change—he would go in to work a little later the next day so that he could have breakfast with his wife and daughter. That next morning, he questioned his choice. There was so much work to do, emails and phone calls to make, and he was still new—would he get in trouble for going in late? "I listened to the inner voice telling me this was important," Mike recalls. "And I stuck to my plan. We had breakfast together, and I went in late."

That day was September 11, 2001. Mike worked on the 96th floor of the North Tower in the World Trade Center. The plane that hit the building not only hit his floor, it slammed into Mike's desk. The only reason he wasn't at his desk on that Tuesday morning was because he chose to have breakfast with his family. "I realized then that every choice—even 'insignificant' changes—can make a huge difference," Mike says.

Mike made another change: choosing to look for the best parts of his current job and find a way to maximize it until he made other plans. "I recreated myself where I was and held myself accountable," Mike says. "It changed how I approached work. And because of that new commitment, I began to focus on management, influence, and coaching."

A year later a friend said, "You'd be a great coach." Those words changed his life. "I didn't even know what professional coaching was," Mike says. "I looked into it and discovered more about coaching. That's when I realized that we need to be discoverers and adventurers in our own lives. Too often, we are making decisions based on a limited life knowledge base, which yields limited vision."

Mike immediately began researching this new world, gained a deeper understanding of possibilities, and found a new perspective. "I became open to the unknown," he says. "I had belief that there was something more out there for me. I also had faith in myself and in my wife, believing we would figure it out. We stepped into the unknown together. It's so important to have support for exploring choice, rather than fear that requires stability."

Building his coaching practice took a couple of years. Mike started by declaring his intention out loud when he was still at his full-time job. "Someone asked what I did, and I told them 'life coach,'" Mike recalls. He started coaching on the side and asked a friend to be his first client, so he could practice. "That helped me find my voice," Mike says. He took two years of coaching training, gained more clients, and had his part-time practice full.

Then Marsh started laying off. "People were going to get severance," Mike says. "I wanted to use that severance money to build my business. So I really wanted to be laid off while many others were afraid." He asked to be laid off and told his boss that he had found his calling. "It was a risk—I could have been fired on the spot with nothing," Mike admits. "Especially since I told them I needed my severance to launch another business." They turned him down. But a few months later, there was another round of lay-offs and Mike was let go.

That summer, the business was building. But when Mike did the math, the numbers didn't add up. "I had not done enough due diligence, and I wasn't covering expenses," Mike says. "I had a 'meltdown' and the fear came back because I wasn't going to make enough money to survive using the business formula I had created." So Mike had to get creative. He called up his old boss and asked to be a part-time consultant. He got a three-month project, which he was able to extend to eighteen months, and that provided the runway he needed to redefine the business in a sustainable way.

Over the next few years, Mike created multiple streams of income, and things were starting to come together. He was doing a lot of paid motivational speaking, which bolstered the coaching revenue. Then the financial crash hit in 2008. Within two weeks, a whole year's pipeline of income got cut as events and external training all got cancelled.

Mike's business was evaporating, and he was living in Westport, CT, which was a beautiful but expensive area. Their two kids were happy, and it was a great community. "Both my wife and I had corporate work experience in our background, so going back into that world was our fallback position," Mike says. He had to detach emotions to think clearly.

Once again, they had to think creatively rather than let the fear completely paralyze them. Their house was their biggest asset, and their top financial priority was to figure out how to keep it. They decided to rent it out, which covered its costs, but it meant that at age forty-two, they had to move back into his childhood home on Long Island with his parents for a year. "We realized we had a choice for how to define our situation. Rather than thinking of it negatively, we did our best to view the situation as a 'life adventure,'" Mike says. "We had to create an open space without judgment or fear. It turned into a happy, joyful year. Our kids were nine and six, and they decided that 'where we are is our home' even though they had to start at a new school."

Mike landed a long-term consulting gig through a friend of the family and relied on that income for a couple of years while the economy recovered. During that first year, he also decided to shift his practice from personal coaching to professional development to better leverage his background. The economy was showing signs of an upswing, and it was time for Mike and his wife to begin thinking about their next move.

"We worked through a lot of options," Mike says. "And we decided to move to the Berkshires in Western Massachusetts. The cost of living was less than in Connecticut, and it was a beautiful, artsy, mountain community. We made sure the kids were part of the house selection. When we told them they would have to move again at the end of that year, they were very resilient. They said, 'We've done it before; we know what we need to do.' I was very proud of them." He also found unexpected benefits to leaving the Manhattan mindset. "Where we live now helps with empathy because the pace is different. It's such a different lifestyle. We're learning to relate to more people in better ways. We've learned more gratitude, and that affects everything else."

Mike rebuilt his practice and now bills himself as "The Human WakeUp Call." He helps other frazzled executives regain perspective and determine their work and life priorities, so they can play bigger in all aspects of their lives. Over the years, he's learned a lot partnering with people who complemented his skills. "I learned that first doing what you expect to teach others is essential," Mike says. "Walk your talk. Realize that ups and downs are part of life. No matter how well you plan and how hard you work, we still fall down all the time. The skill is in learning how to get back up again. Now, I'm accountable to myself, and I know what to do when problems arise."

Mike acknowledges that he's always had a tendency to jump into the unknown. "Now, it's even more so," he says. "I have confidence in what I'm trying to create, and I'm living life from a place of strength and courage. Now, I know my limits, and I'm learning to say 'not now/not yet.' I'm still a work in progress. One lesson I learned is that speaking in front of thousands of people humbles and honors you. I became a better speaker when I gave myself permission to be authentic with my emotions."

Through it all, Mike gained validation of talents and gifts that he had always discounted. "When your mind is set right, you can 'be' anything," he says.

## The Take-Away

Mike's decision to begin shifting his priorities by making one small change—breakfast—saved his life. Your own small steps might not seem to be as consequential, but they still matter, nonetheless. Your own "journey of a thousand miles" can have you walking in circles, arriving at an unknown destination, or showing up somewhere you don't want to go—unless you are mindful of the steps you take and set your intention like your own internal GPS to travel in the direction of your dreams.

As you create your own Fresh Start Success, make mindful, incremental progress an important part of your reinvention. Small changes add up to big shifts.

## Q&A with Mike Jaffe

**Q: What did you learn the hard way?**
A: "When it comes to building a business, the numbers matter. Have faith in a business plan so you have a good formula, but don't be limited by it. Believe in yourself so you can jump into the unknown where the real fun is."

**Q: What one trait is critical to your Fresh Start Success?**
A: "Being able to let go of trauma and loss and stay focused, to believe in myself. Focus is so important. Focus means freedom. Without focus, you waste time. Focus lets us live more effectively."

**Q: If you had a superpower, what would it be?**
A: "To fly. I would love to see the world from that perspective, to have that freedom, and to be able to go on adventures with a broader perspective."

**Q: What role has marketing played in your success?**
A: "Marketing plays an ongoing role. It's the foundation of everything; it's how people find me and how they initially perceive me. I'm on Twitter and Facebook, I have a website, I'm on LinkedIn, and I do YouTube videos. For me,

it's always a balance for how much time I am going to spend on it so I don't lose my focus. I also know I could do more if I spent more time with it, but I only want to share messages that are meaningful. Nobody needs to know (or cares) what I ate for breakfast."

# Reimagine Everything

REMEMBER THE SAYING, "Today is the first day of the rest of your life"? It's true. So as you plan your Fresh Start Success, make this an opportunity to renew everything in your life and make it better.

Did stress, long hours, or too much travel put a dent in your health? Take control of your reinvention and refuse to repeat the things that made you unhappy. Now is a great time to renew your relationships—with the people around you, and with yourself and your hobbies. Start a new exercise program or take classes in something that fascinates you. Rekindle old friendships. Re-think where you live and work, not just for cost-of-living reasons, but for personal satisfaction. Approach networking, collaboration and friendships differently, with an emphasis on giving instead of getting.

This is your time, so make renewal of body, mind, and spirit a priority. You're working hard, but make time to be good to yourself. Look for healthier ways to handle the inevitable stress of making a living by trying new approaches to stress relief, like meditation or a different kind of workout.

Take the chance to change from the inside out. If part of your disillusionment with your old work situation was that it was all about the "Benjamins," take a more holistic approach to your reinvention that builds community, gives back, and pays forward. Explore whatever "spirituality" means to you, so you keep a broader perspective about what really matters in the long run.

Celebrate your new beginning—and declare an end to dwelling on old hurts and disappointments, or to allowing bitterness to hold you back. Forgive yourself and others. Make up for lost time. Rebuild burned bridges. Don't just rethink your work—use this time as a launch pad to question your goals and priorities and make sure they're aligned with what you truly want out of life. Rework your budget and spending habits to go with your new cash flow, which is a great exercise in reprioritization.

Find ways to incorporate the things you love into your work, whether that's travel, fitness, learning, meeting new people, art, music, food—whatever speaks to your heart. Life is too short to relegate the aspects you love into weekends and days off. While you're at it, take a vacation. Give yourself permission to be still. Plan your legacy. If not now, then when?

Do the things you said you would do "sometime." Why not start today? Eat right. Get a physical. Lose weight. Slow down. Breathe. Reconnect. Volunteer and mentor. Contribute. Make a difference. Change the world.

When Gail left her corporate job, our youngest son was still a preschooler. Gail arranged her schedule so that one day a week became her day out with him. They explored local parks and museums, went for long walks, tried new restaurants, searched for the perfect ice cream cone, and went to the dog park. During a period freelancing years earlier, Gail did the same with our older daughters. Almost two decades later, it's amazing how many of those days the kids still remember. It was worth it.

Larry took up pottery when he left corporate life. He had wanted to do something more creative and hands-on for a long time. His prior role in corporate senior management didn't leave much room for art, but his new role working with Gail in marketing and publishing gives him plenty of opportunities to use his abilities and gain satisfaction.

Are you balanced? Are there activities or interests that you need to make time for to help you be more effective? What have you been putting off doing? Now is the time. You'll work plenty of hours bringing your Fresh Start Success to life. Reserve some of that time for yourself to heal, grow, and thrive.

In the process of doing the interviews for the profiles in this book, we asked what single attribute each person credited with enabling their Fresh Start Success. Here's what they said:

Love, open-mindedness, organization, tenacity, attitude, resilience, perseverance, integrity, intentionality, patience, flexibility, focus, confidence, determination, listening, confidence, connections, creativity, drive, curiosity.

Do you see yourself in those words? How many of those terms describe you? These are the attributes you'll want to cultivate in order to walk in the steps of the amazing, successful people you've met in this book and create your own version of success.

Claim your Fresh Start Success by making a brand new start in your work and in the rest of your life. It's time to reimagine everything and rock your reinvention!

## Do you have a Fresh Start Story to tell?

We're looking for true personal stories for upcoming blog posts and books—and yours could be one of them! Fresh Start Success stories tell about a successful professional and personal reinvention. We want to know how you did it!

We're also looking for **Roar Back** stories about turning a business failure into success. Did you hit a brick wall, go down a dead end, see your dreams go up in smoke—and go on to something much better? Were you sure all your plans and goals were never going to happen—and then found a new way to make them reality? Were you ready to give up, walk away, and throw in the towel—and one more push made all the difference? We want to know!

To learn more about sharing your Fresh Start or Roar Back story, go to http://dreamspinnercommunications.com/fresh-start-success-story/

# Next Steps to Rock Your Reinvention

**READY TO DIVE IN?** Feeling a little overwhelmed? It's completely normal to be excited and a bit apprehensive at the same time. We can help.

We've been helping our clients rock their reinvention and create their own Fresh Start Success for more than a decade, and along the way, we've done plenty of adapting and evolving ourselves to meet the changing needs of the market. Between us, we have more than fifty years of combined experience, which includes work for Fortune 10 companies, regional firms, government and municipal entities, small businesses, sole proprietor enterprises, not-for-profit organizations, start-ups, and companies in a wide variety of industries. We can help you—or we'll connect you to the resources that can. Here are some of the ways we work with our clients.

**Coaching.** Need help figuring out your personal branding, how to develop a marketing plan that gets results, how to create scalable business systems, or how to use social media strategically? Want to build your own webinars, events, books, products, coaching programs, and other revenue streams? We specialize in all those topics, and more. We offer a variety of coaching packages designed to meet your needs, tailored to your specific interests.

**Ghostwriting and Publishing**. We've published with Top Five New York publishers, London publishing houses, small presses, and Kickstarter, and also done quality self-publishing. We can consult on traditional publishing and self-publishing and help you get the best results. If you've got a non-fiction book you need help bringing into reality, we're experienced ghostwriters and bring a wealth of publishing background to the project. Our ghostwriting services are perfect for speakers who want to create a "back of the room" book! We also specialize in book marketing to help you get your new book out into the world in a big way.

**Specialty writing.** Blog posts, articles, speeches, video scripts, website copy, newsletters, and more. We take on a limited number of projects as our schedule permits. Ask for a quote.

## The Take-Away

You don't have to reinvent yourself alone. DreamSpinner Communications can help you reimagine your future and shave precious time off your learning curve. Contact us today!

**Website:** www.DreamSpinnerCommunications.com
**Email:** Gail@DreamSpinnerCommunications.com
**Email:** Larry@DreamSpinnerCommunications.com
**Blog:** www.BigDreamsAndHardWork.com
**LinkedIn:** https://www.LinkedIn.com/in/GailZMartin,
**LinkedIn:** https://www.LinkedIn.com/in/LarryNMartin
**Twitter:** www.Twitter.com/GailMartinPR
**Twitter:** www.Twitter.com/DreamSpinnerCom
**Facebook:** www.Facebook.com/30DayResultsGuide

# Appendix
### Biographies of Contributors and
### How to Connect or Learn More

## Abbot, Katana

Katana is a Life and Legacy Coach™ and host of Smart Women Talk Radio with over one million subscribers. She is the founder of The Smart Women Companies™ where she offers coaching, free online resources, and transformational retreats to Costa Rica and Panama. As a CERTIFIED FINANCIAL PLANNER™ professional, her mission for the last 29 years has been to inspire women to take charge of their lives, businesses, and finances. In 2014, she joined MKD Wealth Coaches, LLC, as a Registered Investment Advisor, to support her coaching and consulting clients with financial advice and investment management. Katana is currently writing her next book, *Unlock Your Financial Power: the key to health, wealth & happiness.*

> **Connect with Katana Abbot:**
> **Facebook:** https://www.facebook.com/SmartWomenTalkRadio/
> **LinkedIn:** http://www.linkedin.com/in/katanaabbottsmartwomen
> **Twitter:** http://twitter.com/katanaabbott
> **Website:** http://www.katanaabbott.com
> **Website:** http://www.mkdwealthcoach.com/
> **Website:** http://www.smartwomensempowerment.org/

## Allen, Amber

Amber Allen, CEO and Chief Strategist of Double A Events, is a strategic leader with over sixteen years of experience working with high impact brands and campaigns. Double A Events can be found on the 2015 Event Marketer IT LIST and has created arena events, Times Square takeovers, streaming events, and large-scale corporate retreats. The company focuses on technology, entertainment and video games, targeting the 18-35 year old demographic, creating unforgettable experiences that create massive participation and excitement.

**Connect with Amber Allen:**
**Facebook:** https://www.facebook.com/doubleaevents
**LinkedIn:** http://www.linkedin.com/doubleaevents
**Pixieset:** http://doubleaevents.pixieset.com/
**Twitter:** http://www.twitter.com/doubleaevent
**Website:** http://www.doubleaevents.com

## Bové, Christine

Christine Bové is a speaker, author, and Feng Shui expert. She uses Feng Shui to teach her clients how to create a mindset for success while also helping them organize and beautify their space to create an image that reflects their personal style. Christine is the co-author of *Balance for Busy Moms: A Stress-Free Guide to Tranquility*, and the co-creator of the *Glamour + Metal* documentary on personal branding, as well as being an in-demand speaker and presenter.

**Connect with Christine Bové:**
**Facebook:** http://bit.ly/2dEHDO0
**Pinterest:** https://www.pinterest.com/christinebove/
**Website:** http://www.ChristineBove.com
**YouTube:** https://www.youtube.com/user/rhiroxanne

## Brett Randolph, Lauren

Lauren Brett Randolph is a certified professional co-active coach, as well as an ACC member in good standing with the International Coach Federation. She has been coaching in one form or another for over thirty years. She coaches individuals who have reached a point in life of looking to reclaim passion and purpose, who are hungry for change, and want support to shift toward a new vision. She also teaches the highly acclaimed workshop "Train Your Inner Voice" to college students and teachers, performing artists, and individuals to bring awareness of the negative inner voices and learn how to make conscious choices to follow the more positive empowered inner voice instead.

**Connect with Lauren Brett Randolph:**
**Blog:** http://www.thecartwheelcoach.com/category/blog/
**Facebook:** http://bit.ly/2cXlBZt
**Google+:** http://bit.ly/2dXVcba
**Instagram:** https://www.instagram.com/laurenbrettrandolph/
**LinkedIn:** http://bit.ly/2dEIgXK
**Twitter:** https://twitter.com/cartwheel_coach
**Website:** http://www.thecartwheelcoach.com/

# Dachinger, Debbi

Debbi Dachinger is a media personality whose radio show "DARE TO DREAM" is syndicated on 66 stations. Debbi is a successful motivational speaker and runs the Book Launch Program taking authors to international best-selling book status. Debbi also coaches Radio Mastery Training (private and workshop coaching mediamasteryradio.com) for entrepreneurs, speakers, and authors ready to accelerate their skills and be superb on air. Awards: Broadcasting Industry Lifetime Achievement Award, Who's Who Hall of Fame for Entertainment, Heart and Spirit Award. She is a certified dream coach.

**Connect with Debbi Dachinger:**
**Facebook:** http://www.facebook.com/DaretoDreamRadiotv
**Google+:** https://plus.google.com/+DebbiDachinger/
**LinkedIn:** http://LinkedIn.com/debbidachinger
**Pinterest:** https://www.pinterest.com/debontheradio/
**Twitter:** http://www.Twitter.com/debbidachinger

**Website:** http://debbidachinger.com
**Website:** http://MyBestsellerBook.com
**YouTube:** http://www.YouTube.com/debontheradio

## Darnay, Melissa

Melissa Darnay is the owner of Choose Panama and the author of *Panama Uncorked: Everything You Need to Know to Visit, Live and Invest in Panama.* Choose Panama is a concierge real estate and relocation service for North Americans who want to own a slice of heaven on the Panamanian Riviera. The company offers real estate tours, luxury condo rentals, property management, and traditional real estate services.

### Connect with Melissa Darnay:
**Facebook:** https://www.facebook.com/choosepanamarealestate/
**Website:** http://www.ChoosePanama.com

## De Grosbois, Teresa

Teresa de Grosbois is an international speaker, trainer, and four-time international #1 best-selling author. In service to her mission to change the planet, one grass-roots movement at a time, Teresa also heads The Evolutionary Business Council, a community of emerging thought leaders who focus on teaching the principles of success and prosperity.

### Connect with Teresa De Grosbois:
**Facebook:** https://www.facebook.com/EBCouncil
**Facebook:** https://www.facebook.com/WildfireWorkshops
**LinkedIn:** https://www.linkedin.com/in/teresadegrosbois
**Twitter:** @TeresaDee | @EBCouncil | @WildfireWS
**Website:** http://www.EBCouncil.com
**Website:** http://www.MassiveInfluenceTheBook.com

**Website:** http://www.TeresadeGrosbois.com
**Website:** http://www.WildfireAcademy.com
**Website:** http://www.InfluenceAndSuccess.com


## Dibblee, Jo

Jo Dibblee—a Breakthrough Expert—is determined to be the change she seeks by educating, empowering, and elevating women entrepreneurs via access, connection, collaboration, knowledge, and resources. She is a social entrepreneur who sees it as her responsibility to give back both locally and globally. The founder of Frock Off Inc., Jo is described as a tenacious and fearless philanthropist—a catalyst to change. She works with heart-centered women entrepreneurs who have a big message, product, or service and are ready to amplify their results. Jo is the author of *Frock Off: Living Undisguised*.

Jo is driven by her passion and purpose, which stems from living in hiding for 35 years as a key witness in a murder investigation. She is an international award winning author, speaker, and breakthrough expert. She has been featured in Canadian media nationwide and in *The Huffington Post*.

**Connect with Jo Dibblee:**
**Facebook:** https://www.facebook.com/Jo.Dibblee/?fref=ts#
**LinkedIn:** https://ca.linkedin.com/in/joannvacingdibblee
**Twitter:** http://www.twitter.com/FrockNoMore
**Website:** http://www.frock-off.com


## Edie, Barbara

Barbara Edie, MA, BN, is a best-selling author, writer, and editor who helps entrepreneurs, non-profit organizations, and creative professionals tap into the power of stories to promote their work and expand their businesses. Barbara helps entrepreneurs, authors, and other professionals create their "signature

271

stories" about *why* they do what they do, to connect with their audience, build credibility, and attract the people they came here to serve.

She is the author of #1 Amazon bestseller *Sparking Change Around the Globe: 5 Ways to Make Your Difference in the World* and is currently writing a book about secrets and strategies to turn your vision into reality.

**Connect with Barbara Edie:**
**Facebook**: http://www.facebook.com/barbaraedieauthor
**LinkedIn**: https://www.linkedin.com/in/barbaraedie
**Twitter**: http://www.twitter.com/barbaraedie
**Website**: http://www.barbaraedie.com

## Fink, Sheri

Sheri Fink is an inspirational speaker, five-time #1 best-selling author, and the president of "The Whimsical World of Sheri Fink" award-winning brand. She creates books, products, and experiences that inspire kids of all ages while planting seeds of self-esteem. Her brand is the recipient of the prestigious Gold Mom's Choice Award for the best in family friendly entertainment. Sheri is also the author of the internationally best-selling romance novel, *Cake in Bed*.

**Connect with Sheri Fink:**
**Facebook**: http://www.facebook.com/SheriFinkFan
**Instagram**: http://www.instagram.com/Sheri_Fink
**Twitter**: http://www.twitter.com/Sheri_Fink
**LinkedIn**: http://www.linkedin.com/in/sherifink
**Website**: http://www.SheriFink.com

## Fleming, Dawn

Dawn Fleming is the owner of Energy Transformations, LLC, as well as being an award-winning author and a teacher/speaker. She is a holistic health entrepreneur who helps other practitioners grow their practice and find success doing what they love. Dawn helps her clients to unblock their energy for physical and emotional healing, stress reduction, clarity, and moving forward in life so they can realize their dreams. She is the author of *Creating a Successful Holistic Health Practice, Teaching Workshops Effectively, Navigating the Continuing Education Approval Process.*

**Connect with Dawn Fleming:**
**Facebook**: https://www.facebook.com/dawn.fleming.148
**Blog**: http://www.blogtalkradio.com/twomodernmystics
**LinkedIn**: https://www.linkedin.com/in/dawnfleming
**Twitter:** http://www.twitter.com/DawnFleming220
**Website:** http://www.energytransformations.org

# Goldberg, Marla

Marla Goldberg is an international Psychic-Medium, Certified Consulting Hypnotist, Guided Meditation and Past-Life Regression Expert, professional vocalist and cookbook author for Fortune 500 Companies. She offers private facilitation, workshops and retreats in gorgeous settings specializing in Weight Release through Inner Peace, Developing Intuition, Past-Life Regression and Chronic Pain Remission. Her clients for weight loss with hypnosis are successful women who desire healthier bodies and a more loving relationship with Self- the key to successful relationships with others. Marla believes that everyone has a powerful unique voice and inner gifts to share. She inspires positive change with meditation, music, and more.

**Connect with Marla Goldberg:**
**Twitter:** https://twitter.com/marlameditation
**Pinterest:** http://www.pinterest.com/marlameditation/boards
**Website:** http://marlameditations.com/

## Green, Tamara

Tamara Green, LCSW, is a psychotherapist and mediation facilitator. She is also a Loving Relationship Expert and the author of *Transform Your Life Using The 7 Sacred Flames: Daily Guided Meditations*. She is an author, speaker, and coach who has helped thousands of women meet and marry their soul mates—all while falling madly in love with themselves in the process. Trained as a Love Mentor® by Diana Kirschner, PhD, individual and couples psychotherapist, meditation facilitator and hypnotherapist, Tamara's coaching combines years of professional training with her gifts as an energy healer, intuitive, and seer to serve as a catalyst for deep emotional healing.

**Connect with Tamara Green:**
**Blog**: http://www.tamaragreen.me/blog/
**Facebook**: https://www.facebook.com/TGreenLoveExpert
**Google+:** http://plus.google.com/u/0/+TamaragreenMe/posts
**LinkedIn**: https://www.linkedin.com/in/tamaragreen4u/
**Pinterest**: http://www.pinterest.com/TamaraGreen4u/
**Twitter**: https://twitter.com/tamaragreen4u
**Website**: http://www.tamaragreen.me/
**Yelp**: http://www.yelp.com/biz/tamara-green-lcsw-new-york
YouTube: https://www.youtube.com/user/TamaraGreen4u

## Gritsenko, Oksana

Oksana Gritsenko is the Founder and CEO of Joyfulness at Solful Gifts, Inc., mind transformation coach, and creator of the "Know Your True Self" program. Solful Gifts, Inc., is a company with mind substance, based on passion and deep beliefs of its founders. It offers a variety of integrative services created to guide individuals toward personal transformation and self-actualization on multiple levels. Its mission is to help others discover happiness and embrace the art of joyful living.

**Connect with Oksana Gritsenko:**
**Facebook**: https://www.facebook.com/SolfulGifts
**LinkedIn**: https://www.linkedin.com/company/solful-gifts-inc-
**LinkedIn**: https://www.linkedin.com/in/oksanagritsenko
**Website**: http://www.SolfulGifts.com

## Gupta-Krishnan, Poonam

Poonam Gupta-Krishnan is the Founder and President, Government Technology Foundation, Inc.; CEO, Iyka Enterprises, Inc.; and Chief Technology Officer, Diversity MBA.

Poonam is a relentless technology innovation champion and entrepreneur and a social leader. The Government Technology Foundation creates synergies between government, technology companies, and academia by providing an educational and collaborative platform where executives in these fields can meet, share best practices, and develop worthwhile collaborations. Iyka Enterprises, Inc. is a data management company focusing on big data analytics.

**Connect with Poonam Gupta-Krishnan:**
**Facebook**: https://www.facebook.com/IykaEnterprises
**LinkedIn**: https://www.linkedin.com/in/poonamgupta
**Twitter**: https://twitter.com/Iyka_Enterprise

## Hassler, Christine

Christine Hassler is a life coach, speaker, and author. She is the author of *Expectation Hangover, The 20 Something Manifesto*, and *20 Something, 20 Everything*. As a speaker, retreat facilitator, and life coach, Christine's goal is to ease suffering. Christine believes once we get out of our own way, we can show up to make the meaningful impact we are here to make.

**Connect with Christine Hassler:**
**Facebook**: https://www.facebook.com/christinehasslerpage

**Instagram**: http://www.instagram.com/christinehassler
**LinkedIn**: https://www.linkedin.com/in/christinehassler
**Twitter**: http://www.twitter.com/christinhassler (Note: no 'e')
**Website**: http://www.christinehassler.com

## Hobbs, EdD, Stephen (Steve)

Stephen Hobbs, EdD, guides professionals and entrepreneurs to create Well-Living Workplaces™ with involvement of their staff, volunteers, and/or customers. And in doing so, all fully express their Life Leadership Legacy. He is a philanthropist for programs involving children and trees. In addition, he is a prolific author of articles, book chapters, and books including his latest books *Help Them Help YOU Manage-Lead* and *Unbounded Dimensions: Manage and Lead the Organization of Work Using the Wiggly-T Dance Model.*

**Connect with Steve Hobbs:**
**Blog**: http://www.wellthmovement.com/wellth-blog
**LinkedIn**: https://www.linkedin.com/in/stephenhobbscalgary
**Twitter**: @wellthlearning; @writetoshade
**Website**: http://www.wellthmovement.com
**YouTube**: https://www.youtube.com/user/wellthlearningTV

## Ida, Wendy

Wendy Ida (pronounced ee'da) also known as *America's #1 Expert on Looking Fit, Fierce & Fabulous after 40* is an internationally recognized best-selling author, speaker, TV host, life transformation coach, and fitness expert. She is also a two-time *Guinness World Record Holder* and nine-time award-winning National Fitness Champion. Wendy is on a mission to transform and rebuild the lives of women (and men) around the world. She is also the author of *Take Back Your Life: My No-Nonsense Approach to Health, Fitness and Looking Good Naked.*

**Connect with Wendy Ida:**
**Blog**: http://wendyida.com/blog/
**Facebook**: http://facebook.com/WendyIdaFitness
**Instagram**: https://instagram.com/wendyidafitness
**LinkedIn**: https://www.linkedin.com/in/wendyidafitness
**Twitter**: http://twitter.com/wendyida
**Website**: http://www.wendyida.com
**YouTube**: https://www.youtube.com/user/WendyIdaFitness

## Jaffe, Mike

Mike Jaffe is a nationally-recognized speaker, seminar leader, executive coach, author, and founder of The Mike Jaffe Company, a global leadership development corporate coaching firm providing socially-responsible companies a scalable, single-vendor solution for transforming the human side of leadership. Mike is committed to championing programs that bring perspective, tools, and support to the workplace, enabling increased professional success and accountability together with a better quality of life. He recently served as the president of The Coach Initiative, an organization that offers coaching support to not-for-profit projects around the world that focus on the betterment of the human condition and the human spirit. Mike is also the author of *Wake Up! Your Life Is Calling.*

**Connect with Mike Jaffe:**
**Facebook**: https://www.facebook.com/MikeJaffeCompany/
**Website**: http://www.HumanWakeUpCall.com

## Jendza, Lisa

Lisa Jendza is a successful spa owner, an expert in body wraps, and the developer of Glow Natural Cosmeceuticals. Lisa Jendza is a contributing author and speaks to business owners about the *Boutique Business Model.*

**Connect with Lisa Jendza:**
**Facebook**: http://www.facebook.com/glownaturalinc
**Facebook**: http://www.facebook.com/lisajendza
**Facebook**: http://www.facebook.com/newyoubodywraps
**LinkedIn**: http://www.linkedin.com/in/lisajendza
**Pinterest**: http://www.pinterest.com/glownaturalinc
**Pinterest**: http://www.pinterest.com/newyoubodywraps
**Twitter**: http://www.twitter.com/glownaturalinc
**Twitter**: http://www.twitter.com/lisajendza
**Twitter**: http://www.twitter.com/newyoubodywraps
**Website**: http://www.glownaturalinc.com

## Kelly, Grace

Grace Kelly is a success coach, and was nominated as coach of the year 2015 in the UK. Grace's blog, CityGirl Confidence™, was selected by *Forbes* as one of the top 100 Best Websites for Women, and her expertise has been featured in *The Sunday Times, Zest*, and *Soul and Spirit*. Grace offers private coaching programs and international retreats in destination locations around the world.

**Connect with Grace Kelly:**
Facebook: https://www.facebook.com/CityGirlGrace?fref=ts
Twitter: https://twitter.com/CityGirlGrace
Website: https://www.citygirlconfidence.com

## Kessler, Karen

Karen Kessler is a social entrepreneur launch expert and the CEO of ChooseRESULTS.

ChooseRESULTS is narrowly focused on entrepreneurs launching or re-launching in the social entrepreneur space and helps them capture the skills needed for the highest human potential for self and other. Karen's signature programs include Road to RESULTS: Entrepreneur Mastery for those who want to fill their wallet and their soul.

### Connect with Karen Kessler:
**Blog**: http://www.chooseresults.ca/blog/
**Website**: http://www.chooseresults.ca/
**LinkedIn**: https://ca.linkedin.com/in/karenkessler
**Facebook**: http://www.facebook.com/KarenAnneKessler
**Google**+: https://plus.google.com/+KarenKesslerCR/

## Manyon, Lisa

Lisa Manyon is the President of Write On Creative. She's known as The Business Marketing Architect and creator of a simple 3-step "Challenge. Solution. Invitation.™" framework to create marketing messages with integrity as featured in Inc. Magazine and best-selling books Wonder Women and Engage. Lisa is a speaker, trainer, consultant, writer and award-winning blogger. She specializes in reverse engineering your most powerful solutions into profitable revenue streams via web strategy, messaging and content strategy plans known to help create million dollar results. She received the People's Choice Award at the California Women's Conference and serves on the Leadership Team of the Women Speakers Association.

### Connect with Lisa Manyon:
**Facebook**: https://www.facebook.com/WriteOnCreative
**LinkedIn**: https://www.linkedin.com/in/lisamanyon
**Twitter**: https://twitter.com/WriteOnCreative
**Website**: http://www.writeoncreative.com

## McRill, Sharon

Sharon McRill is owner and president of The Betty Brigade, an expanding relocation and organizing company based in Ann Arbor, MI. The Betty Brigade helps busy professionals with moving, home staging, organizing, selling their unwanted belongings—virtually anything clients need done when they're moving but have no time to do themselves.

**Connect with Sharon McRill:**
**Facebook**: http://www.facebook.com/TheBettyBrigade/
**Instagram**: https://www.instagram.com/TheBettyBrigade/
**LinkedIn**: https://www.linkedin.com/company/the-betty-brigade
**Pinterest**: https://www.pinterest.com/thebettybrigade/
**Radio Show**: http://www.blogtalkradio.com/bettybrigade
**Twitter**: https://twitter.com/bettybrigade
**Website**: http://bettybrigade.com/
**Website**: http://www.trustbetty.com
**Website**: http://www.bettyrealsale.com
**YouTube**: https://www.youtube.com/user/TheBettyBrigade

## Mininni, Lisa

Lisa Mininni, MSA, MCBC, is a hardwiring expert. She travels the globe educating small business owners, entrepreneurs, and business leaders on their biological hardwiring. Wiring dictates the type of environment in which you are best equipped to thrive and succeed, and the kind of environment you prefer to live and work. Your hardwiring drives you in business and is primarily unconscious. Hardwiring and how you run your business systems are deeply connected. Lisa shows you how to make those connections so you increase your profits to levels you didn't think were possible.

Lisa is the best-selling author of *Me, Myself, and Why?*, *Get More Clients Now!*, and co-author of *Leading Women*.

**Connect with Lisa Mininni:**
**Book**: http://www.memyselfandwhy.com
**Facebook**: http://www.facebook.com/excellerateassociates
**LinkedIn**: http://www.linkedin.com/in/lisamininni
**Twitter**: http://www.twitter.com/lisamininni
**Website**: http://www.excellerateassociates.com

# Monson, Faith

Faith Monson achieves success using proven coaching techniques with clients to develop and implement a customized, results-oriented plan to achieve specific, targeted goals.

Faith also offers business consulting services, including business assessments, market and competitive evaluation, recommendations to clarify and enhance personal and business strengths, fresh ideas for better visual marketing, public relations strategies, and interviewing/sales training.

Faith is the author of two eBooks—*Creating Possibilities, How to Realize Your Personal Power to Succeed and Empower Yourself and Your Career* and *Opening Doors, Reinvent Yourself & Realize Your (Business) Potential*—and more than seventy published articles. All are available in her success coaching library on her website.

**Connect with Faith Monson:**
**Blog**: http://www.bigdreamsandhardwork.com
**LinkedIn**: http://www.linkedin.com/in/faithmonson
**Twitter**: https://twitter.com/faithmonson
**Website**: http://www.faithmonson.com

## Moran, Sheevaun

Sheevaun Moran has helped over 15,000 people achieve their epic life and success. She is an author of several books, a master energy coach, the creator of the Energetic Solutions, Inc.® Success System, and is devoted to teaching entrepreneurs, CEOs, and leaders universal success principles with proven step-by-step "How-To's" to break through and create success. Through her Conscious Conversations for CEOs, Innovator's Circle, Unleash Infinite Prosperity, Epic Life Conference programs and dozens of products, Sheevaun unleashes within you clarity, simplicity, and profits to live exponentially. She's been named Female Entrepreneur of the Year and has been featured in media including *The Wall Street Journal*, CBS, ABC, and many others.

**Connect with Sheevaun Moran:**
**Website**: http://www.sheevaunmoran.com

## Oberlin, Loriann

Loriann Oberlin, MS, LCPC, is a licensed clinical professional counselor with offices in North Potomac and Easton, Maryland. She sees clients of all ages and families, including couples using Gottman Method Couples Therapy. Ms. Oberlin is the author of ten non-fiction books, including *Surviving Separation & Divorce*, *The Angry Child*, and *Overcoming Passive-Aggression*. Under the pen name Lauren Monroe, she's written women's novels *Letting Go: Book One of The Maryland Shores* and *Second Chances: Book Two*. A third will complete the trilogy.

**Connect with Loriann Oberlin:**
**Facebook**: http://www.facebook.com/lauren.monroe.novels
**Website**: http://www.laurenmonroenovels.com
**Website**: http://www.loriannoberlin.com

## Peterson, Debbie

Debbie Peterson is the owner of Money Counts, a financial planning company with a different approach. Money Counts offers clients access to personal cash flow management strategies that are intended to help them enjoy the money they have now—as well as to provide savings for retirement. Through individual consulting sessions, the Money Counts team helps clients understand how to unleash their money's hidden potential—and obtain more of what *they* want— with the money they already have.

> **Connect with Debbie Peterson:**
> **Facebook**: http://bit.ly/2dynUUn
> **LinkedIn**: https://www.linkedin.com/in/deborah-peterson-34403249
> **Twitter**: https://twitter.com/MoneyCountsInc_
> **Website**: http://www.moneycounts.biz

## Ratliff, Danielle

Danielle Ratliff, LMBT/RDN, is the owner of Serenity Now Massage Therapy. Danielle is a licensed massage and bodywork therapist and a registered dietitian. Serenity Now Massage Therapy is "The Premier Therapeutic Massage Studio of Lake Norman." Each of her therapists is certified in neuromuscular therapy (NMT) to more effectively treat soft tissue injuries and chronic pain.

> **Connect with Danielle Ratliff:**
> **Blog**: http://serenitynowcornelius.com/resources/blog
> **Facebook/Business**: https://www.facebook.com/SerenityNowMassageTherapy
> **Facebook/Personal**: https://www.facebook.com/danielle.ratliff.9
> **Google+**: https://plus.google.com/110654203364158757481/posts?hl=en
> **LinkedIn**: https://www.linkedin.com/in/danielle-ratliff-a5936047
> **Twitter**: http://www.twitter.com/SerenityNowLKN
> **Website**: http://www.serenitynowcornelius.com

## Richards, Sherri

Sherri Richards is the owner of Rise Consulting. She is a business consultant with a rare combination of finance, marketing, distribution, and operations experience both nationally and internationally. Her true gift is her love of creating and telling the whole story. The fun is taking an idea, developing the business plan with its pieces and parts, then bringing it to life in a holistic, profitable and sustainable way.

### Connect with Sherri Richards:
**Facebook**: https://www.facebook.com/mymoneyexperience
**LinkedIn**: https://www.linkedin.com/in/sherririchards
**Twitter**: http://www.twitter.com/Risemme
**Website**: http://www.mymoneyexperience.com

## Sandhriel, PhD, C.H, Cha~zay

Cha~zay Sandhriel is the founder of Core Freedom Academy, an online personal development course site with over 12,000 students. She is also an international speaker who has shared the stage with Robert Kiyosaki, author of *Rich Dad Poor Dad*, and was a Learning Annex instructor for many years. Cha~zay has written several books and most recently published *The Four Gateways*. She's a frequent radio guest and the host of her own podcast, *The Core Freedom Show*. She's a Reiki master, a trained grief and suicide hotline counselor and certified hypnotist. Cha~zay has a PhD in metaphysical science and a second PhD in holistic life coaching.

### Connect with Cha~zay Sandhriel:
**Facebook**: http://facebook.com/drchazay
**Google+**: http://www.plus.google.com/+Corefreedomhangout
**LinkedIn**: https://www.linkedin.com/in/corefreedom
**Pinterest**: https://www.pinterest.com/corefreedom/
**YouTube**: https://www.youtube.com/user/BlueprintForLove

## Shattuck, LeeAnn

LeeAnn Shattuck is an automotive enthusiast, speaker, writer, radio and television host, and champion race car driver. LeeAnn owns a unique car buying service dedicated to helping women through the entire car selection and buying process. LeeAnn is passionate about educating women about cars and empowering them to make informed decisions when purchasing, selling, and servicing automobiles. Known around the world as "The Car ChickTM", LeeAnn has been featured on national radio and television programs and regularly co-hosts the internationally syndicated radio show, *America's Garage*, and the internet channel, *Car Chick TV*. She is currently producing and co-hosting a new reality show about restoring classic cars, called *Rust Rescue*.

> **Connect with LeeAnn Shattuck:**
> **Blog**: http://www.TheCarChick.com/blog/
> **Facebook**: https://www.facebook.com/The-Car-Chick-762875857071361/
> **LinkedIn**: https://www.linkedin.com/in/leeannshattuck
> **Twitter**: https://twitter.com/chiefcarchick
> **Website**: http://www.TheCarChick.com/
> **YouTube**: http://www.CarChick-TV.com

## Simpson, Pierette

Pierette Domenica Simpson's career has evolved from teaching foreign languages for 37 years to becoming an author, speaker, documentarian, screenwriter, actress, and producer.

In 2014, she founded an international project creating cultural bridges between the two sister cities of Detroit and Turin, Italy: Project DeTur. Recently, Pierette produced a docufilm (documentary with re-enactments) that was filmed near both cities. It is based on her publications, *Alive on the Andrea Doria! The Greatest Sea Rescue in History* and *I Was Shipwrecked on the Andrea Doria: The Titanic of the 1950s*.

**Connect with Pierette Simpson:**
**Facebook**: https://www.facebook.com/andreadoriathemovie/
**Facebook**: https://www.facebook.com/pierette.simpson
**LinkedIn**: https://www.linkedin.com/in/pierette-simpson-77a0785
**Teaser**: https://www.youtube.com/watch?v=sXmtDbw5B2w
**Trailer**: https://www.youtube.com/watch?v=IyFUiRrE230
**Website**: http://www.andreadoriamovie.com
**Website**: http://www.Iwasshipwreckedontheandreadoria.com
**Website**: http://www.pierettesimpson.com
**Website**: http://www.projectdetur.com
**YouTube**: https://www.youtube.com/user/Pierette


# Sklar, M.D., Susan

Dr. Susan Sklar is a nationally recognized Harvard-trained physician who is dedicated to figuring out the root cause of her patients' symptoms. She is a fierce health detective who believes that you can age gracefully and feel great while doing so. She utilizes the cutting-edge science of functional medicine to support your body to heal itself through diet, lifestyle, and appropriate supplementation.

After a 25-year career as an obstetrician/gynecologist, she started a second career in the field of anti-aging and restorative medicine. She started the Sklar Center for Restorative Medicine in 2007 as an answer to the unmet needs of men and women who want to feel good in midlife and maintain health long term. She sees private patients at her center in Long Beach, California.

**Connect with Susan Sklar:**
**Facebook**: https://www.facebook.com/SklarCenter/
**Website**: http://www.sklarcenter.com
**Yelp**: http://bit.ly/2dRyUX1

## Watson, Gail

Gail Watson co-founded Women Speakers Association in 2011, committed to a vision of a world in which women are empowered to authentically express themselves; to build a thriving, prosperous business; and feel a part of something greater. A world in which women take ownership of and step into being the leaders that they are using their voice to powerfully inspire others, thus causing transformation in the lives of their clients, their companies, communities, and the world.

### Connect with Gail Watson:
**Facebook** Group: http://www.wsafacebookgroup.com
**Facebook**: http://www.facebook.com/womenspeakersassociation
**Twitter**: http://www.twitter.com/womenspeakassoc
**Website**: http://www.womenspeakersassociation.com

## Wezowski, Patryk

Patryk Wezowski is the producer of *Leap*, the world's first documentary about the coaching profession, and together with his wife, Kasia Wezowski, authored the best-selling *The Micro Expressions Book for Business*. As the founder of the Center for Body Language, the World's #1 Body Language Training for Business, Negotiations and Branding, he and Kasia developed over a dozen non-verbal communication training programs tailored for sales, recruitment, leadership, and negotiations. Their methodologies and conversation strategies are being taught in local languages by fifty international representatives in twenty countries. They make movies that touch millions of lives and support entrepreneurs to make their creations come to life through crowdfunding.

### Connect with Patryk Wezowski:
**Facebook:** https://www.facebook.com/WezowskiFan
**Google+:** https://plus.google.com/+PatrykWezowski1
**IMDB:** http://www.imdb.com/name/nm5862650/?ref_=fn_al_nm_1

**LinkedIn:** http://be.linkedin.com/in/wezowski
**Twitter:** https://twitter.com/pwezowski
**Website:** http://wezowski.com/
**YouTube:** https://www.youtube.com/c/PatrykWezowski1

## Woodie, Lisa

Chef Lisa Woodie is the owner of Homemade Fresh Chef Service. Her company specializes in planning and preparing meals that are personalized to each client's tastes, preferences, and dietary requirements using food from nature, not science. The business philosophy is that food is fuel for your body, and food choices can affect your energy, productivity, and overall wellness. During regularly scheduled cooking sessions in each client's home, the chef prepares, packages, and labels multiple personalized meals, leaving them in the refrigerator or freezer. The chef brings groceries and equipment, provides simple reheating instructions, and cleans the kitchen when finished. Homemade Fresh also provides chef service for personal and business events.

**Connect with Lisa Woodie:**
**LinkedIn:** https://www.linkedin.com/in/lisawoodie
**NAWBO 2015 Rising Star Award Winner:** http://bit.ly/2dS4Pfq
**Podcast:** http://bit.ly/2dA1RZG
**Website:** http://www.homemadefresh.net
**Yelp:** http://www.yelp.com/biz/homemade-fresh-chef-service-charlotte

## Woodworth, Wendy

Wendy Woodworth is a "Guide by Your Side" who exclusively helps women who want to Dance With Life Again—at their own pace—in an era where so many women have lost their sense of belonging and feel they don't matter. Wendy empowers women to take important steps toward achieving prosperity.

At age 45, Wendy found herself divorced, with four children to get through university, and responsible for sixteen staff members, and her mother, all financially dependent on her to keep moving forward. Wendy soon realized that she knew how to survive, but she didn't know how to LIVE. Her life changed when she began to invest in herself in creating a vibrant, mutually supportive community of BraveHeart women.

**Connect with Wendy Woodworth:**
**Facebook:** http://facebook.com/BraveHeartWomenChapter
**LinkedIn:** https://www.linkedin.com/in/WendyWoodworth
**Twitter:** http://www.twitter.com/WendyWoodworth1
**Website:** http://www.WendyWoodworth.com
**YouTube:** http://bit.ly/2cX25fE

www.ingramcontent.com/pod-product-compliance
Lightning Source LLC
La Vergne TN
LVHW051224080426
835513LV00016B/1397